July 12, 2013

Dear Jack.

A small token of
respect + gratitude.

Warmly,

Aaron

Abrahamic Religions

ABRAHAMIC RELIGIONS

*On the Uses and
Abuses of History*

AARON W. HUGHES

OXFORD
UNIVERSITY PRESS

OXFORD
UNIVERSITY PRESS

Oxford University Press is a department of the University of Oxford.
It furthers the University's objective of excellence in research, scholarship,
and education by publishing worldwide.

Oxford   New York
Auckland   Cape Town   Dar es Salaam   Hong Kong   Karachi
Kuala Lumpur   Madrid   Melbourne   Mexico City   Nairobi
New Delhi   Shanghai   Taipei   Toronto

With offices in
Argentina   Austria   Brazil   Chile   Czech   Republic   France   Greece
Guatemala   Hungary   Italy   Japan   Poland   Portugal   Singapore
South   Korea   Switzerland   Thailand   Turkey   Ukraine   Vietnam

Oxford is a registered trademark of Oxford University Press
in the UK and certain other countries.

Published in the United States of America by
Oxford University Press
198 Madison Avenue, New York, NY 10016

© Oxford University Press 2012

Library of Congress Cataloging-in-Publication Data
Hughes, Aaron W., 1968–
Abrahamic religions : on the uses and abuses of history / Aaron W. Hughes.
p. cm.
Includes bibliographical references and index.
ISBN 978–0–19–993464–5
1. Religions—Relations.   2. Abrahamic religions.   3. Abraham (Biblical patriarch)
I. Title.
BL410.H84 2012
201'.4—dc23
2012005605

ISBN 978–0–19–993464–5

1 3 5 7 9 8 6 4 2
Printed in the United States of America
on acid-free paper

For my parents,

William and Sadie Hughes

in gratitude

Contents

Abrahamic Religions

Introduction

ON THE COLD morning of February 25, 1994, which just happened to coincide that year with the Jewish holiday of Purim and the Muslim month
of Ramadan, an American-born physician dressed as an Israeli soldier
made his way, as tens of thousands of Jewish and Muslim worshippers
had before him, to the cave of Machpelah in Hebron. There, at the tomb
of Abraham, Jews and Muslims prayed awkwardly with one another as
they had for centuries. On common ground, each invoked the God of
Abraham in the traditional manner prescribed by their respective traditions. On this particular morning, however, Dr. Baruch Goldstein raised
and pointed his machine gun at the crowd and began to shoot indiscrim-
inately at the Muslim worshippers. Screams of horror pierced what had
just a few seconds earlier been the calm melody of prayer. By the time the
screams had finished, twenty-nine Muslims were dead, another one hundred and twenty-five were injured, and the perpetrator, beaten to death by
the remaining crowd, lay crumpled on the ground.[1]

This tragic event marks the ambiguity of Abraham in the modern world.
Perceived by many as the common denominator of Judaism, Christianity
and Islam, the so-called "real" Abraham remains elusive. An ahistorical
figure, some contend he holds the seeds for historical reconciliation. A
symbol of ecumenicism, Abraham can just as easily function—as Baruch
Goldstein so painfully reminds us—as one of division and exclusivity.
This dialectic of history and myth, inclusivity and exclusivity, is the true
progeny of Abraham as the three monotheistic religions have sought to
define themselves and their relationship to one another.

Traditionally each of the three monotheisms perceives itself to be the
authentic heir of what it constructs as Abraham's true message. Many in the
twentieth century, by contrast, have increasingly conceived of Abraham as
a central figure with which to imagine and designate a perceived commonality or a wistful paternity among the three monotheisms at a time when
they have become increasingly at odds with each another. Since the fateful
attacks of September 11, 2001, we increasingly witness the term "Abrahamic

religions" invoked to delineate a set of qualities that many imagine as the point of departure for interfaith conversation and understanding.

But what exactly are "Abrahamic religions"? Like our understanding of Abraham, the category "Abrahamic religions" is vague and nebulous. Although the term has become increasingly omnipresent in both popular and academic literature, its actual meaning nevertheless remains obscure. Sure we can say that Judaism, Christianity, and Islam are "Abrahamic religions," but then what? When we use this omnibus term to designate these three religions, do we facilitate analysis or curtail it? Yet before we can even answer such questions, we need to back up and ask several others: Whence does the term "Abrahamic religions" derive? When was the term coined? Who created it and for what purposes? What sort of intellectual work is it perceived to perform?

In order to answer these and related questions, *Abrahamic Religions: On the Uses and Abuses of History* explores the creation and dissemination of this category. Part genealogical and part analytical, this study seeks to call into question the appropriateness and usefulness of employing "Abrahamic religions" as a vehicle for understanding and classifying data. In so doing, it can be taken as a case study that examines the construction of categories within the academic study of religion, showing how the categories we employ can become more an impediment than an expedient to our ability to understand.

Most works devoted to "Abrahamic religions" take their existence for granted and proceed to uncover a set of phenomenological similarities among them. It is not uncommon, for example, to see studies devoted to "Abrahamic" notions of monotheism or faith, or to more modern virtues such as peace and justice. The present study, by contrast, is not interested in elucidating such aspects of "Abrahamic religions" or contributing to the increasingly popular "Abrahamic religions" discourse, but in analyzing where the term came from and why we still insist on employing it. My general argument is that definitions of "Abrahamic religions" tend to rely on a series of qualifiers that amount to little more than a string of vague caricatures. Many of these (e.g., faith, covenant, revelation, chosenness) are theological, all are ahistorical, and the end result is that our employment of the constructed category "Abrahamic religions" needs to be rethought.

***

The "Abrahamic covenant" is often referred to as the origin of monotheism. Judaism, Christianity, and Islam all developed strong theological notions of covenant and all three make connections between their prophetic figures—Moses, Jesus, and Muhammad, respectively—and Abraham. In the broadest of terms: for Jews, Abraham's willingness to enter into a covenant with God, marked by the act of circumcision, established his chosenness, something that was handed down from Abraham to Isaac, from Isaac to Jacob, and from Jacob to his twelve sons and, from them, to the ancient Israelites and then to the Jewish people. For Christians, the relationship between God and Jesus in the New Testament is modeled on that of Abraham and Isaac in the Old, further legitimating the giving of the new covenant to Jesus's followers.[2] And in Islam, the relationship between Abraham and Muhammad is also crucial since, as a lineal descendant of Abraham, the latter becomes genealogically privy to the institution of prophecy.[3]

Through the mythic figure of Abraham three diverse religious traditions seek to legitimate themselves and, in the process, establish their authenticity by invoking the claim that they alone are Abraham's true, spiritual descendants. The present study is neither interested in adjudicating these religions' claims nor studying them in any detail. On the contrary, its purpose is to examine how and why, in recent years, the category "Abrahamic religions" has emerged as a vague referent and as an ecumenical term to explain the myths, structures, and historical interactions among these three religions. As used today, the term is a modern creation, largely a theological neologism. Although I shall eventually conclude that we should abandon using the term, the problem is actually much deeper. Our employment of "Abrahamic religions" is not simply a terminological mistake, but primarily a categorical one. Rethinking both the term and category must take the form of developing a new conceptual language that avoids positing discrete religious traditions interacting with and borrowing from one another, and that instead envisages complexity and porosity between manifold and overlapping subgroups within and among "religions."

Rather than claim that the category "Abrahamic religions" names some historical phenomenon, I instead argue that it functions simultaneously as a form of wish fulfillment and ecumenicism. Like many of the terms and categories we employ in the academic study of religion, it is artificial and imprecise, a modern projection that we then transcribe onto the historical record. The danger of employing such generic categories is that they blur our understanding of how diverse cultural formations— not three monolithic and essentialized religions—have historically intersected and thought with one another, defining themselves and others in the process. The desire to envisage Judaism, Christianity, and Islam as having the same "father" or as belonging to the same genus has resulted from deliberate or strategic misunderstanding and subsequently further magnifies it.

Although, as I shall demonstrate in chapter 3, the term originated in nonacademic circles, it has as of late become an academic one. Increasingly it is playing a role in the various ways that scholars of religion conceive of what was more traditionally called "Western" religions or even the "Judeo-Christian" tradition (now expanded to include Islam), both of which are equally imprecise. My interest in this monograph is in its *academic* use and abuse. I should make it clear at the outset that I have no quarrel with nonacademics who want to use a romantically conceived or imagined "Abraham" to encourage interfaith trialogue; if such a trialogue creates meaningful exchanges among Jews, Christians, and Muslims at the grassroots level, all the better. My main objection, and the subject of my study, is the invocation of "Abrahamic" as a heuristic principle that claims to do analytical work when it comes to understanding phenomena constructed as "religious" within the academy.

The "Abrahamic religions" discourse opens a window onto the manufacture and dissemination of historical myths. If we perpetuate a set of half-truths to facilitate interfaith trialogue or if we use the historical record solely to create a story that has contemporary relevance for us, then we cease to be transparent about the way we use our data, and we cease to be honest to ourselves and to one another. If theologians or scholars want to engage in ecumenical conversation, they should be clear that this is what they are doing. To invoke academic disciplines such as Religious Studies or History to facilitate such an agenda is to use these disciplines, with their respective critical discourses, in the service of something else. Too much of the academic discourse devoted to "Abrahamic religions" in recent years either buys into or seeks to justify ecumenical agendas.[4]

There exist many monographs that seek to tell us about "Abrahamic religions," but none of which reflects theoretically on the very term or category. The novelty of this study is that it presents a second or higher-order examination of this category, seeking to explore when, where, why, and how it developed. For "it is a truism," to use the words of Bruce Lincoln, "that there is much at stake in the words people use and in how they happen to use them."[5] Despite this, however, we rarely interrogate their meanings or histories. One of the primary aims of this study is to provide a metanarrative that contextualizes and, I trust, undermines the uses to which the narratives of "Abrahamic religions" have been put. It is not simply the case that this term was created to replace the less inclusive term "Judeo-Christian" in recent years. Rather the term, like all terms, carries in its wake a host of unchecked assumptions that, unless interrogated, threaten to undermine critical analysis. Too many of the words that we use in the academic study of religion, as I shall discuss in detail in chapter 5, are not innocent, but vectors of larger concepts.

My problem is not with the data, but with a category that functions as the guiding and organizing principle of data. It is not simply the case that we must replace "Abrahamic religions" with another, less ideologically loaded, term. Nor is it just a matter of words and semantics. Rather, I suggest that this critique gets to the very heart of how we organize data. The conceptualization of Judaism, Christianity, and Islam as monoliths that cohabit within the same religious genus (i.e., "Abrahamic religions") results from conceptual misunderstanding and, in the process, further exacerbates it. "Abrahamic religions," "religions of Abraham," "Abrahamic covenant," and "Abrahamic faiths" are all terms that denote a worrisome nebulousness. All are artificially constructed and all connote, in various ways, a vague sense of ecumenicism that implies something like the following: "If these three religions could only realize that they are all siblings who share the same father, Abraham, they might all just be able to get along in the modern period."

Such a statement, and the hermeneutics to which it gives rise, is highly misleading and inappropriate within the academic study of religion. It assumes something essential about the collection of historically disparate "Abrahamic" sources, and implies a genetic commonality to a diverse set of conceptions and practices that arose in various times and places as responses to various stimuli. This shared essence and other commonalities that flow from it are subsequently used to structure these three religions in ways that are both potentially unhelpful and misleading. What, for example, does a fifteenth-century Jewish cabalist from Salonika share with a twenty-first-century Sufi sheikh in, say, Pakistan? To claim that they both represent mystical currents pulsing through the "Abrahamic religions" does not tell us much. What is necessary, on the contrary, is to study "thickly" each of these two individuals in their immediate historical, social, cultural, religious, and intellectual contexts. Only then, perhaps, *may* it be possible to make some second-order generalizations and comparisons/contrasts between them. My concern, however, is that this is not done because the generic and monolithic "Abrahamic religions" potentially levels all historical and cultural differences.

Making "Abrahamic religions" my exemplum, the extended argument of this monograph amounts to a case study in the construction of categories in the academic study of religion, showing how, unless we are self-conscious, our use of categories can curtail understanding. Like many of the categories we employ in the academic study of religion, "Abrahamic religions" is of a decidedly modern provenance and is most likely not sufficiently justified as a strategy of categorization.

The data, the manifold phenomena that have come collectively to be called "Abrahamic," are a truly fascinating assortment of diverse religious imaginings. What the category "Abrahamic" threatens to do is collapse these difference in the quest for some sort of vaguely defined commonality, thereby ignoring the specifics of cultural interactions at particular historical moments for the sake of an artificially constructed universal. It is not helpful when three religions are routinely treated as though they are best understood when considered to be essentially the same, possessing the same ancestry, the same essential structures, the same religious disposition, and the same habits.

History

"History," to use the words of Arthur McCalla, "is not history when it is the history of religions."[6] In what follows, I make frequent appeals to "history" and the "historical record" as the more sober-minded counterpoint to the study of religion, something that is paradoxically known as the "history of religions."[7] I certainly do not mean to hold "History" up as the gold standard discipline against which those of us working in Religious Studies ought to measure ourselves.[8] Nor do I intend to use "History" as a vague referent with which to criticize those with whose interpretations I happen to disagree. However, I do think that detail-oriented and disinterested historical work provides one of the key antidotes to certain essentializing tendencies within our discipline in general, and that associated with "Abrahamic religions" in particular. This is because history forces us to localize and contextualize our data, thereby preventing us from making overarching generalizations. When we study the social, cultural, and legal interactions among Jews, Christians, and Muslims in ninth-century Baghdad, for example, we study particular groups of Jews, Christians, and Muslims interacting with one another at a particular time and in a particular place. We do not study, in other words, three generic mono-theistic religions interacting with one another ahistorically. The study of historical particulars ideally prevents the invocation of ahistorical catego-ries and all of the quasi-theological baggage they carry.

When I appeal to the "historical record" then, I refer to nothing more than primary sources, and the relevant intellectual and social contexts out of which they emerge. We must accordingly be wary of postulating that religions possess essences that move—Hegelian-like—throughout history, manifesting themselves in various times and places. Such a phe-nomenological model, one still in vogue among many who work with "religious" data, potentially ignores the conflict and creativity that goes on as various actors and groups seek to define and legitimate themselves by appealing to concepts that they understand as "authentic religious teach-ings." The issue, of course, is not that they are "authentic," but the ways in which they are imagined to be. The historical record forces us to pay attention to matters such as these, cautioning us from forcing categories and other heuristic models on concrete particulars.

This certainly does not mean that we cannot nor should not theo-rize or analyze our datasets, and simply content ourselves with descrip-tive analyses. The point I wish to draw attention to here is the distortion that emerges from the collision of historical particulars and ahistorical categories. It is this collision that I refer to in my subtitle as "the uses and abuses of history." Many invested in the "Abrahamic religions" dis-course, whether supersessionist or ecumenical, make vague and often uninformed appeals to history both to justify and legitimate their largely ahistorical claims. Both Christian and Muslim theologians in the pre-modern world (and many to this day), for example, have had no qualms about saying history was on their side when they argued that Jesus represented the true fulfillment of the covenant of Abraham or that Muhammad appeared to restore Abraham's original religion. But these are *not* historical claims. They are the stuff of theological dogma and must be contextualized as such.

In like manner, when contemporary ecumenicists appeal to the "Golden Age" of tolerance witnessed in a place such as tenth- and eleventh-century Cordoba in Muslim Spain, they are rarely interested in the particulars of the interactions among these three religions "on the ground." On the contrary, they make appeals to categories that carry much valence in the modern world (such as "tolerance"), but that clearly would have had little or no meaning in the time in question. Again, as an ahistorical category,

"Abrahamic religions" is invoked to delineate a set of qualities that can subsequently be used in the quest for interfaith understanding. However, the term is still every bit as ahistorical and essential as its supersessionist predecessors. The claims of both supersessionists and ecumenicists are predicated on historical myths. Only by returning to the historical record can we begin to rethink our conceptual modeling used to interpret and explain the contours of the manifold interactions of various groups.

Caricatures, Clichés, and Misunderstandings

Although there exist certain family resemblances or commonalities among the three religions, there exists no compelling reasons for creating an omnibus canopy under which manifold Judaisms, Christianities, and Islams neatly cohabit. Their resemblances or commonalities have nothing to do with a shared essence or with a religious patrimony. Rather, many of the similarities that we perceive in these three religions are the result of real historical interactions. For example, that Paul would emphasize the Abrahamic roots of Jesus's message or that Muhammad would perceive himself as the restorer of the original "religion of Abraham" (*millat Ibrāhīm*) is not an essential property that clearly reveals their "Abrahamic roots," but an ideological move to legitimate the new in light of the old. Or, when in the modern world these three religions are invoked in various military conflicts such as the Middle East, it is not helpful to say that this is a "family squabble."[9]

My goal in dismantling the category "Abrahamic religions" is certainly not to deny the undeniable fact that these three traditions have intersected, interacted, and struggled with one another throughout history. My objection is when we try to account for such relations by invoking essentialist and monolithic traditions that admit of little or no nuance. Instead, I argue that we must find new conceptual language to explain both the particulars and the diversity of such interactions. The generic, amorphous, and increasingly politically correct "Abrahamic religions," I maintain, prevents us from understanding the complex nature of contact and cross-pollination. Positing a perceived common or shared origin may result in overlooking the particulars of historical interactions because we have already convinced ourselves that we can reduce such complex interactions to a common source, that is, to Abraham.

It is perhaps worth pointing out early in this study that the term "Abrahamic religions" has absolutely no historical precedent. It is, as I mentioned earlier, a theological neologism. The premodern world literally had no such term for these three religions since the category is largely a modern construction. This means that none of the religions that are now classified as "Abrahamic" have ever used this term to refer to themselves prior to the last twenty years and, because of this, they most certainly have never used this term before this period as a shared rubric with which to engage in dialogue with one another. If anything, these three religions have tried to force their understanding of Abraham on each other, killed one another in his name, and imagined themselves and themselves alone as the true recipient of the Abrahamic covenant.

In the past several years the term "Abrahamic religions" has become so protean that it really has no meaning whatsoever. We witness, for example, "Abrahamic" interpretations of pluralism, of gender, of the environment, and so on.[10] But this desire for commonality actually levels diversity both between and within these traditions. A common and omnibus rubric, in other words, threatens local traditions, putting at risk all those many particularities that do not neatly fit a hermeneutic that has been created for other purposes.

In the place of such wide-ranging diversity we often find caricatures and clichés based on vague and indefinable traits. We are told, for example, that "Abrahamic religions" put a lot of stock in traits such as monotheism, ethics, and faith. Such a narrative, however, sidesteps or completely overlooks the thorny issues of how each of these traits were created, the various ways in which each has been imagined, the contexts in which they were created, and how they often emerged based on complex interactions with "non-Abrahamic" traditions.

Certainly serious work into these three religions must involve a certain amount of caricature.[11] We make certain generalizations for the sake of appreciating something in one tradition or data set with that in another. But, as J. Z. Smith reminds us, we must realize that we are doing this for the sake of *our* own theoretical interests. We must be cautious of transcribing our own interests onto the data we examine and, from there, onto the natural world. There is the omnipresent danger, in other words, that the caricatures that we use in our own work might well become fixed as clichés that inhibit understanding.

There certainly exists an inexhaustible assortment of sources, movements, and submovements within Judaism, Christianity, and Islam. However, the constant repetition of clichés and caricatures such as those mentioned above risk subsuming them under artificially constructed

rubrics. Continual references to what "Abrahamic religions" believe or pro-
fess about any given topic, or features that characterize "Abrahamic religions" by making them distinct from so-called "non-Abrahamic" religions
have created the impression of a generalized historical and social unity for
which there exists no evidence and against which there is much.

Dislocating Essences

This is certainly not to make the claim that each of these three religions—
Judaism, Christianity, and Islam—exist in hermetically sealed vacu-
ums. On the contrary, as I alluded to above, it makes much more sense
to break each of these religions down so that the very terms "Judaism,"
"Christianity," and "Islam" do not represent three discrete essences, but
become canopies under which multiple Judaisms, Christianities, and
Islams cohabit. Once we do this, we begin to witness the fixed and often
heavily patrolled borders between these three discrete traditions begin to
break down and even collapse. On the microlevel, we begin to encounter subgroups from each of the three religions that resemble one another
more closely with respect to particular features than they do other subgroups within the same religion. It is unfortunate that much of our intellectual energy is expended on what is going on at the macro level that we
often lose sight of what is happening at the microlevel.[12]

If essentialist terms such as Judaism, Christianity, or Islam add a lens
of distortion to the particulars of how subgroups within each of these
three religions interact with one another, even vaguer terms, such as
"Abrahamic religions," add an additional one. It is in the overlapping and
complex interactions between Judaisms, Christianities, and Islams that
we encounter various struggles, skirmishes, and the desire to imagine
manifold identity formations. To reduce these complexities to the singular of each tradition, let alone to move a step further and use a name that
subsumes within it all three monolithic traditions, is decidedly unhelpful.
As a typological category "Abrahamic religions" is of extremely limited
use not only because it is historically inaccurate, as I suggested above, but
also because it increasingly functions as a laborsaving device that is con-
ducive to anachronism, caricature, and eisegesis.

Rather than use vague terms such as "Abrahamic" or other simplistic
designations to fit an already selected body of data, it is high time to think
about creating a new theoretical language to account better for the fluidity between "religions" and the borders that separate them. Rather than

say, for example, that Judaism, Christianity, and a nascent Islam existed in seventh-century Arabia, it might be more useful to try to specify which types or subgroups of these larger, less helpful generic terms existed. It may well be the case that the traditional words we employ to describe such interactions are not even helpful.

New models must be based on more suitable and less problematic categories for sorting through these and other data. Only by engaging in thick analyses based on particular historical interactions is it possible to get an adequate sense of how these religions have struggled with, thought with, and defined themselves against one another. Once this occurs, of course, it should become clear that general and leveling terms such as "Abrahamic religions" are of very little academic utility.

"Abrahamic": From Theology to Academy

Chapters 2 through 4 tell the story of where our modern category came from. From its polemical origins in Christian and Muslim theological writings that were used to show their respective claims to a variously constructed pristine Abrahamic message and to discredit the claims of their rivals, Abraham represented an ancient authenticity. Jews claimed to be the direct descendants of Abraham, Christians to be his spiritual heirs, and Muslims to be the true practitioners of Abraham's original religion. All these claims, however, are predicated on establishing legitimacy in an environment of rival and competing claims of religious superiority. Note that no religion in the premodern world invokes Abraham or "Abrahamic" to denote commonality or interfaith relations. Although I shall explore this in greater detail in the following chapter, suffice it to mention in the present context that Abraham is so important in rival claims to legitimacy because he exists prior to Moses and the revelation of the commandments on Mount Sinai. Both Christians and Muslims, in other words, perceive Abraham as living prior to the reception of the Law and, thus, as living before the earliest articulation of Judaism. Abraham, in other words, can neatly and anachronistically be constructed as a pre-Jewish Christian or a pre-Jewish Muslim.

Increasingly in the middle of the twentieth century several voices in Europe—responding to the horrors associated with the Second World War, the colonialist legacy, and problems between Jews and Arabs in the newly formed State of Israel—began to search for a way forward. Abraham was now held up by many as the common origin of the three monotheisms

and a representative of a shared heritage in the fight against the cata-
strophic effects of secular materialism. Most symbolic of this change in
orientation is the fact that some of the documents associated with the
Second Vatican Council—Vatican II—began to speak of an "Abrahamic
heritage." While still acknowledging the superiority of the Church, for
the first time we clearly witness Abraham as the focal point for interfaith
trialogue.

After the attacks of September 11, 2001, the full-scale "Abrahamic religions" discourse was created. No longer perceived to be the shield against
the forces of irreligion or materialism as it had in the 1950s and 1960s,
it now became an ecumenical term to promote peaceful relations among
the three religions at a time when they were perceived to be increasingly
hostile to one another. Taken as an antidote against the "clash of civilizations" thesis proposed by the likes of Bernard Lewis and Samuel
Huntington,[3] "Abrahamic religions" was meant to show the common
origin and history these three religions share with an eye toward their
future coexistence.

Although I shall explore these issues in much greater detail in the
pages that follow, the point to underscore here is that all of the instantia-
tions of the term "Abrahamic" mentioned above—from the supersessionist to the ecumenical—were and are largely theological. Whether to argue
for the superiority of one's own religion or to provide an interfaith space
wherein the three religions can expatiate on common ground, the term
has always been invoked with a theological agenda. Despite this, we continue to use the term as if it denotes some sort of historical referent.

"Abrahamic Religions" as Exemplum

Yet, as chapter 5 reveals, this genealogy is perhaps not unique to the category "Abrahamic religions." In the introduction to *Imagining Religion*,
J. Z. Smith argues that, for the self-conscious student of religion, no data
set is inherently interesting.[4] Data, facts, philological study, and so forth
only become interesting when we connect them to larger and more fundamental issues within the academic study of religion. It is these larger
questions that enable religionists to communicate with one another and
not simply stake out their own territory in various subfields within various area or ethnic studies.

I follow the lead of Smith in what follows and conceive of my data
set—that is, "Abrahamic religions"—as connected to the uses, misuses,

and abuses to which history can be put within the academic study of religion. Frequently for those interested in doing historical work within the study of religion there looms the confrontation with those who study the same data but who want to filter it through an interfaith, ecumenical, or ahistorical prism. Too often there is a tendency within academic circles to conflate fact with fiction, thereby mistaking salvation history with history. In this respect "Abrahamic religions" functions as an exempli gratia, or "e.g.," of the tension between the study of history and the study of religion, between trying to study the past on its own terms and reading into it what we would like the past to have been.[15]

In so doing, I use "Abrahamic religions" as a microcosm through which to examine some of the ways in which the discipline of Religious Studies forms its categories. This categorical formation is not solely an intellectual endeavor, but is based on a host of political, ideological, and theological agendas. Unless we work through the genealogical heritage of our categories, preferring instead to see them as natural terms that simply reflect and name phenomena in the world, we risk distortion. Such an undertaking will ideally enable us to free ourselves from the shackles of liberal Protestant theologizing, which has largely defined the field since its origins in the late-nineteenth and early twentieth centuries.

So many of the terms that we employ—from the disciplinary ones such as "religion" and "experience" to more recent ones, like "Abrahamic religions"—are not value-neutral. On the contrary, they emerge at particular historical moments and, as such, reflect these moments and their concerns. The unfortunate corollary of this is that, even if we recognize or acknowledge their particularity, we tend to assume that they represent universal and cross-cultural characteristics. It is extremely important to our disciplinary wellbeing that we reflect upon the terms we use, all of which have histories and genealogies. Unless we do this, we risk repeating past mistakes and mistaking the constructed for the real.

Since it is of fairly recent provenance, "Abrahamic religions" ideally permits us to illumine the processes and assumptions of our disciplinary and categorical formations. For this reason I provide an extended meditation on the term as an exemplum of how we imagine, create, disseminate, and maintain our categories within the academic study of religion. The results, I trust, will be of interest even to those not directly working in the area of the so-called "Abrahamic religions."

Beyond "Abrahamic Religions"

Boundaries that we now assume to be clearly defined and patrolled were not always that way, as is explored in the final chapter. Rather than apply categories that we think of today as disinterested and objective, we ought to recognize that they are often the end products of much conflict and contestation. All of the three religions that comprise the category "Abrahamic religions"—"Judaism," "Christianity," and "Islam"—have been and indeed still are highly contested. Intellectual and/or comparative focus should be directed not at the potential for peaceful coexistence among these three essentialized religions, but at the points at which they overlap, often becoming indistinct from one another in the process. My interest here is in the shared and often liquid borders between various subcultures that exist within each "religion." How do they go about perceiving themselves (and others), and defining themselves (and others) in the process, in the creation of various overlapping identities?

It should be clear by now that I am not seeking to replace the term "Abrahamic religions" with a better one. My problem is not the term but, to reiterate, the category and the way that this category claims to perform intellectual work, when in point of fact it levels various data in such a manner that we miss out on the dynamic and creative work of self- and other-making. Rather than witness three essentially discrete traditions interacting with one another, we need to begin the process of rethinking our notions of exchange and interchange, especially when it comes to understanding what occurs along the porous boundaries of these three traditions. Rather than see "Jews," "Christians," and "Muslims" working with or against one another, we need to imagine a set of shared cultural vocabularies or semantics that various subcultures within each of the so-called religions either share or resist at particular historical moments.

Only when we begin to engage in such intellectual activity will we be able to get a better sense of how "religions" interact with one another. Rather than use categories developed in theological circles, we must develop and sharpen our own that emerge from witnessing the particulars of historical exchanges and interchanges.

I

What Are "Abrahamic Religions"?

AS THE AMERICAN public was beginning to recover from the trauma of 9/11, a small book appeared bearing the title *Abraham: A Journey to the Heart of Three Faiths*. In it, Bruce Feiler, a well-known journalist and *New York Times* best-selling author, sought to chart a path of global reconciliation among Jews, Christians, and Muslims. In the place of traditional interfaith slogans and dicta, he boldly proclaimed that what we most needed was a "foundation," a bedrock, something that would embody "the monotheistic ideals of faith in God and righteous behavior toward humanity."[1] Such a foundation was necessary, Feiler opined, because it had the potential to take us back in time, to an ideal "that existed *before* the religions themselves existed."[2] What the world most needed, in other words, was Abraham.

Wittingly or not, Feiler was here giving expression to an ecumenical discourse that has rapidly been picking up steam over the last few decades. Since this discourse regards Abraham as the progenitor of Judaism, Christianity, and Islam—the father of the so-called "Abrahamic religions"—it not surprisingly also perceives him functioning as the model for subsequent interfaith coexistence. This is not the Abraham in whose name or understanding three rival monotheisms have been excluding (and killing) one another for millennia, but a newly repackaged interfaith Abraham who fulfills the modern role of peacemaker.

In the same year that Feiler's book appeared, *Time* magazine put Abraham on its front cover, with the title "The Legacy of Abraham." The lead article proclaimed that "excluding God, Abraham is the only biblical figure who enjoys the unanimous acclaim of all three faiths, the only one referred to by all three as Father."[3] Since the attacks of 9/11, organizations throughout the United States and the world have been engaging in "Abrahamic lectures," "Abrahamic summits," and "Abrahamic salons."

The common denominator of these events, as well as such books and magazine articles, is to get people from different faiths to gather together to discuss issues of commonality. Tens, perhaps even hundreds, of thousands of people throughout the Western world have convened in the name of Abraham, now held up as the source of the three religions and as the common heritage of Jews, Christians, and Muslims. Abraham, according to this paradigm, is "the seed of hope" for reconciliation among his "children."[4]

This interfaith conversation has, for reasons to be discussed in the pages that follow, crossed over into the academic study of religion. With an increasing consensus, "Abrahamic religions" has become an intellectual category. We now have, for example, endowed chairs of Abrahamic religions, courses devoted to teaching their so-called "common origins" and subsequent development, academic conferences convened in the name of this patriarch, and so on. The result is that "Abrahamic religions" is increasingly perceived both to name a historical reality and to perform real analytical work. The many uses of the adjective "Abrahamic"—whether to refer to religions, a covenant, faith, or other such phenomena—are perceived to delineate something natural in the world. This reverse hermeneutic essentially uses a category, one that was invented for the sake of interfaith awareness, and subsequently projects it onto the historical record. It can then be located in this record—in places such as the "interfaith utopia" of "Golden Age" Spain—and held up as an exemplar for modern readers to try to emulate.

"Abrahamic religions" here functions as an exemplum of a larger issue in the academic study of religion: how do we create and use terms and categories? What do these terms and categories contribute to disciplinary formation? Unless we are cautious of whence our categories derive, if we simply import interfaith vocabulary and assume that it then performs analytical work, our attempts to understand religion as a social and cultural practice become highly problematic.[5] Within this context, "Abrahamic religions," like so many of the categories we employ in the academic study of religion, is both grounded and invested in quasi-theological and ecumenical desires.

It is accordingly necessary for us to shift focus from *what* and *why* we study, which has received the overwhelming energy of our disciplinary focus, to *how* we study. That is, what words and concepts do we use (and not use) to isolate and compare our data? As Jonathan Z. Smith constantly reminds us, it is part of our job as scholars to "expose the set of tacit understandings which inform, but are rarely the objects of, our corporate discourse about religion."[6] Attention to words and categories is crucial to this enterprise because these, more than anything else, are ultimately responsible for how we bring our objects of study into existence.

If we just use the terms and categories that religious actors use to describe what they are doing or if we simply recycle religious terms and employ them as if they were analytical signifiers, our enterprise risks distortion. If we assume, for example, that "religion" is a valid cross-cultural category, or that to each religion there is an eternal essence that undergoes temporal metamorphoses, we potentially overlook the various conflicts and contestations of rival ideologies that seek to impose their understandings and interpretations on others. The academic study of religion, in other words, should not be about facilitating interfaith or multicultural understanding, but about attempting to understand the uses and abuses of religion in specific cultural contexts.

That which we imprecisely label as "Abrahamic religions" comes at a cost, and if we continue to use this term (which I do not think we should), we must be absolutely clear and transparent about what it is and is not, what it can and cannot do. Like so many of the terms we use in the academic study of religion, it has become such a protean label that it has lost, if it ever had, any reliably identifiable meaning. The term has come to mean, both among popular and scholarly audiences, too much and, as a result, far too little. Often employed in contemporaneous discourse as a replacement for the equally vague "Western" or "Judeo-Christian" religions, "Abrahamic" is far too generic and imprecise. What counts as an Abrahamic religion? Obviously those who employ it tend to refer to the triumvirate of Judaism, Christianity, and Islam. But what, if anything, do these three religions have in common other than a belief in God and the notion that each later manifestation legitimates its claim to superiority based on supersessionist arguments. Certainly at particular historical moments two or three of these religions, or parts thereof, have intersected with one another, whether creatively or destructively. But to argue from this that there exists some core of "Abrahamness" that all three share is highly contentious.

"Abrahamic religions," as used in much contemporary literature, is an interfaith term meant to show historical commonality and imply future reconciliation. However, it does not follow from this that it ought to be employed as either a historical or a heuristic category. Rather than use it as something to enumerate a set of features—for example, creation, revelation, and redemption—that each of these religions is perceived to share, we need to acknowledge and appreciate difference. By invoking the adjective "Abrahamic," it seems to me we level or flatten difference for the sake of an overarching unity or sameness. To say, for instance, that there exists an "Abrahamic" notion of revelation or an "Abrahamic" conception of scripture says very little beyond the fact that religions perceived to have their origins in Abraham possess a scripture that many take to be the transcript of divine revelation. It does not tell us, for example, about interpretive strategies and the various material conditions from which such strategies emerge.

Perhaps most importantly there is very little to no historical evidence that these three religions ever believed that they shared a common understanding of scripture or anything else for that matter. If anything, adherents of these religions have accused and persecuted one another precisely for their perceived misunderstandings. To say now, in the present, that there exists a common or shared "Abrahamic" framework is grossly inaccurate. And while it might certainly make some sense to do this, say, at an "Abrahamic salon," or to encourage interfaith dialogue, it makes absolutely no sense to employ it as an academic or even quasi-academic term.

***

On the face of it, Abraham might seem an unlikely protagonist to be the "father" of three religions. He was, for instance, someone who sold his wife into prostitution, someone who impregnated his slave, and, once she gave birth to a son, cast them both out into the wilderness to die. At the behest of a dream, he took his other son up to the mountains and would have killed him were it not for some sort of an act of divine intervention. Yet, despite these actions, all three religions hold Abraham up as the exemplar of faith and courage. My interest in what follows is not in this individual, however, but the adjective to which his name gave rise, that is, "Abrahamic."

I think the term "Abrahamic" is less about the mythic figure of Abraham, whose story is initially recounted in the book of Genesis, than it is about the fact that he predates the specifically Israelite/Jewish revelation at Mount Sinai. Although any pre-Mosaic character could ostensibly be used (e.g., Adam, Enoch, Isaac), the extended narratological focus that Genesis puts on Abraham makes him a perfect candidate for subsequent and rival interpretations. Since he is not a Jew, a Christian, or a Muslim, partisans of each subsequent denomination can shape and manipulate him as they see fit. For Jews, he can be read as upholding the later Jewish virtue of covenantal obligation; for Christians, Abraham becomes the model of faith; whereas for Muslims, Ibrahim, as he is called in that faith, becomes the paradigm of submission to God's will. All three traditions, then, locate in Abraham their origins and subsequently find in him the end point of their quest for legitimation. When these three virtues— covenantal obligation, faith, submission—were put together, the modern myth of Abraham as the father of all monotheistic believers arose.[7]

Although he originally appears in the Hebrew Bible, Abraham does so before Moses and the revelation that determines the specifics of what Israeliteness (and, subsequently, Jewishness) means. Although he is the recipient of a covenant that establishes him as the father of a great nation, the biblical narrative nowhere names this nation specifically (but certainly implies that it will be Israel). Abraham also appears in the New Testament and the Quran, only now as the shining exemplum of faith and obedience to God. A foreshadower of both Jesus and Muhammad, Abraham is sub- sequently crafted into a religious ideal for one and all. This is what makes him such a malleable figure. This malleability also seems to be behind the modern desire to make him into the ideal for interreligious reconciliation.

All three religions have historically sought to imagine Abraham in their own image and thereby fashion themselves as his true spiritual heir. This is not the same thing, however, as saying that "Abrahamic" religions, for example, possess a set of "shared beliefs and values."[8] Or, as others might frame this modern ecumenical discourse, that "each of the three Abrahamic religions envisages a world in which human beings would actively promote actions orientated toward peace and justice. These actions are expected to be both moral and efficacious, and they rule out the possibility of using unethical means, such as violence, or at least unqual- ified violence."[9] Nor, it seems to me, can this appellation account for their perceived "common roots, their evolution over time...and their striking resemblances and their equally striking differences."[10] If anything, what Judaism, Christianity, and Islam do is construct three rival versions of Abraham, claim that their construction is not only the most valid but the only valid one, and, in the process, discredit the constructions of their rivals. These three religions actively construct Abrahams in specific his- torical contexts. What they do not do is inherit an interfaith Abraham. The patriarch Abraham, in other words, has been used historically more to exclude than to include, to kill rather than to establish peace.

If it is ideally the goal of terms and categories to make the natural world clearer and easier to sort out, what happens when we employ terms that do the opposite? We are frequently told, for example, that "Abrahamic religions" share equally—as the quotations in the previous paragraph demonstrate—vague concepts such as monotheism, faith, and ethics that can presumably be used to distinguish them from other religions (often referred to as the "Eastern" or "non-Abrahamic" religions). This caricature, like all caricatures, involves both essentialism and distortion. The result is that we risk making something like "Abrahamic religions" into a cliché that prevents us from adequately understanding or being able to classify the data in question. The goal of our analyses should not be greater simplification, but an appreciation of complexity and the messiness that goes with it, and the creation of new taxonomic models to classify it adequately, if imperfectly.

Naming Abraham

At the heart of this book resides not the figure of Abraham, but the adjective to which his mythic persona would eventually give rise: "Abrahamic." Before proceeding, however, it might be worthwhile to provide a basic overview of both the general myth of Abraham and the subsequent narrative permutations that it would undergo.[11] What we know about Abraham emerges from several narrative sources, beginning with the account found in Genesis 11:31–25:18, as well as later expansions supplied by rabbinic commentators including various midrashic collections. Owing to the fact that he is also upheld as the progenitor of both Christianity and Islam, we also encounter him, albeit with less extensive narrative focus and with different emphases, in the New Testament, especially within the letters of Paul, and scattered throughout the Quran. Because of Abraham's importance to these two later traditions, there is also much said about him in subsequent Christian and Muslim theological writings. To get a full sense of Abraham in these respective traditions is a scholarly desideratum, and such a study, if done historically as opposed to theologically, would ideally provide tremendous insights into the rival constructions of Abraham. Needless to say, such a study is beyond the purview of the present volume.

Abram, as he was originally called prior to God's injunction to change his name to Abraham in Genesis 17:5, was a nomadic patriarch. His entrance into scriptural history is associated with the departure from his idolatrous kith and kin in search of the one true God of monotheism:

> The Lord said to Abram, "Go forth from your native land and from your father's house to the land that I will show you.
> I will make of you a great nation,

And I will bless you;
I will make your name great,
And you shall be a blessing.
I will bless those who bless you
And curse him that curses you;
And all the families of the earth
Shall bless themselves by you." (Gen. 12:1–3)[12]

What God here offers Abraham is a covenantal relationship. In exchange
for continued fidelity, both he and his offspring will be rewarded materially and spiritually. As they make their way to the land of Canaan,
Abraham and his wife, Sarai (later to be called Sarah, at the same time
that Abram changes his name to Abraham), encounter many hardships.
However, not once does Abraham appear to doubt the initial call that
told him to leave his ancestral home for a new land promised to him and
his offspring. Since they have no children, we witness very early on in
the narrative a struggle over inheritance—a struggle, according to some
commentators and readers, that can be found reverberating until today.
Unable to bear children, Sarah suggests that Abraham father a child
with her Egyptian maidservant, Hagar. Sarah, however, comes to regret
her suggestion and subsequently treats Hagar harshly, at which point
the latter runs away. In the desert, an angel of the Lord appears to her
and says:

I will greatly increase your offspring,
And they shall be too many to count...
Behold you are with child
And shall bear a son;
You shall call him Ishmael.
For the Lord has paid heed to your suffering.
He shall be a wild ass of a man;
His hand against everyone,
And everyone's hand against him;
He shall dwell alongside all of his kinsmen. (Gen. 16:10–12)

Hagar returns to Abraham's household and subsequently gives birth to
a son, whom not surprisingly she names Ishmael. God again appears to
Abraham and informs him that Sarah, now ninety years old, will herself

become pregnant with a son, subsequently to be named Isaac. In the
words of Genesis:

> Sarah your wife shall bear you a son, and you shall name him
> Isaac; and I will maintain my covenant with him as an everlasting
> covenant for his offspring to come. As for Ishmael, I have heeded
> you. I hereby bless him. I will make him fertile and exceedingly
> numerous. He shall be the father of twelve chieftains, and I will
> make of him a great nation. But my covenant I will maintain with
> Isaac, whom Sarah will bear to you at this season next year. (Gen.
> 17:19–21)

After Isaac's birth, undoubtedly worried about inheritance rights, Sarah
asks Abraham to dismiss Hagar and Ishmael, which Abraham does with
a heavy heart. The next morning, Hagar and Ishmael leave and wander
off into the Negev, a desert where presumably they will die. Neither per-
ishes, however. God, upon seeing them, sends an angel, who supplies
them with a well of water.[13]

Skipping ahead to the Quran, we read that Abraham did not simply dismiss Ishmael and Hagar from his house, but in fact traveled with them to
the Arabian Peninsula via the Negev desert. There Abraham and Ishmael
built the Kaaba, the cubed, stone house that to this day stands in the heart
of Mecca (see Quran 2:125).[14] Another Arabo-Islamic narrative tradition
has Abraham and Ishmael rebuild that Kaaba, which had originally been
built by Adam, the first man (and, by Muslim accounts, the first *muslim*). Although later generations of Muslims would subsequently identify
Ishmael as the father of the Arabs, there is little evidence that Muhammad
made this connection, "much less," in the words of F. E. Peters, "that
either he or his followers were blood descendants of Abraham."[15] At this
point, Abraham apparently returns to his family and the further events
of the Genesis narrative unfold, although the later Islamic tradition tells
us that Abraham would also make occasional visits to Ishmael and his
family in Mecca.[16]

When we return to the Genesis account and pick up Abraham's story
there, we next encounter one of the most dramatic scenes in Western literature,[17] the divine call to Abraham to sacrifice his son Isaac.

> God put Abraham to the test. He said to him, "Abraham," and he
> replied "Here I am." And He said, "Take your son, your favored

one, Isaac, whom you love, and go to the land of Moriah, and offer him there as a burnt offering on one of the heights that I will point out to you." (Gen. 22:1–2)

Abraham and Isaac set out three days later at daybreak, and make their way to the land of Moriah as directed by God. Once there, Abraham asks Isaac to carry the wood on the pretext that it will be used to sacrifice a sheep for a burnt offering. Once father and son arrive at the appointed place,

> Abraham built an altar there; he laid out the wood; he bound his son Isaac; he laid him on the altar, on top of the wood. And Abraham picked up the knife to slay his son. Then an angel of the Lord called to him from heaven: "Abraham! Abraham!" And he answered, "Here I am." And he said, "Do not raise your hand against the boy, or do anything to him, for now I know that you fear God, since you have not withheld your son, your favored one, from Me." (Gen. 22:9–12)

Although the Quran also recounts this story (in Quran 37:102–113), it nowhere specifies which son Abraham intended to sacrifice. Indeed, the early Muslim commentary tradition debates which son the Quranic narrative refers to.[18] Some, most notably al-Tabari, argue that the son was in fact Isaac, whereas the majority opinion, the one that ultimately carried the day, is that the unnamed Quranic son is in fact Ishmael, presumably related to the fact that Muslims in the generations after Muhammad increasingly identified Ishmael as the ancestor of the Arabs. This connection was so important because it not only established the prophetic pedigree of Muhammad, but also made monotheism part of the Arab birthright.

Finally, at the age of 175, Abraham breathed his last breath. According to tradition, he was buried with his wife Sarah at the Cave of Machpelah. At his funeral we are told that both Isaac and Ishmael were present (Gen. 25:9) in an act of perceived reconciliation. The second-century BCE *Book of Jubilees* informs us that just before his death Abraham gathered all his children and grandchildren around him and told them that they should continue to observe the ritual act of circumcision, maintain ritual purity, and refrain from marrying any of their children to the Canaanites, the sworn enemy of the ancient Israelites.[19]

Today in Hebron, about twenty-five miles south of Jerusalem, one can still visit and pay one's respects to Abraham at the place believed to be the Cave of Machpelah. There, Jews and Muslims have prayed alongside one another, in their different ways, until one Purim/Ramadan morning in 1994 when, as we saw in the Introduction, Baruch Goldstein, a radical Jewish settler originally from Brooklyn, opened fire and killed twenty-nine Muslim worshippers. To this day, Hebron remains a lightning rod of the Palestinian–Israeli conflict, and the shrine to Abraham—reflective of its larger context—has become a complex amalgam of religious devotion, sectarian violence, and delicate political negotiation.

The Importance of Abraham

Since all three of these religions now either refer to themselves or are referred to by others as "Abrahamic," it is necessary to inquire into what exactly it is about the figure of Abraham that makes him the perceived symbol of commonality. Is it simply because he appears in the books regarded as sacred by Jews, Christians, and Muslims? Is Abraham important because he shows obedience to God? Is there something about his persona that somehow structures the subsequent theological elaborations within and between these three traditions?

Surely there are many other shared individuals from the religious myths of Judaism, Christianity, and Islam that also represent the same virtues he does? For example, we could easily point to Moses in Judaism, Jesus in Christianity, and Muhammad in Islam. It seems most likely, however, that Abraham draws significance from his "chronological" placement. Since he exists prior to the Mosaic revelation at Sinai, Abraham becomes a figure or a trope that later monotheists can use to legitimate themselves without literally buying into the Jewish message of chosenness. Because he is prior to the religion of ancient Israel articulated by Moses at Sinai, Abraham can accordingly be imagined or constructed as not only upholding Christian or Muslim values, but as being an actual (pre-Jewish) Christian or Muslim. It is for this reason that we frequently hear contemporary appeals to Abraham as a figure of commonality—and thus of reconciliation—among the three religions, a role that other biblical figures quite simply cannot perform.

Connecting Abraham

Judaism, Christianity, and Islam all trace their roots back to Abraham. To do this, however, they must discredit the claims of their rivals. Although it may seem natural to posit that Judaism has the strongest claim on Abraham because he appears originally in the Hebrew Bible, both Christianity and Islam assert that they are Abraham's true spiritual heirs. The subsequent story among these rival accounts is not one of peace and reconciliation, as ecumenicists would have us believe, but one of disjuncture and displacement, of loss and betrayal.

As descendants of Abraham, through his son Isaac and grandson Jacob, Jews connect their chosenness to the covenantal promise that we have already encountered between God and Abraham in Genesis 12:1–3. For Jews, realizing that the tradition is anything but a monolith,[20] Abraham, especially in his response to what the later rabbinic tradition referred to as the *Akedah* or binding (of Isaac), proves his obedience to God. It is this obedience that is subsequently upheld as a virtue of devotion, especially devotion to the Law.

Early Jewish followers of Jesus, later to become known as Christians, also claimed to be following in the footsteps of Abraham. They put their faith in Jesus as the promised Messiah in the same manner that Abraham put his faith in God, so much so that he was willing to sacrifice his own son. If Jews see in Abraham the model for obedience (i.e., to the Law), Christians see in him the paradigm or prototype of faith. As articulated by Paul in his letter to the Romans:

> For this reason it is by faith so that it may be by grace, with the result that the promise may be certain to all the descendants—not only to those who are under the law, but also to those who have the faith of Abraham, who is the father of us all....Against hope Abraham believed in hope.... He did not waver in unbelief about the promise of God but was strengthened in faith, giving glory to God. He was fully convinced that what God promised he was also able to do. [This] was not written only for Abraham's sake, but also for our sake, to whom it will be credited, those who believe in the one who raised Jesus our Lord from the dead. He was given over because of our transgressions and was raised for the sake of our justification. (Rom. 4:16–25)[21]

Abraham here becomes a foreshadower who prefigures God's plan to have his own son, Jesus, die on the cross as a substitute or sacrifice for humanity. Abraham's willingness to give up his own son Isaac is seen, in this view, as a precursor to the willingness of God the Father to sacrifice his only son. Similarities are also noted between the submission of Isaac and Jesus during their ordeals: both choose to lay down their own lives in order for the will of God to be accomplished. Both stories also portray the participants carrying the wood for their own sacrifice up a mountain.

For Muslims, who regard submission (*islām*) to God as the foremost religious virtue, both Abraham and Ishmael submit their wills to God, showing that they are not afraid to sacrifice everything to the divine Will. In this respect Muslims regard Abraham as among the first *muslims* and, as such, he provides the paradigm for modern Muslims. The Quran, for example, states that

> Abraham was neither a Jew nor a Christian, he was a man of pure faith; one who surrendered [i.e., was a *muslim*]. He was not one of those who associate others with God. (Quran 3:67)[22]

According to subsequent Quranic commentary, the biblical Mount Moriah, the place where Isaac was to be sacrificed, is identified with Marwah, a mountain near the Kaaba. To this day, Abraham's willingness to submit to God is celebrated and commemorated by Muslims during the holy day known as *eid al-adha* ("the Feast of the Sacrifice"), which takes place at the end of the *hajj* or annual pilgrimage to Mecca. During the festival, those who can afford it sacrifice or pay to have sacrificed a ram, cow, sheep, or camel. The sacrificial meat is eaten and what remains is distributed to the poor.

The Struggle over Inheritance

From the above account, several salient features begin to emerge. First, when these disparate narratives concerning Abraham are put together they form a putative "Abrahamic" narrative. Although this narrative nowhere exists in its entirety, each subsequent iteration of it seems to depend on its precedents. The New Testament account, for example, could not exist without the Old Testament version, and the Quranic account depends, at least rudimentarily, on those found in both the Old and New Testaments. Second, even though this grand, tripartite Abrahamic myth nowhere exists as a coherent narrative, it has been imagined and invoked in recent years either as proof of, or to prove, the existence of something referred to as "Abrahamic religions," the "religions of Abraham," or the "Children of Abraham." Third, despite the perceived existence of some common Abrahamic bond, the three religions conceive of Abraham in mutually exclusive ways. Let me take up each of these features in turn.

First, the fact that we nowhere have a full-blown or mutually consensual account of Abraham that incorporates elements from all three traditions means that we are on flimsy historical ground, at least when it comes to ascertaining some sort of shared heritage. No Jew or Muslim, for example, could agree with the Christian claim that the sacrifice of Isaac prefigures the sacrifice of Jesus. In like manner, neither Jew nor Christian could agree with the Muslim commemoration of sacrificing animals during the hajj pilgrimage. Moreover, neither Jew nor Christian would assent to the Quran's assertion that not only was Abraham the person who built the Kaaba in Mecca, he was actually the first Muslim. Nor would Christian or Muslim agree that the myth of Abraham supports claims of Jewish chosenness, since both Christians and Muslims have much at stake in maintaining the universality or inclusivity of some constructed Abrahamic covenant.[23]

Second, even if we did take the various myths associated with Abraham from these diverse religious traditions and say they represent the "Children of Abraham," we are still no better off. The fact of the matter is that there is no historical precedent for Jews, Christians, or Muslims reading or endorsing the treatments of Abraham found in rival traditions. When Jews and Muslims have had good relations in, say, eleventh-century Cordoba, they did not do so under the auspices of Abraham or a perceived common Abrahamic heritage. On the contrary, they did so owing to real historical, legal, socioeconomic, and political reasons.

Third, all three religions use the figure of Abraham for their own purposes and they do so polemically. Both Christianity and Islam, for example, use Abraham to legitimate themselves on ideological grounds, not on ecumenical ones. Christians, Jews, and Muslims have all engaged in violence, even murder, on the basis of interpretations of Abraham that they have created for themselves. If Jews have used the covenant established between Abraham and God as proof of their chosenness and their subsequent religious and emotional attachment to a piece of land in the Middle East, both Christians and Muslims have used Abraham to deny such claims. Abraham, according to their readings, becomes either the first Christian or the first Muslim, but certainly not a Jew.

Another way of saying all of this is that there is no historical precedent for reading the Jewish, Christian, and Muslim myths that deal with the figure of Abraham or Ibrahim together in the ways that many want to align them today. The question we have to ask ourselves, a question that will form the heart of the remainder of this study, is what extra-historical and ideological forces have contributed to the creation or formation of the trope of "Abrahamic religions" and the various discourses that emerge from it?

The objection could be raised: the point is not that they share common stories, but that Judaism, Christianity, and Islam all seek their origins in the same individual. It is precisely this common perception that unites them. While this might be a nice motto or slogan for interfaith dialogue or trialogue, "Abrahamic religions," "the children of Abraham," or whatever else we want to call it, has very little grounding in the historical record. My concern, to reiterate, is that this largely ecumenical term has become an academic one and that the latter has absolutely no intellectual or analytical value.

From Abraham to "Abrahamic Religions"

In recent years we have seen a shift from the person "Abraham" to the term "Abrahamic religions." This shift is not simply grammatical, from noun to adjective, but primarily semantic. If Abraham is an individual lurking in the mythical background of Judaism, Christianity, and Islam, he becomes synonymous with a set of perceived values that all of these religions have shared and continue to share in the living present. In his foreword to F. E. Peters' *The Children of Abraham*, for example, John Esposito—indicative of this new approach—writes that the relationship among these three religions can be understood using a "family model." For him,

> family in the history of religions, as in the ordinary lives of many, is a source of strength, nurturing love, and security, but also of conflict and violence. Biblical and Quranic stories such as those of Cain and Abel, Isaac and Ismail underscore this truth. Despite—some would even argue because of—close family resemblances, relations between Judaism and Christianity, Christianity and Islam, Judaism and Islam have often been characterized by tension, conflicts and persecution.[24]

There are numerous problems with such a statement. First, when family is invoked in the history of religions, and it is unclear how Esposito is actually using this term, it is usually done in the narrower context of "family resemblances."[25] That is, the history of religions is not composed of families of religions—for example, vague and reified notions of "Abrahamic" or "Western" religions on the one hand, and "Eastern" ones on the other—but, invoking Wittgenstein, of terms or concepts that lack an essential core in which the meaning of words is located. Family resemblances, at least in religious studies discourses with which I am familiar, refer to the use of a particular word or category through "a complicated network of similarities, overlapping and criss-crossing."[26]

The twin acts of classification and definition, staying with Wittgenstein for a little longer, are ultimately based on selection and choice, as opposed to simply and passively recognizing qualities thought to reside in an object or set of objects. A set of family resemblances presupposes that no one characteristic is possessed by all members of a group (e.g., Judaism, Christianity, Islam) but, instead, that a series of traits must be present, each to varying degrees, among its members. If Esposito is, in fact, invoking the technical term "family resemblances" to describe the interactions between the three religions here, he nowhere provides us with the traits that govern his taxonomic schema. Possessing a myth of Abraham cannot be the only prototype that one uses for group membership. We cannot simply look at a given phenomenon, describe its main features, and then generalize from these to establish a definition of what one would expect other cognate or adjacent phenomena to possess.[27]

Whether or not this technical discussion (and critique) is lurking behind Esposito's invocation, he perseveres with his metaphor of family relations by suggesting that they provide "strength, nurturing love, and security" to its members. Nowhere, however, does he elaborate how the religions that he argues constitute the "family" of Abraham provide this for one another. Does Judaism, as the so-called "oldest," offer its younger "siblings" nurturing love? At any time in the historical record, prior to our generation, has this motif of family love been used to describe the dynamics and relationships among these three religions?

Not only does Esposito emphasize the positive, he also contends—extending the family metaphor—that these "siblings" also have disagreements. The Crusades, the Inquisition, the Holocaust—to give a few examples—can, in this worldview, be reduced to family squabbles.[28] This view is very difficult to maintain and it is precisely such difficulties that proponents of "Abrahamic religions" must confront and, it seems to me, that they ultimately cannot. Esposito, however, certainly makes his intentions known at the end of the paragraph that I just quoted when he states that these sibling rivalries "have been stumbling blocks to religious pluralism and tolerance."[29] Values such as "pluralism, "tolerance," and "coexistence," however, are not scholarly, but ecumenical. And it is in this latter sense that Esposito uses and endorses the term.

If I have spent a significant amount of time discussing Esposito's comments, I have done so because they are indicative of so much of the ahistorical wistfulness that surrounds our modern, invented "Abrahamic religions." This term is subsequently used as a category that is perceived to describe a reality and as a heuristic device to perform real intellectual work. If Esposito's remarks were unique, they would not be worth focusing on. But because his comments are metonymic for an entire discourse, it is necessary to examine their tacit assumptions.

The Institutional Study of Abrahamic Religions

It is now customary to talk about "Abrahamic religions" as if they were a natural phenomenon. Professorships are established to study them,[30] institutes to chart them,[31] and conferences to exchange and disseminate information about them.[32] The concern of the following chapters is how all of this happened, and what sort of larger political and ideological forces are lurking behind our terms. Unless theorized, however, such terms risk becoming little more than the objects of some interdenominational or ecumenical fantasy. None of the endowed chairs, institutes, or conferences just mentioned, however, is interested in interrogating this term. For them "Abrahamic religions" is as firmly embedded in the world as any other religious phenomenon.[33]

In a world filled with strife among the three monotheisms, "Abrahamic" becomes the romantic or ecumenical adjective that unites them, both historically and religiously. Perceived to exist beyond the conflicts of today, always just out of reach, "Abrahamic" becomes a quasi-theological, quasi-mythic essence that has very little historical precedent. It is incumbent upon us to inquire into the diverse political, intellectual, and social processes that have contributed to the creation of this term. If not, the term "Abrahamic religions" risks becoming, like so many of the other words we employ in the academic study of religion, a stereotype or a cliché. And, with sufficient repetition, such stereotypes can be mistaken as natural qualities immune from historical scrutiny.

What Makes a Religion "Abrahamic"?

Thus far we have witnessed the manifold permutations that the story and interpretive framework of Abraham has undergone by the three religions now referred to as "Abrahamic." We have also witnessed that, from a historical perspective, each of these three religions has more likely wanted to exclude or murder rival religionists owing to their perceived misinterpretations of Abraham than sit down and engage in reconciliation over some sort of shared patrimony or ancestry. One could say that, historically, the goal has not been to talk about Abraham, but to try to force other religions to accept a rival Abraham.

Despite this, we today feel quite comfortable using the rubric "Abrahamic religions" to designate a shared something, whatever that might be—for example, a sense of scripture or law, a monotheistic heritage, or a structure. The historical minimalization characteristic of this discourse redefines and reconstructs these religions as creeds and not as the products of social, economic, and ideological actors.[34] In our desire to find a set of commonalities among these three religions we have removed them from history and instead constructed an artificial rubric— "Abrahamic"—that largely consists of the methods that are supposed to elucidate it.[35] The problem here, reflective of many of the problems endemic to the academic study of religion, is to study individuals simply as if they were believing and disembodied minds. To do this, according to Russell McCutcheon, is to ignore the manifold ways that human actors divide themselves along other taxonomic structures.[36]

So what is an "Abrahamic religion"? Although the term in its plural usage—"Abrahamic religions"—is used to denote religions that trace their ancestral origins back to the patriarch Abraham, it is by no means clear what is being referred to. Why "Abrahamic"? Why not "monotheistic"? Why not "faith-based"? What, in other words, is it about the figure of Abraham that makes him the linchpin for all three of these religious traditions? Although I have intimated above why I think he is so important, the pages that follow will attempt to flesh this argument out in greater detail.

This brings up the related question, what did the religion of Abraham look like? Does the religion that he practiced represent some ur-religion that, if we could only return to it, holds the magical key to unlocking contemporary problems among Jews, Christians, and Muslims? Is it our goal, as Bruce Feiler contends, to get back to this ur-religion "that existed *before* the religions themselves existed."[37] This religion, as invented as it is impossible to verify, represents the symbol of inclusivity, tolerance, and equanimity that does not exist today in any of the three religions imagined to emerge from it. Implicit is that if we could get back to this ur-religion, we might not even need the three monotheisms because they all represent bastardizations of the true Abrahamic faith.

A set of real tensions emerges from this relationship between specific Abrahamic religions on the one hand and some vaguely constructed original Abrahamic faith on the other. It is a relationship, moreover, that can neatly fit with a certain phenomenological approach to religion, one wherein an essence is articulated and then located in diverse phenomena (that is, religions) as various manifestations.[38] This essence/manifestation framework often leads to the examination of reams of data, signified as unproblematic or existing naturally in the world, that are perceived to be united by means of a specifically or essentially "religious" valence.

When applied to "Abrahamic religions," we also encounter an essence of what "Abrahamic" is assumed to denote (for example: faith, obedience, and submission to God; a certain theological structure predicated on belief and ethics) and then the subsequent discovery of this in each of the three religions. The historical record, including an anti-essentialist and disinterested approach to it, is largely ignored because it threatens to get in the way of either a good story or an ecumenical agenda. The result is that there is a tendency when discussing "Abrahamic religions," as with religion itself, to historical revisionism.

Conclusions

This chapter has attempted to set the stage for those that follow by providing and subsequently interrogating the basic story of Abraham as it appears in the three religions. The goal in doing this was not to create an ecumenical story of common origins and shared heritages, but to reveal some of the reasons behind its mythopoeia. In fact, a shared "Abrahamic" myth that spans the three traditions nowhere exists. This is primarily because each subsequent iteration of the story implies that previous religions either misinterpreted or corrupted the true message of Abraham. As a result, the accounts of Abraham witnessed here revolve around exclusion and supersessionism, as three different religious traditions simultaneously seek to define themselves as the true descendants of Abraham.

Despite this, some in the contemporary world insist on pointing to Abraham as laying the seed for future coexistence. I have tried to argue that those who do this engage in an eisegesis whereby they read their own ecumenical desires into the material in question. The result is less about following the intricacies of various conflicts and coexistences, adoptions, and adaptations among various subgroups within the three religions than about creating an overarching and generic narrative. In order to challenge this model, the following three chapters provide a genealogical study of the various ways in which the term "Abrahamic religions" has been used and abused over the millennia.

2

My Abraham Is Better Than Yours

TWO MAJOR REFERENCE works devoted to the study of religion book-end the twentieth century. Although James Hastings' twelve-volume *Encyclopaedia of Religion and Ethics* (1908–1927) and Mircea Eliade's sixteen-volume *Encyclopedia of Religion* (1988; 2nd ed., 2004) provide different windows for quantifying and classifying religious data reflective of their dates of publication, neither provides an independent entry for the term "Abrahamic" or "Abrahamic religions."[1] This certainly does not mean that the term is simply a post-1988 invention, however.[2] As the present chapter will demonstrate, the term has had a lengthy history, albeit one largely confined to the realm of supersessionism and the related genre of interreligious polemics.

Before the Second World War, when the adjective "Abrahamic" was invoked it was done so to imply that only one religion—not surprisingly, the religious denomination out of which any particular author wrote—was the true heir to the Abrahamic covenant. This is not to imply that the academic discipline of Religious Studies is immune from theologizing,[3] and that it is for this reason that "Abrahamic" did not find its way into either Hastings' or Eliade's encyclopedias. Rather, if the omission of "Abrahamic" from these two reference works tells us anything it is that the academic study of religion in the twentieth century tends to eschew matters of explicit supersessionism and interreligious polemics, and that Abraham and "Abrahamic religions" used as a positive and inclusive term is largely a post-1988 phenomenon. As the following two chapters will demonstrate, the contemporary use of this term is equally theological; the only difference is that the theology favored in Religious Studies today is primarily of the liberal and ecumenical variety as opposed to that of explicit supersessionism.

The present chapter is the first of three devoted to the genealogy of the term "Abrahamic." The present chapter analyzes the term from its origins in Pauline literature until roughly the first half of the twentieth century. Although Paul, as far as I am aware, never used the adjective "Abrahamic," he certainly spoke of "the covenant of Abraham" and of "Abraham's off-spring" to denote spiritual fulfillment in Jesus. Until roughly the mid-twentieth century I cannot find a single instance of the term "Abrahamic" in which it is used positively. Either it is invoked in this Pauline sense or, among Orientalists, to demonstrate the derivative nature of Islam. For example, circumcision or pilgrimage is "Abrahamic," that is, it is not something introduced by Islam in the seventh century c.e., but some-thing that Islam's framers "derived" or "stole" from other "Abrahamic" (i.e., monotheistic) sources. Certainly the adjective is still used today by some (whether Jew, Christian, or Muslim) to demonstrate the superiority of either the "old" or "new" covenant; however, this is primarily confined to non-liberal theology. Its use in the contemporary period, the subject of the following chapter, has largely shifted from supersessionism to ecu-menicism. This seemed to occur after the mid-twentieth century for a variety of reasons, not the least of which was the emergence of Vatican II and the desire to end religious intolerance. Following these two chapters, I examine the various uses to which "Abrahamic" has been employed to classify religions both in the past and especially in the post-9/11 world.

What quickly emerges from these three genealogical chapters is that the term "Abrahamic" has always been used apologetically and/or ideologically. Although it has been invoked to denote the superiority of Christianity over Judaism, of Islam over Christianity and Judaism or, in the modern period, of some vaguely defined set of shared essential and phenomenological traits, none of these uses is historically grounded. Despite this, all those who use "Abrahamic" or "Abrahamic religions," both in the past and in the present, have no problem invoking the term as if it accurately demarcated some form of historical reality.

Pauline Origins

On February 6, 1812, Adoniram Judson and five other New Englanders were commissioned to set sail, as the first American foreign missionar-ies, to convert the "heathens" of the globe to the religion of Abraham. Contributing to and facilitating their desire to go out and spread the "good word" was the Reverend Dr. Samuel Worcester, pastor of the Tabernacle

Church in Salem, Massachusetts, and one of the leaders in the growing world mission movement.[4] Indeed it was from Worcester's church that Judson and his colleagues—the so-called "Brethren"—were commissioned as missionaries. In 1807, five years before Judson and his colleagues set sail for Burma and other exotic locales, Rev. Dr. Worcester published a treatise entitled *Two Discourses on the Perpetuity and Provision of God's Gracious Covenant with Abraham and His Seed*. Therein he expressed an opinion that had been articulated by Paul in the first century C.E.: "the Abrahamic covenant and church, are to be accounted the true church of Christ."[5] Within this pithy yet theologically loaded statement we encounter numerous themes that will reverberate throughout this chapter. These include the perceived existence of a pristine "Abrahamic" church (alternatively imagined as religion); its fulfillment or restoration in a later prophetic leader (whether Jesus or Muhammad); and the exclusive right of those doing the imagining to lay claim to it.

Although Worcester's use of the term "Abrahamic" in 1807 represents one of its earlier iterations in the English language, it would not be going too far to say that the relationship between Abraham and Jesus has played a formative role in the creation of Christian identity soon after the latter's death. Moreover, it is a relationship that continued to power the engine of such identity for the next two millennia. In his letter to the Galatians,[6] for example, Paul informs his audience that Abraham's faith was not the sole inheritance of the Jews, but the birthright of all those who have faith and believe in the same manner that Abraham did. "So, you see, those who believe are the descendants of Abraham," writes Paul in Galatians 3:7, in his desire to begin the process of transferring the contents of the ancient covenant to those who have faith in Jesus from those Jews who remain so blinded by the confining strictures of their legalism that they are unable to see or recognize the Truth.

Paul's message was that the Abrahamic covenant had not been superseded, but fulfilled, in Jesus. The one covenant that Paul, not to mention much of the later Christian theological tradition, argued had been replaced and supplanted was the one established with Moses on Mount Sinai. It was this latter covenant, according to them, that represented the set of legalistic and ritualistic norms that kept Jews in spiritual bondage. The covenant that God established with Abraham, on the contrary, was an authentic expression of religious devotion centered on the faith of Abraham and his true, spiritual descendants (and not necessarily his literal ones).

Abraham's faith, as articulated in the non-Pauline letter to the Hebrews, enabled him to leave his home in Ur, to believe that he would have children even in his old age, and be willing to sacrifice his son to the God of monotheism (Hebrews 11:8–17). It is Abraham's faith, according to the authors of this epistle, which foreshadows that of Jesus. Only now the table is turned somewhat since Jesus has become the sacrificial son, the one whose death is meant as an atonement for the world; and it is faith, not the Law, that now represents the virtue of the true believer. The covenant that God strikes with Abraham neither finds fulfillment in the Mosaic covenant at Sinai nor in Judaism, but lives eternally in the believers in Jesus, who now become the true descendants of the "children of Abraham." The stubborn Jews have, for all intents and purposes, been written out of the covenant.

Paul picks up this theme in his allegory of Hagar and Sarah in Galatians 4:21–31, wherein he connects the Jews to the biblical figure of Hagar. Although Paul certainly intends this kinship to be disparaging to the Jews, it is interesting to note that centuries later Muslims will be more than happy to call themselves the descendants of Hagar. Returning to his letter to the Galatians, Paul distinguishes between Hagar, who "was born according to the flesh," and Sarah, who "was born through the promise." Hagar, bearing children for slavery, symbolizes terrestrial Jerusalem, for she and her children "are in slavery" to the Law. Juxtaposed against her is Sarah, who corresponds to the celestial Jerusalem, and who lives in freedom, thereby functioning as the mother of Jesus's followers. Picking up the theme of inheritance from the Abrahamic story of Genesis, Paul exhorts his listeners to "drive out the slave and her child; for the child of the slave will not share the inheritance with the child of the free woman" (4:30). This exhortation "to drive out the slave and her child" would reverberate through the centuries, finding another major articulation in 1095 when, from his palace at Clermont, Pope Urban II invoked it in his papal bull which justified the First Crusade as meant to "drive out" the infidels from the Holy City of Jerusalem.

If we have seen what Paul tried to do in his writings, it is perhaps worthwhile to pause momentarily and see what he decidedly does not do. He makes no appeal to some vague concept of shared inheritance with Jews. Nor does he seek to engage Jews except to convince them of the error of their ways. What we witness, as we shall see again when we get to Islam, is the desire to prove an earlier monotheism (or monotheisms) as incorrect or as the bastardization of an original Abrahamic covenant, church, and/or religion. The origins of the term "Abrahamic" thus emerge from the polemical desire to exclude and to demonstrate superiority over rival claimants.

The notion of Jesus and his followers as the ultimate recipients of the Abrahamic covenant is the bedrock of Christian identity. To show this, those who believe in the new covenant of Jesus had to claim that the covenant of Moses, returning to the Reverend Dr. Samuel Worcester, "has been blotted out and nailed to the cross."[7] For Worcester, the church established by Jesus and the one that he himself administered in Salem, Massachusetts is the one and only true church. He writes,

> So plain it is, that the church under the Christian dispensation is only the ancient, Abrahamic, church continued and enlarged according to the promises, made to Abraham and his seed; and that this church, and, of course, the covenant by which it was originally formed, is to be continued down to the latest generations.[8]

Worcester's words here are by no means unique. However, his use of the term "Abrahamic," as should be clear from the aforementioned statements, is not used in the manner that we are accustomed to see or hear it invoked today. In fact, Worcester uses it in the opposite manner, and this is precisely the way in which the term "Abrahamic" will be employed until, roughly, the Second World War. However, even though the term would then begin to take on a decidedly different meaning in response to a variety of historical stimuli associated with the aftermath of World War II, this does not necessarily mean that the older and more exclusive use of the term, as we shall see near the end of this chapter, completely disappears.

The Abrahamic covenant is the crucial feature in the argument for Jesus's, and by extension, Christianity's, superiority over Judaism. For Paul, as indeed for so many who will come after him, the covenant made to Abraham in Genesis 12 was not based on the Law, which would only come later at Mount Sinai, but on the promise: "For if the inheritance comes from the Law, it no longer comes from the promise; but God granted it to Abraham through the promise" (Gal. 3:15). It is for this reason that an important trope in this theological writing is the notion that there existed a pristine and spiritual Abrahamic faith that Jesus has come to restore. This, of course, is a way for Paul to justify the claim, as we have seen already, that the followers of Jesus, not the Jews, represent the true

Israel. As such, it is the former and not the latter who are the authentic and spiritual descendants of Abraham.

Muhammad's Millat Ibrāhīm

This trope of a pristine Abrahamic religion was picked up, consciously or unconsciously it is impossible to tell, by the architects of early Islam. There we encounter the term *millat Ibrāhīm* (the "religion of Abraham"); note its use in the singular and not the plural. In fact, this use of the term throughout the Quran might well be one of the first times that we encounter the phrase "religion of Abraham," even though it is certainly implied in Pauline and other early Christian writings. Within the Quran, *millat Ibrāhīm* is used at least ten times to refer explicitly to the original religion of Abraham. The early followers of Muhammad are exhorted to "follow the religion of Abraham" (Quran 3:95), where the latter is described as "an intimate friend [*khalīl*]" of God (Quran 4:125). Islam, we are informed in several verses, is nothing more or less than the religion of Abraham restored (e.g., Quran 16:123; 22:78). This *millat Ibrāhīm* is also referred to as the correct path (*sirat mustaqīm*) and the correct religion (*dīn qiyām*) in Quran 6:161.

Like the "Abrahamic" faith of Jesus and his followers, the term in the Quran also has a polemical intent. Originating in a monotheist environment populated by various subgroups of Jews and Christians, Muhammad and the subsequent creators of the Islamic foundation narrative (e.g., storytellers, hadith collectors, early theologians, historians) made claims that Islam superseded both Judaism and Christianity. The way they went about this was not unlike what we witnessed above in Paul and the subsequent Christian theological record: to demonstrate that what existed before somehow, at some point in time, went wrong and, as a result, became gravely misunderstood. In order to do this, as David Powers has persuasively argued, the Islamic claims of supersession cannot be understood apart from the dynamics of the foundation narratives of Islam's two predecessors.[9]

One of the major ways that this was done was by arguing that earlier scriptural accounts of revelation had been falsified. According to the Quran and subsequent Muslim theology, Jews and Christians failed to preserve the original contents of their respective revelations which, over time, were subjected to textual distortion (*tahrīf*). The fundamental tenet of Islam, by contrast, is that the Quran represents the pure, unadulterated

account of revelation and that it has always been immune from such textual distortion.[10] According to Islam, then, various mistakes crept into
the Old and New Testaments with the result that these two texts ceased
to remain reliable sources of the divine will. It is for this reason that God
sent Muhammad to the Arabs. This is why it was so important that, from
the perspective of early Islamic salvation history, Muhammad be a lineal descendant of Ishmael, and thus a member of the Abrahamic family to which the office of prophecy had been entrusted. The purpose of
Muhammad's mission was nothing more or less than to restore the original, uncorrupted version of earlier revelations.[11] It is on account of this
perceived textual distortion, moreover, that early Muslim theologians did
not attach these earlier revelations to the Quran in the same way that
Christian theologians attached the Old Testament to the New, an act that
was predicated on the notion that the former foreshadowed the latter.

In terms of Abraham, this translates into the notion that he be the
lineal ancestor of Muhammad, referred to as the so-called seal of the
prophets (khātam al-nabiyyīn; cf Quran 33:40).[12] Equally important, however, it also means that the religion Abraham was perceived to be a pure
form of monotheism, a form that was corrupted by subsequent Jews
and Christians, and something that Muhammad sought to restore. The
Muslim notion of "Abrahamic" religion, then, is not unlike its expression
in Pauline literature: a purity built on faith, an expression of authenticity,
that surpasses anything that came before it.

According to Quran 3:67, "Abraham was neither a Jew nor a Christian,
but a man of pure faith [hanīf]; one who surrendered [i.e., was a muslim].
He was not one of those who associate others with God." The verb translated here as "surrendered" comes from the root "to surrender" (s-l-m),
which is interchangeable, in Arabic, with "to become a Muslim;" indeed
the word Islam (i.e, "surrendering") comes from the same root. The word
hanīf in this verse is used to refer to the pure monotheistic worship of
Abraham that Muhammad was subsequently charged to reinstate. It was
also a technical term used to refer to individuals before Muhammad who
lived in the Age of Ignorance (or the period before the revelation of the
Quran), but who rejected idolatrous practice in favor of the pure monotheism of Abraham. Muhammad, then, was a hanīf, an "Abrahamian" as it
were, before his prophetic call.

In the second sura of the Quran, Abraham is described not simply
as a hanīf, but as a Muslim: "When his Lord said to [Abraham], 'Submit
[aslim],' he said, 'I have submitted [aslamtu] to the Lord of the created

beings" (Quran 2:131). Relating verses such as this to the concept of *tahrīf*, or the corruption introduced to earlier scriptures, we can see that, for Muslims, both Jews and Christians sought to co-opt Abraham into one of their own, manipulating their scriptures in such a way as to remove Abraham's "Muslimness" from the annals of monotheism. This would also include the removal of verses, subsequently preserved in the Quran, that mention Abraham's and Ishmael's restoration of the Kaaba, and their prayer to God that He would make their progeny into a great nation from whom would descend a messenger to recite His revelations (Quran 2:125; cf. 14:35–40; 22:26–29).[13]

Once again, from this brief overview of Quranic materials, we witness the polemical intent of the term "Abrahamic." In the visceral world of religious polemics and in the need to define oneself and one's group in the face of others, we see "Abraham" and "Abrahamic" as responsible for the creation and maintenance of difference. Both Christians and Muslims need Abraham—hence the desire to establish the Abrahamic lineage of Jesus and Muhammad—to legitimate their messages. In order to establish their Abrahamic bona fides, however, it is also necessary to denigrate those of their rivals. As I have mentioned time and again in this study, Abraham and/or Abrahamic is not used in any of these sources as a multifaith or interfaith term to show similarities between Judaism, Christianity, and Islam. On the contrary, when it is invoked it is always done so to show that only one of these traditions lays claim to the true and authentic message of Abraham. The others are either corrupt or based on misreadings.

Early Christian Polemics

One of the earliest external sources written by an observer to the unfolding events on the Arabian Peninsula concerning the rise of Islam was the seventh-century Armenian bishop and chronicler Sebeos. In an interesting passage, one worth quoting at length, he informs us that

> In that period a certain one of them, a man of the sons of Ishmael named Muhammad, a merchant, became prominent. A sermon about the Way of Truth, supposedly at God's command, was revealed to them, and [Muhammad] taught them to recognize the God of Abraham, especially since he was informed and knowledgeable about Mosaic history. Because the command had come from

On High, he ordered them all to assemble together and to unite in faith. Abandoning the reverence of vain things, they turned toward the living God, who had appeared to their father, Abraham. Muhammad legislated that they were not to eat carrion, not to drink wine, not to speak falsehoods, and not to commit adultery. He said: "God promised that country to Abraham and to his son after him, for eternity. And what had been promised was fulfilled during that time when [God] loved Israel. Now, however, you are the sons of Abraham, and God shall fulfill the promise made to Abraham and his son on you. Only love the God of Abraham, and go and take the country that God gave to your father, Abraham. No one can successfully resist you in war, since God is with you."

This account, one of the first narratives of Muhammad to survive in any language, confirms that Muhammad perceived himself to be a prophet in the line of Abraham and that he preached a message centered upon the religious message of his prophetic descendant. Descent from Abraham was necessary to establish Muhammad's prophetic pedigree because the early architects of Islam—familiar, according to Sebeos, with Jewish foundation narratives—knew that if Muhammad was a descendant of Abraham he became part of the family to which the office of prophecy had been entrusted by God. Interestingly, this account also informs us that Muhammad established a community of Arabs and Jews based both on a common Abrahamic descent and a monotheistic message.[14]

Whereas later Muslims envisaged Muhammad as the final prophet in the Abrahamic line, the so-called "seal of the Prophets," this claim did not go unnoticed in the larger world of the Near East. John of Damascus (ca. 676–749), a Christian polemicist of the Late Antique period, for example, writes that this Abrahamic descent is a ruse:

There is also the still-prevailing deceptive superstition of the Ishmaelites, the forerunner of the Antichrist. It takes its name from Ishmael who was born to Abraham from Hagar, and that is why they are called Hagarenes and Ishmaelites.[15]

Here John of Damascus seeks to dismantle the claims that Muslims are actually descendants of Abraham—a claim, of course, that would weaken the Christian community of which he himself was a part. Ishmael, after all, was the first-born son of Abraham and, as such, had a strong claim to be his father's heir.[16] John of Damascus goes on to recount the lies that the Muslims have invented for themselves in order to maintain this "deceptive superstition." Before the rise of Muhammad, whom John considers to be a false prophet, he argues that the Arabs worshipped Aphrodite and that the stone in the Kaaba that Muslims kiss to this day is nothing other than the head of a statue of Aphrodite, upon which, he informs his readers, one can still see the traces of the sculpture.[17]

In his *Refutation of the Quran*, Nicetas of Byzantium (842–912), another Christian polemicist, argues that God's promise to Abraham explicitly denies Ishmael and his descendants a place in the divine covenant.[18] Rather, Nicetas informs Muslims that if they truly want to be the sons of Abraham, then it is necessary for them to renounce both Muhammad and the Quran. Although Muslims claim to worship the God of Abraham, according to him, they can never truly understand this God who is the Father because they reject the Son. Like the Jews, the Muslims ignore the faith-based aspect of the Abrahamic covenant and instead engage in the corporeal act of circumcision.

Moving beyond the Byzantine world and the Late Antique period, we also encounter, for lack of a better term, an "anti-Ishmael" polemic in the medieval West.[19] Much of the polemical material from this period, not unlike its antecedents, sought to disable the claim that Muslims are the true descendants of Abraham. Obviously they cannot be so in the Christian imagination because this pride of place is preserved for their own believers. Perhaps the most famous of all polemical uses of the Abraham myth is supplied by Pope Urban II's papal bull, already witnessed above, issued at Clermont in 1095, which ushered in the First Crusade the following year. In it he justified the coming chaos by quoting, in Latin translation, the words of Sarah to Abraham: *"Ejice ancillam et filium eius"* ("Cast out the slave-girl and her son!").[20] With the Crusades more knowledge about Islam and Muslims was gradually brought back to the Christian West, and in 1143 Robert of Ketton (ca. 1110–ca. 1160) completed the first Latin translation of the Quran, sponsored by Peter the Venerable, Abbot of Cluny. In the translation, entitled *Lex Mahumet pseudoprophete* ("The Law of Muhammad, the false prophet"), Ketton refused to translate the word "Muslim" or its related verbal forms when it came to Abraham, further denying the Muslims any claim whatsoever to the biblical patriarch. For example, he truncated and translated the latter half of the verse mentioned above—Abraham was "a *hanīf*, one who surrendered his will [i.e., was a muslim]. He was not one of those who associate others with God."—as *vir Dei et non incredulous vixit* ("He was a faithful man of God and did not live as an unbeliever").[21]

Such accounts are multiple in the medieval period. One final example comes by way of San Pedro Pascual (1227–1300), who, in his *Sobra el seta mahometana*, made fun of Muslims' purported Ishmaelite ancestry. Why, asked Pascual, would Muhammad claim descent from Abraham's cursed and disinherited son? Engaging in a fanciful interpretation, Pascual figured that Muhammad—whom he called *demoniacus*—was born three hundred generations after Jesus and that if one removed the final zero from this number, one would be left with the number thirty, equivalent to the thirty pieces of silver said to be paid to Judas Iscariot to betray Jesus.[22] The connection, of course, is that Muhammad, like Judas, betrayed the true religion.

This is certainly not to say, however, that it was only Christians who engaged in polemical discourses with Muslims, although it was Christian polemicists who did seek to make the most of undermining the Abrahamic claims or pretensions of both Jews and Muslims. Despite the fact that many of the later polemical exchanges between these "Abrahamic religions" would focus on concepts other than the patriarch, suffice it to say that improper interpretation of the Abrahamic message was certainly in the background of virtually all such exchanges. Christians would frequently attack Muslims for the distortions that the Quran introduces into biblical stories and motifs (which, not surprisingly, are taken to be the authentic versions). Muslims, in turn, would accuse Christians (and Jews) of distorting their own scriptures, thereby removing them from the true religion of Abraham (i.e., Islam). Polemical attacks from both sides would, of course, have their violent manifestations throughout much of the Middle Ages.

Muslim Polemics: Abd al-Jabbar's The Critique of Christian Origins

Christians were not the only ones who engaged in polemics over the patriarch Abraham. The need to uphold one's own interpretation of Abraham and to discredit rival interpretations was, as we have seen, foundational to all pre-twentieth-century usage. Jews, perhaps not surprisingly, tended to engage less in this polemical activity, no doubt owing to their liminal and often precarious status within the rival empires of Islam and Christianity. Muslim theologians, however, actively engaged in this practice, directing their energies to refuting the major principles of Christianity, especially the notion of the Trinity and the divinity of Jesus.[23] One of the major genres of Islamic theology (*kalām*) was that of heresiography, wherein authors would list the main heresies, both internal (e.g., Shi'ism) and external (e.g., Judaism, Christianity), to Islam. Within this context, one of the most important works seeking to refute Christianity was *The Critique of Christian Origins* by Abd al-Jabbar (d. 1025).[24] This treatise meant to show that Muslims are the ones who truly understand Jesus and that true Christianity, that is, Islam, has been falsified by the likes of Paul and Constantine. Concerning Abraham, Abd al-Jabbar writes of Christians that they

> [c]onsider people such as Abraham and the prophets—blessings of God upon them—whose teachings and intentions are known. Yet they depart from them with [their] speculative interpretation and questionable expressions. Their teachings follow a conclusion that is not supported by a rational interpretation of revelation. For the knowledge that Christ, in monotheism, was in the model of Abraham, Moses, Aaron, David, and Muhammad—blessings of God upon them—cannot be doubted by one who knows....[25]

According to this passage, Abd al-Jabbar accuses Christian theologians of going against the simple meaning of their own texts, both the Old and New Testaments. Such texts, when properly understood, make it clear that Jesus is nothing more than a messenger and a prophet in the same monotheistic model as Abraham and eventually Muhammad. Christian theologians, however, engage in fanciful speculation in their desire to prove that Jesus is God, and, as a result, they ultimately distort this because Jesus, like Muhammad, was but one link in a larger prophetic chain. According to this position, Muslims actually understand Jesus better than Christians do.

Abd al-Jabbar is also critical of Christians who use other languages as opposed to Hebrew, which he mistakenly calls the "language of Christ" (*lugha al-masīh*). Whereas Jews retain the language in which their revelatory book was sent down and Muslims still read the Quran in its original language, Christians are uninterested in preserving the language that Abraham or Jesus spoke. The result, according to him, is that Christian theologians are careless and unconcerned if mistakes slip into their interpretations. In a passage from a section entitled "Christians avoid Hebrew, the language of Christ, in order to hide their errors," he is particularly critical of the fact that none of the Gospels were written in Hebrew, but rather in Greek. Hebrew, after all,

> is the language of Christ, which he and his companions spoke, the language of Abraham the close friend of God [al-khalīl]....God addressed them in Hebrew, but these [Christians] abandoned it....They turned to many languages that Christ and his companions did not speak...such as [that of] the Romans, Syrians, Persians, Indians, Armenians, and other foreigners. Thus they disguised and plotted in order to cover up their shame and to achieve leadership, the object of their desire....If that were not so, they would have adhered to the language of Abraham, of his offspring, and of Christ, by whom the demonstration [of religion] was established and to whom the Books were sent down.[26]

Abd al-Jabbar here engages in a classic example of showing how later Christian thinkers "tampered" (tahrīf) with their scriptures in order to gain power for themselves by hiding Jesus's original message (that is, Islam) from later followers.

The Critique of Christian Origins represents but one example of the polemics that Muslims engaged in with Christianity. Whereas a lot of Muslim polemics do not focus explicitly on the figure of Abraham, Abd al-Jabbar does so briefly to show that, reinforcing the Quranic position described above, Islam is tantamount to the restoration of the original Abrahamic religion that Christians (and Jews) had, but ultimately corrupted. In order to do this, he must argue that Jesus, like Abraham, was a Muslim and that the message that both brought was Islam. Understanding Abraham, as we saw in the previous section, is contingent upon projecting one's own religious message, and the virtues that coincide with it, onto him.

Orientalist Polemics

In 1862, Sir William Muir (1819–1905), the Scottish Orientalist and future president of the Royal Asiatic Society, published the fourth volume of his *The Life of Mahomet*. In 1878, he abridged the four volumes into one entitled *The Life of Mahomet from Original Sources*. Whether in their original or abridged form, Muir's goal—like many of his generation who shared his profession—was not to demonstrate the ecumenical nature or shared heritage between Islam and its "sister" religions, but to show the newer religion's ultimate dependence upon them. In this Muir follows a long line of his predecessors who sought to, if not actually discredit Islam, show its derivative nature. Islam, for many associated with the European Orientalist tradition, was a corruption, a garbled version of existing monotheisms.[27]

It is within this context that Sir William Muir could invoke the adjective "Abrahamic." In the posthumously published 1923 edition, based on the third edition of 1894, he writes that "once the loose conception of Abraham and Ishmael as great forefathers of the race was superimposed upon the superstition of Mecca, and had received the stamp of native currency, it will be easily conceived that Jewish tradition and legend would be eagerly welcomed and readily assimilated with native legend and tradition."[28] For him many of the religious rituals that Muhammad used were not original, but copied from other monotheisms in the area. Muir refers to these other monotheisms by the vague name "Abrahamic races" or "Abrahamic tribes."[29] Even those customs or rituals that might not have an immediate precedent, he writes, probably derived from some "Abrahamic" practices in the area. Muir writes, for example, that the

> rite of circumcision is hardly to be mentioned as an institution of Islam. It was current among the Arabs as an Abrahamic ceremony, and continued (without any command in the Kor'ān) to be practiced by the followers of Mahomet.[30]

Here Muir's invocation of the term "Abrahamic" is based on his quest to find precedent for a Quranic teaching or Muslim practice in one of the other monotheisms on the Arabian Peninsula. There is never any desire to ascertain the formation of diverse identities (whether "Jewish," "Christian," or "Muslim"), but only the need to show the derivative status of Islam and Muhammad.[31] The goal of Orientalists of the nineteenth century was to demonstrate the anarchic nature of the Quran by finding the original sources which had been usurped by Muhammad. This story of the Euro- and Christocentric roots of the modern study of the Orient has been told many times before[32] and does not need to be retold here.

Within the context of the present study, let me mention that on some levels Orientalists provided the cover of objectivity with which to engage further in religious polemics. In his treatment of the legend of Abraham in the Quran, for example, Christiaan Snouck Hurgronje (1857–1936) argues that in the period before the migration to Medina, the so-called *hijra*, Muhammad likely only had vague and confused notions of Abraham. Once in Medina, however, where Muhammad would have encountered a fairly large population of Jews, he created an Abraham based on political expediency and only then encouraged the Jews of Medina to return to this "religion of Abraham" (i.e., *millat Ibrāhīm*).[33] When they did not he began the process of forming his own religion based on an amalgam of practices and beliefs that he invented in the spirit of his imagined Abraham.

If I can generalize about the Orientalist imagination of Abraham and "Abrahamic," of which I have here provided but a glimpse, it is to say that when invoked it is done so in the spirit of reductionism. "Abrahamic" is invoked to show that a particular Islamic custom, belief, or practice is unoriginal and derives its ultimate origin from another religion, be it Judaism or Christianity. It is certainly not used in an ecumenical sense, but is done so as a continuation of the polemical encounters and exchanges of the premodern period.

The Use of "Abrahamic" in the Eighteenth and Nineteenth Centuries

In 1757 there appeared in the pages of the *Monthly Review* a "Review of *The Covenant of Grace, and Baptism the token of it, explained upon Scripture principles* by John Taylor DD of Norwich." Taylor (1694–1761) was a dissenting minister, theologian, and the author of a Hebrew–English and English–Hebrew lexicon.[34] His work on original sin, in particular, influenced the likes of Jonathan Edwards and John Wesley. Here the unnamed reviewers write in point form what they consider to be some of the key features of the book:

> 3. That whereas the covenant of *peculiarity* (by which is meant that mentioned in Gen. xv. 18, and which is annexed to the Abrahamic covenant) gave the Jews alone a right to the land of Canaan, the Abrahamic covenant included *all nations of the earth*, though God did not see fit to reveal and publish it to them....
>
> 4. That the Abrahamic covenant was *confirmed*, or ratified of *God in Christ*. This is proved particularly from Gal. iii.[35]

As we see in this excerpt, "Abrahamic" is used to open up the Genesis narrative so that a covenantal relationship between God and the ancient

Israelites can now be expanded to refer not just to the Israelites, but to "all nations of the earth." Yet Taylor and his anonymous reviewers conveniently argue here that for some reason God did not see fit to mention this at the time of the initial covenant. It is only in the later revelation, symbolized by Jesus and the giving of the "new" covenant, that we are provided with the hermeneutic keys to unlock the "old" one. Once read in this manner, the Abrahamic covenant now becomes open to all, witnessed as early as Paul's Epistle to the Galatians, through the salvific power of Jesus and through the faith of the individual believer. To prove their point, the above reviewers end their comments with the proclamation: "Go and baptize *all* nations in the name of the Father, Son, and Holy Ghost."

On the topic of nineteenth-century exclusivity, we witness the desire of theologians to connect the new covenant to the Abrahamic one, in a way that is meant to bypass the Sinaitic, or Mosaic, one. Witness, for example, the 1811 title by Daniel Dow, DD—pastor of the Congregationalist Church in Thomson, Connecticut, and Corporate Member of the American Board of Foreign Missions—which nicely sums up this use: *A Dissertation on the Sinaitic and Abrahamic Covenants: Shewing the Former to be Only Temporary, the Latter Everlasting.*[36] Therein he writes that

> They differ in respect to their duration. The Sinaitic Covenant was only temporary; *imposed till the time of reformation* [Heb. 9:10]; but after that, this ministration of death was abolished. It decayed; it waxed old; it vanished away. But the Abrahamic Covenant is everlasting. The law which was four hundred and thirty years after, could not disannul it. It extends to all believers, and, consequently must endure forever.[37]

Here we witness the straight line that many Christian theologians were content to draw between Abraham and Jesus. This was based, of course, on the interpretive strategy afforded to them by the New Testament and by their concomitant desire to deny any Jewish claims to the covenantal relationship. The Sinaitic covenant, which defined Judaism, is here implied to be legalistic and annulled. The language used to describe it in the above passage, for example, relies on adjectives such as "old" and "decayed."

Abraham, as seen earlier in this chapter, was necessary to legitimate Jesus and his message. Not only does Abraham foreshadow the coming of Jesus, he paved the way for the fulfillment of the old covenant in the new. In his *Household Consecration* of 1836, Nathaniel E. Johnson, Pastor of the Third Free Presbyterian Church in New York City, who published his volume "to communicate to his fellow Christians his views and feelings respecting the consecration of households to God,"[38] writes in a chapter entitled "The Abrahamic Covenant" that in the opening pages of the book of Genesis, God was busy

> developing the truth of his law, and the arrangements of his grace. He ordered the whole current of human affairs in view of the advent of Christ. This great event, on which the interest of the world depended, was now to be connected with the posterity of Abraham, and a nation was to be provided as a cradle for the Saviour, and a nursery for the Church. For this purpose, and in view of all results consequent upon the establishment of Christianity, Abraham was called to go out from his native land, a lonely pilgrim, yet an heir of glorious promises.[39]

In fairly typical fashion, Johnson here reads everything contained in the Old Testament, but especially in the book of Genesis, as an elaborate foreshadowing of the Advent of Jesus. "Abrahamic," for him and for so many others, has nothing to do with Judaism or inclusivity, but refers solely to Christianity (of course, not surprisingly, to their own particular denominations) and the desire to show that Jews and Judaism have no place within the covenantal relationship. Abraham is, once again, used as a rhetorical tool for exclusion and deprivation.

It is certainly worth pointing out that none of the individuals engaged in the supersessionist arguments examined in this section are interested in Islam or Muslim claims to be the true representatives of the "religion of Abraham." This is most likely owing to the fact that, other than Orientalists, most theologians in the eighteenth and early nineteenth centuries neither knew Muslims nor anything about Muslim claims to Abraham. Rather, their polemical energy devoted to Abraham was aimed solely at Judaism and the so-called "old" covenant. Jews have no idea, the argument went, how to read their own religious text, which has largely been superseded by a new hermeneutic and a new covenant. For an explicit connection between Abraham and Jesus, witness an anonymous article entitled "The Covenant of Scripture" from *The Danville Quarterly Review*, published out of Danville, Kentucky, in 1862. The author writes,

> In so far as circumcision emblematized the work of God upon the heart, it is superseded by baptism; and in this regard baptism

is called Christ's circumcision (Col. ii: 11), and may be said to come in the place of circumcision. We come into the Abrahamic covenant, *not by circumcision, but by Christ.* We are united to him by a living faith, so far as it is outward, by baptism. The circumcision is eternal in him, and we are circumcised in him . . . baptism is the seal of the covenant with us, and that by it we are one with him (that is outwardly and ceremonially), that he is Abraham's seed, and heirs according to the promise. If we are faithful, then are we the children of faithful Abraham. But faith does not unite us to Abraham, but to Christ, and he unites us to Abraham.[40]

The Quarterly, as one of the mouthpieces of the Presbyterian Church in the United States, in this passage reflects the Christian notion that baptism and the circumcision of the heart replaces or supersedes fleshly circumcision. It is only through Jesus, in other words, that the believer truly understands and is united with Abraham.

We should not assume, however, that this invocation of the term "Abrahamic" has been completely replaced in the contemporary world by an ecumenical and interfaith approach. Although this transformation from supersessionism to ecumenicism will be the subject of the following two chapters, and is primarily the way many tend to invoke the term today, the former still lives on, especially in Christian publications. For example, Keith H. Essex writes in *The Master's Seminary Journal* in 1999 that

The promises of the covenant are unconditional . . . the NT [points] out that Jesus Christ, Abraham's seed, will make possible the final fulfillment of that covenant in the future.[41]

This use of the term "Abrahamic" today is certainly not mainstream, at least in circles associated with the academic study of religion. The mission statement of *The Master's Seminary* that produces this journal is, after all, "to advance the kingdom of the Lord Jesus Christ by equipping godly men to be pastors and/or trainers of pastors for excellence in service to Christ in strategic fields of Christian ministry."[42] I do, however, mention it as a way to show that the genealogy recounted in this chapter is still alive and well in certain modern circles and itself has not been superseded by the ecumenical claims of liberal theology.

"Abrahamic" and the Pedobaptism Debate

Between the fifteenth of November and the second of December 1843 there occurred a debate between one Reverend A. Campbell and one Reverend N. L. Rice in Lexington, Kentucky. The debate, transcribed in 912 pages, was published in 1844 under the title *A Debate Between Rev. A. Campbell and Rev. N. L. Rice on the Action, Subject, Design and Administrator of Christian Baptism; Also, on the Character of Spiritual Influence in Conversion and Sanctification, and on the Expediency and Tendency of Ecclesiastic Creeds, as Terms of Union and Communion: Held in Lexington, KY., From the Fifteenth of November to the Second of December, 1843, a Period of Eighteen Days.* The second point of debate—entitled "The Infant of a Believing Parent is a Scriptural Subject of Christian Baptism. Mr. Rice affirms. Mr. Campbell denies"—was held on Monday, November 20 at ten o'clock in the morning. This particular debate focused on the question of whether or not the institution of infant baptism (pedobaptism) should exist.

Their discussion begins with the Abrahamic covenant and revolves around the issue of whether or not baptism is the spiritual and supersessionist continuation of Abraham's practice of circumcision which was a sign of his covenant with God. Reverend Rice begins by claiming, "I maintain that the church was organized in the days and in the family of Abraham; when God entered into a covenant with the father of the faithful to be a God to him and to his seed."[43] Reverend Campbell denies what he calls the "nationalistic" (i.e., through the nation of Abraham) interpretation of Reverend Rice and instead argues that none can enter Christ's church unless "born again" or "born from above." For him, "circumcision, requir[es] no moral qualification, communicate[s] no spiritual blessings."[44] Instead he claims that "circumcision was the door of entrance into the church under the former dispensation [i.e., the Abrahamic]; baptism is the door under the present dispensation"[45] and, as evidence, he adds, "how many baptized infidels are there in the bounds of all the Pedobaptist communities."[46]

This exchange reveals yet another iteration of the adjective "Abrahamic" in its pre-ecumenical history. Beginning, as far as I can tell, in the late-eighteenth and early nineteenth centuries we begin to see monographs, such as the one by Jacob Jones Janeway (1774–1858), Director of the Princeton Theological Seminary from 1813 to 1830, and again from 1840 to 1858, entitled *Letters Explaining the Abrahamic Covenant: With a View to Establish, on the Broad and Ancient Basis, the Divine Right of Infant*

Baptism and the Question Relative to the Mode of Administering this Christian Ordinance: Addressed to the Members of the Second Presbyterian Church, in Philadelphia,[47] or his older contemporary, Reverend F. G. Hibbard, one of the most respected voices in the Methodist Episcopal Church, writing in 1856 and assuming that "infants are in a regenerated state."[48] He claims,

> There is no *assignable reason* for such a change. If infants had a right to the blessings of the Abrahamic covenant anciently, they have the same right now. If they were eligible to the *"token"* of that covenant—circumcision—anciently, they are eligible to the *token* of the same covenant—baptism—now.[49]

If these examples have all been from the side arguing for the importance of pedobaptism (with the exception of Reverend Campbell), surely it is worth looking at the polemic from the other side. On the last "Lord's Day of August 1864," Elder Jonas Hartzel arose before the executive members of the Christian State Missionary Baptist Meeting in Columbus City, Iowa, to speak "in an extemporaneous discourse" about the nature of covenant and its culmination in the figure of Jesus Christ. So impressed was the executive committee that they asked Elder Jonas to write up his speech and provide it to them for publication, "believing it to be a valuable contribution to Christian literature, on a most important subject."[50] The result was the publication in 1865 of *A Dissertation on the First and Third Abrahamic Covenants, The Covenant at Horeb, and the New Covenant. Their Differential Peculiarities.* Elder Jonas writes, for example, that the old covenant "took the whole nation in the aggregate...each had to bear the iniquity of the others, for the good of the whole."[51] The new covenant, on the contrary, was one based on "personal experience":

> The new covenant could only take the house of Israel, and the house of Judah in their individual capacity, and as there is no proxy obedience in this it took every man upon his own responsibility; and as its promises are spiritual it did not allow one man to bear the iniquity of another, as this would have involved guiltless eternal suffering; and as this suffering would have to be inflicted in a future life, it would be neither retributive nor disciplinary, but vindictive.[52]

As we have seen many times already, there is certainly nothing new about a Christian author invoking the term "Abrahamic" as a way to talk about

Christian supersessionism. Indeed, prior to the twentieth century the term is only used in such a sense. Elder Jonas, however, impressively ties together a number of features that constellate in the genre: the supersessionism of the old by the new covenant; the superiority of the metaphysical sign of the covenant (baptism) over its physical sign (circumcision); and the primacy of the individual over the collective. But for the good sense of Paul, writes Elder Jonas, the "grievous Jewish yoke would have been put upon the neck of the disciples...and [this] saved the church from universal Judaizing."[53]

At the end of his work, Elder Jonas makes an "Appeal to the Pedobaptist Clergy," in which he writes to Methodists, Presbyterians, Lutherans, and those of other Protestant denominations who insist on the practice. Unsurprisingly, he is not at all interested in Catholicism, a "popish" tradition far outside of the Protestant mainstream. In the Appeal, he makes the following comments,

> In word you have discarded the popish doctrine of "baptismal regeneration," but in your doctrinal standard and in your practice you hold to a kind of semi-infant baptismal regeneration by means of sprinkling a few drops of water on the face of an infant in the name of the Father, Son, and Holy Spirit. You have assigned eligibility for gospel blessings to the flesh, which belongs *only* to faith. In this you have placed the infant of a day upon an equality with the instructed believer in Christ, and elevated that which is born of the flesh, to that which is born of the Spirit.[54]

Protestant denominations, much like the Roman Catholic Church, are here implicitly accused of "Judaizing." They mistake the spirituality and the individuality of the credobaptist (one who is baptized on faith) for what, Elder Jonas implies, is a form of physical circumcision. For it is the individuality of the act, as we saw above, that defines the true believer in Jesus.

The pedobaptism/credobaptism debate witnessed in this section again shows how the term "Abrahamic" emerges from theological polemics. It does not refer to a historical reality, but a perception of the way things ought to have been. Is the Abrahamic covenant superseded or not? Although all Christian thinkers could agree that it was superseded and that the sign of the Abrahamic covenant—physical circumcision—was no longer necessary, they still debated the meaning of baptism. Was it to be done to infants or only to those who are "instructed believers in Christ"? The preceding debates show that the term "Abrahamic" was used polemically both interreligiously and intra-religiously.

Conclusions

The genealogical survey presented in this chapter clearly reveals that the noun "Abraham" and the adjective derived from it, "Abrahamic," are anything but ecumenical. They are, on the contrary, vehicles of exclusion based on the ideology of superiority. When they are invoked before the twentieth century, it is done solely as a way to show one's religious rivals the error of their ways and to claim that there is only one true and authentic way to understand Abraham. I say "show" in the previous sentence because none of the examples in this chapter *demonstrated* a claim so much as argued a position based on prior faith commitments. "Abrahamic," in other words, is never invoked objectively, but always religiously. Despite this, all who insisted on invoking the term made appeals to some vaguely constructed historical record. In all of the uses examined in this chapter, it is never applied in a value-neutral manner.

The examples that I chose to showcase here come from a variety of sources—ancient, medieval, and modern; some by well-known scholars and others from more obscure journals and even anonymous authors. The goal in cásting my net as wide as possible was to show the manifold venues in which this term has been employed and that, despite this variety, all uses can basically be reduced to the same polemical principle. The historical permutations of the term "Abrahamic" surveyed in this chapter all convey the same intent: Abraham is a mirror wherein each religion sees its own reflection. In order to admire this reflection, furthermore, anything that impeded it had to be excised and deemed inauthentic or a later invention.

It is also worth noting that of all the examples examined here not one has a positive valence. That is, none of these individuals are interested in showing commonalities or affinities. This is not selectivity on my part. In examining the term "Abrahamic" over the course of two millennia, in a variety of languages (Hebrew, Greek, Arabic, Latin, English), not once could I find it deployed in an ecumenical or interfaith sense. This might not be so surprising because, as we shall see shortly, ecumenism and interfaith dialogue are decidedly modern virtues and not necessarily premodern ones. In this latter sense, "Abrahamic" has functioned as an important trope to disable, dependent upon the author in question, the claims of Jews, Christians, Muslims, credobaptists, and pedobaptists.

In the modern period we shall see something quite different. It is to this period that I now turn.

3

From Supersessionism to Ecumenicism

DURING THE COURSE of the second half of the twentieth century the term "Abrahamic" underwent a surprising metamorphosis. Although the concept of Abraham's patrimony had been employed for the previous two millennia as a weapon in the arsenal of interreligious polemics, the last sixty years have witnessed it become increasingly associated with interfaith conversation. No longer invoked to exclude other religions by claiming sole spiritual proprietorship of an obscure biblical patriarch, "Abrahamic" has now been enfolded within the larger desire to envisage a set of commonalities among diverse religious heritages. Exclusivity gave way to inclusivity, and the ecumenicism of Abraham suddenly replaced the supersessionism that had traditionally been made in his name. Now we begin to witness the creation of an "Abrahamic religions" discourse, one that encourages us to imagine something positive, a common faith or "spiritual" bond that Jews, Christians, and Muslims share in the present and are perceived to have shared in the distant past. No longer the marker of a faith-based or religious superiority, the term has now become synonymous, both in the scholarly and popular imagination, with interfaith "trialogues," something that can be carried out against the backdrop of liberal theologizing.

The year 1995 might well have signaled a symbolic high point of this metamorphosis, for this was the year in which the Library of Congress introduced "Abrahamic religions" as one of its official Subject Headings. According to its official guide, "Abrahamic religions" was created to catalogue "works dealing collectively with Judaism, Christianity, and Islam, and sometimes other monotheistic religions, that discuss an underlying, common heritage traceable to the patriarch Abraham."[1] This "common heritage" is what is new and, despite the Library of Congress's surety and confidence, it is by no means obvious that such a heritage exists. Many of the works that fall under this Subject Heading, as I will show in the following chapter, are primarily ones of ecumenical theology and rarely, if ever, works devoted to historical analysis. The year 1995, however, is symbolic in that it presents us with a taxonomic category and, with it, the official justification to delineate a phenomenon imagined to exist naturally in the world. The present chapter seeks to chart some of the historical reasons that led to the eventual formation of this ahistorical Subject Heading. In so doing, it examines this sea change in the conception of Abraham, showing the manifold ideological and theological reasons behind its deployment.

This theme of religious coexistence and interfaith dialogue or trialogue has, not surprisingly, become especially popular in the aftermath of the terrorist attacks of September 11, 2001. Since then we readily encounter books with ecumenical titles such as *Heirs of Abraham*,[2] *The Tent of Abraham*,[3] *Abraham's Children*,[4] and *Building Interreligious Trust in a Climate of Fear: An Abrahamic Trialogue*.[5] The present chapter seeks to tell the story of how a term that was used solely in a pejorative and exclusive sense transformed into this new one of interfaith dialogue. Within the space of a century we encounter a near-complete reversal in usage. *The Tent of Abraham*, for example, is a far cry from titles that appeared in the previous chapter, such as *An Inquiry, Proving Infant-Baptism to be Untenable, As Well From the Abrahamic Covenant, As From the Scriptures At Large. Containing Also an Investigation of the Principles Which Bind Christians to Unite and Forbear with One Another*.[6] What were some of the external stimuli that led to this transformation? The answers to such a question, however, will again reveal that the term "Abrahamic religions" remains firmly entrenched in apologetics.

The argument of the present chapter is that scholars of Islam in the early and mid twentieth century—most notably those associated with the "school" of Louis Massignon—played an important initial role in this change of usage. Subsequently picked up by the Second Vatican Council in the 1960s, "Abrahamic" increasingly became a central trope to imagine and designate a commonality or a wistful paternity among three monotheisms at a time when they were increasingly at odds with one another. The 1940s and 1950s witnessed, among other things, the horrors of the Holocaust, the aftermath of the Second World War, the formation of the State of Israel and concomitant Israeli–Arab wars, and increasing troubles in the European colonies of North Africa, especially French Algeria. "Abrahamic" now became a convenient category both to point to a shared heritage and also, increasingly in the years following, to include Muslims in a manner that the more traditional, yet equally artificial,[7] rubric "Judeo-Christian" could not. And while the addition of "Abrahamic" to this increasing ecumenical vocabulary may well make us feel more multicultural, the replacement of one vague term with another does not help us understand any better the historical interactions of discrete religious traditions, each of which is in possession of its own complex set of characteristics that display tremendous temporal and geographical diversity.

Despite the fact that this chapter charts the metamorphosis and rehabilitation of the term "Abrahamic," I wish to argue that even in its new, transformed state, it is just as theologically and ideologically loaded as those usages examined in the previous chapter. The difference, of course, is that now it is used in a liberal and inclusive sense whereas in the past it was used to demark exclusivity and to argue that one's own religion possessed some unique claim to Abraham and his covenantal message. The fact remains, however, that there is no common "Abrahamic" religion. The "Abraham" of "Abrahamic religions" is a theological invention, now increasingly the product of an ecumenical, as opposed to supersessionist, imagination. What we do possess is a mythic story in Genesis that has been picked up and elaborated upon by Jews, Christian, and Muslims. This is a story that, as the previous chapter tried to argue, has provided the seeds of dissent and destruction for well over two millennia. Now, on the contrary, it is imagined as the harbinger of peaceful coexistence.

Those seeking an ecumenical Abraham, much like their supersessionist counterparts, are on unstable historical terrain. Those interested in reclaiming this Abraham for interfaith dialogue are not motivated by historical study, even though they may try to make certain appeals to it. Rather they imagine variously constructed romanticized and pristine periods of interfaith interaction. They subsequently create a set of words and categories based on their own contemporary concerns and desires, and then read these into various historical and textual sources. For example, many interested in the project of reclamation point to the "interfaith utopia" of Muslim Spain (the subject of chapter 6),[8] however, their portrayal is romantic and their interest is largely political: to remember a time of cultural and artistic *convivencia* and to conjure up hope that it may return again to the moment that Jews, Christians, and Muslims realize their shared inheritance and will presumably stop killing one another.

Yet in order to understand how we get to the ecumenical Abraham and the hope placed in "Abrahamic" as the symbol of peaceful coexistence in the contemporary period, we must turn to the first half of the twentieth century, for it was ultimately in French colonial outposts in the Middle East and North Africa and in the back rooms of the Vatican that our modern sense of "Abrahamic" was born. There Abraham was imagined, constructed, and reimagined to fit the needs of an interreligious dialogue that was gradually picking up momentum in the mid-twentieth century.

Louis Massignon and His Circle

The biography of Louis Massignon (1883–1962) is among the more interesting of early twentieth-century Orientalists. Combining a love and a passion for Arabic culture, the religion of Islam, and his own Catholic tradition, he ultimately translated them into one another's categories. A convert to Catholicism,[9] Massignon ultimately and paradoxically understood Islam through the lens of Jesus's life and crucifixion. Despite his commitment to his own religion, he was a vocal critic of French colonialism in North Africa and did much to elucidate Islam to Western audiences. In his desire to facilitate good relations between Christians and Muslims he was one of the earliest to appeal directly to the figure of Abraham. His reading of Abraham, especially in his role as the spiritual ancestor of the three religions, would have a direct influence on some of the key figures within the Second Vatican Council.

After receiving the equivalent of a doctorate in Paris, Massignon became involved in French colonial administration as a translator and, based on his knowledge of both Arabic and Islam, became part of the Sykes-Picot Agreement in 1917 that was responsible for delineating the British and French spheres of influence in the aftermath of the collapse of the Ottoman Empire. From 1917 to 1919, Massignon served as the assistant to Georges Picot, the High Commissioner of Palestine and Syria. After this, Massignon returned to Paris and was eventually appointed to the Chair of Muslim Sociology at the Collège de France, a position that he held until his retirement in 1954.

It is not the scholarship of Massignon that concerns me here—for example, his impressive magnum opus, a four-volume biography of the twelfth-century mystic al-Hallaj who was crucified on account of his antinomianism—but his relationship to Catholicism. It is the latter that ultimately drew him to the figure of Abraham.[10] Upon his return to Paris, for example, he became a Franciscan tertiary (lay member) and interestingly took "Ibrahim" as his spiritual name.[11] On February 9, 1934, on a trip to Egypt, he prayed at the abandoned Franciscan church in Damietta, the place where Francis of Assisi met the Sultan in 1219 and where he was said to have offered to demonstrate his faith in a trial by fire.[12] Based on his experience there, Massignon subsequently founded the Badaliya, an association of Arab and other Christians who desired to show the relevance of Jesus for Islam not by seeking proselytes, but by substituting (*badaliya*) themselves for Muslim souls and working for the betterment of Muslim society.[13] Shortly thereafter, Massignon also arranged for delegations of Muslims to attend and participate in the annual festival and pilgrimage in Brittany devoted to the Cult of the Seven Sleepers of Ephesus, a group of individuals who also appear in the Quran where they are known as the "folk of the cave."

In 1949, Massignon, with the permission of Pope Pius XII became a Melkite Greek Catholic, which allowed him to remain in the Roman Catholic Church but to take the Byzantine liturgy in Arabic. In January of 1950, the married Massignon was ordained as a priest in the same church (Greek Catholic priests are allowed to marry).[14] This act enabled Massignon to offer his own life in a salvific act in order to make reparation for others.[15] In retrospect, Massignon's activities with Muslims might well strike us as patronizing or insulting. This, however, was not his intention and he was clearly deeply committed to improving Christian–Muslim relations. His retirement from the Collège de France, for example, coincided with the Algerian War of Independence. These years witnessed him protest publicly against French atrocities in North Africa (for which he was publicly attacked in the street in 1958 and injured). He also visited North African prisoners and, in addition, ran adult literacy classes for North African workers. Many times after his retirement he was criticized for "lapsing into politics" at academic conferences.[16]

Interfaith dialogue was very important to Massignon. Using the metaphor of Abraham, he believed in the peaceful coexistence of Jews, Christians, and Muslims in the Middle East. Although not opposed to the foundation of the State of Israel in 1948, he was however opposed to the displacement of Arabs in the region at that time. He was especially critical of French involvement in Morocco and he sought a peaceful solution to the war in Algeria. It is within this context of coexistence that Massignon published his *Les trois prières d'Abraham: seconde prière* (The Three Prayers of Abraham: The Second Prayer) in 1935.[17] This work, an extended meditation on Abraham's prayer for Ishmael, connects the blessings of Abraham in the Genesis account to Muhammad, his message, and subsequent generations of Arabs. Although Muhammad certainly possessed the faith of Abraham, according to Massignon, he did not go as far as Jesus and, for this reason the Quran denies Jesus's Incarnation and death on the Cross.[18] Although Muslim faith is real and heartfelt, in Massignon's opinion, it needs to be completed by Christian charity. Massignon concludes the work by claiming that, to use Neal Robinson's words, "The rift between the three Abrahamic religions will not finally be healed until Christ returns and, as Muslims themselves believe, Jerusalem once more becomes the direction of prayer."[19]

Roughly fifteen years later, in 1949, Massignon published a smaller version of this work entitled *"Les trois prières d'Abraham, père di tous les croyants"* (The Three Prayers of Abraham, Father of All Believers).[20] As in the earlier treatise, he again offers a theological account of the prayers of Abraham in the book of Genesis and their relevance today. He writes, responding to the possibilities of the newly formed State of Israel, that all three traditions must have respect for one another and for the "Holy Land" that they all share through their common Abrahamic inheritance. In a passage worth quoting at length, Massignon explains,

> Like history, the geography of today brings us closer to Abraham by focusing our attention on a high place of humanity which began with his own....Here is the physical return of the two inimical brothers to the chosen place of their resurrection (the al-Aqsa mosque for Muslims, the Temple for the Jews, only 150 meters apart on the same *Haram*); and only 350 meters from the Anastasis or Qiyama (The Holy Sepulcher) of the Christians, who, because they have not yet developed sufficient consciousness of their "Abrahamic adoption," are not yet concerned about returning to Jerusalem to await the Parousia of the Lord. Nevertheless, there in Jerusalem the Christians have Arab witnesses of their faith and the geographical convergence of the pilgrims of the three Abrahamic faiths in one and the same Holy Land, trying to find there that justice which Abraham through his threefold trial found in his God, led a year ago to a horrible war. Why? Because the Christians have not yet fulfilled their complete responsibility toward their brothers in Abraham. Because they have not yet explained to them how to love the Holy Land, which is one of the two terms of the promise to Abraham.[21]

This passage is important for a number of reasons. First, it represents the symbolic halfway point on our genealogical journey. Far beyond the unpalatable supersessionism of the previous chapter, we are still not at the end of the journey where "Abrahamic" emerges as a truly ecumenical and seemingly value-neutral term. Although Massignon is certainly much more ecumenical and dialogic than the individuals encountered in chapter 2, he still contends that the other "Abrahamic religions" need Christianity for some sort of spiritual completion or fulfillment. This, for lack of a better term, Catholic supremacy is something that we will also encounter in the following section, when I examine the use of Abraham and "Abrahamic" in some of the documents associated with Vatican II. Second, and this is a new development, Massignon links the three religions to Abraham and uses this common source to explain some of the commonalities among them. Third, and perhaps most importantly from the contemporary perspective, Massignon stresses this "Abrahamic" bond in a time of war, when Jews and Muslims were engaged in conflict within the newly formed State of Israel. Abraham, in other words, is offered as a symbol of peace and hope in the midst of internecine squabbling.

Two years after Massignon's essay, in 1952, there appeared in Paris a special edition of the journal *Cahiers Sioniens* entitled *Abraham: Père des croyants* (Abraham: Father of the Believers).[22] There had certainly been attempts at interfaith conversation before this, but they had primarily consisted of just Jews and Christians. In 1947, for example, Jules Isaac, an author and French survivor of the Holocaust, and Paul Demann, a Catholic priest, convened a formal dialogue of Jews, Catholics, and Protestants in Seelisberg, Switzerland. Massignon's significance is that he introduced Muslims into these conversations and he did so, moreover, using the figure of Abraham. *Abraham: Père des croyants* is unique in that, following in the footsteps of Massignon, it represents one of the earliest interfaith attempts to examine the figure of Abraham. Noticeable is the fact that it was not simply written from a Catholic perspective. For example, one of the contributors is a Jew, P.-J. de Menasce, a specialist in Arabic and Islamic philosophy, who wrote an essay entitled "*Traditions juives sur Abraham*" (Jewish Traditions about Abraham) and another, an Arab, Youakim Moubarac, a Marionite priest interested in interfaith dialogue, has an essay entitled "*Abraham en Islam*" (Abraham in Islam). However, despite these two essays the other seven essays are primarily devoted to the figure of Abraham in the New Testament, in the Christian liturgy, in the Christian tradition, and in Kierkegaard. Also notable is the fact that the person responsible for the piece on Islam, while an Arab, is not a Muslim. Muslims, in other words, are not given a voice of their own in the earliest examples of this genre. In his preface to the volume, Son Eminence le Cardinal Tisserant nevertheless strikes the ecumenical and theological tone of the essays to follow:

> At a time when neopagan materialism forces us to compromise and let go of our spiritual values, the example of Abraham's faith can give courage to all those who can admire it. Jews, Christians and Muslims are united in their invincible confidence in the absolute power of He who grants it to those who request.[23]

Abraham here is offered as an antidote to the spiritual malaise of Europe, something particularly apropos in the immediate aftermath of the Second World War. France—in its post-Vichy era, in the aftermath of the Holocaust, and at a time of growing conflict with its North African colonies (especially Algeria)—is in dire need, Cardinal Tisserant believes, of a symbol that can heal wounds among diverse peoples and religions. Abraham, for him, as for Massignon, provides the way out of the malaise. It seems to me that this is one of the major reasons behind the gravitation of Massignon and the contributors of the above volume to this ancient patriarch. An ahistorical Abraham ultimately presents an escape from history.[24]

****

During his years as Chair of Muslim Sociology at the Collège de France, Massignon trained many of the next generation of French and Arab Islamicists, including Henry Corbin, the Egyptian Abd al-Rahman Badawi, and the American-born George Makdisi. Although I shall examine Massignon's influence on the Catholic Church and its policy of Abrahamic and interfaith dialogue in the following section, let me briefly turn now to one of his American protégés. Born in St. Cloud, Minnesota, and educated at Saint John's Abbey, Princeton, and Harvard, James Kritzeck (1930–) would go on to become Professor of Oriental Studies at Princeton and a member of the Center for Theological Inquiry at the same institution. Influenced by Massignon, Kritzeck in 1965 published a slim volume entitled *Sons of Abraham: Jews, Christians, and Moslems.* This is one of the earliest uses of the newly redefined term "Abrahamic religions" in the United States. In this book, Kritzeck's goal is to introduce American audiences to "a few of the best recent invitations to a dialogue with Islam on the part of Catholic Christians."[25]

Kritzeck subsequently describes the recently deceased Massignon as "an active participant in all recent efforts at promoting Christian–Muslim understanding, and...the greatest figure of our age in the line that goes back to Peter the Venerable and St. John Damascene."[26] Given the strife in the Middle East and well aware of the "burden" of peaceful coexistence, Kritzeck—not surprisingly, given what we have seen so far and given the title of his book—holds up Abraham as the starting point of "dialogue among the sons of Abraham":

> It stands to reason that the dialogue of which we are speaking cannot be legislated. It has nothing whatever to do with politics. It cannot seek or enjoy the arena of the United Nations. It can never be a confederation or a conclave. It can never use the ballot. No philanthropic foundation can set it up. No advertising campaign, however skillful, can promote its aims or guarantee its solvency. It must have many beginnings, and they must all be humble.[27]

Reminiscent of the "Abrahamic salons" envisaged by Bruce Feiler that we encountered at the beginning of chapter 1, Kritzeck here seeks a heartfelt and grassroots set of exchanges among members of the three religions. A necessary prerequisite for Abrahamic recognition is that members of the three religions engage in meaningful dialogue with one another. This is an early example of what will become in the 1990s and 2000s a virtual cottage industry. At the end of the book, in particular, Krtizeck argues that there must "be further efforts among Jews, Christians, and Moslems to understand one another better, and to realize more fully both their common traditions and their common debts. This realization will enable them better to know, to love, and to serve the God of Abraham, Isaac and Jacob."[28]

Vatican II

James Kritzeck ends his *Sons of Abraham* with appeals to recently published documents stressing interfaith dialogue associated with the Second Vatican Council (1962–1965). He quotes at length from the Latin of some of the documents that had not yet been issued as official translations.

Kritzeck's interest in and use of Vatican II documents, however, is not simply one of coincidence. Linking Kritzeck and Vatican II is Louis Massignon, someone whom the former had already described as the towering figure of Muslim–Christian dialogue. Although Massignon had passed away during the first session of the Council in 1962, his presence, or more precisely his conception of Abraham and dialogue, would reverberate through a number of the documents that the Council ultimately produced. In this respect Vatican II—especially the documents concerned with relations between the Church and other religions, *Nostra aetate* and *Lumen gentium*—would carry on Massignon's legacy and further contribute to the transformation and rehabilitation of the term "Abrahamic."

Pope John XXIII convened the Second Vatican Council in 1962 in order to address the nature of the relationship between the Church and the modern world.[29] When he died a year into the Council, Pope Paul VI was elected as his successor. Interestingly, the latter was not only sympathetic to Islam, but was both a confidant of Massignon and a member of the Badaliya.[30] The latter, it will be recalled, was founded by Massignon as a way for Catholics to offer their lives for Muslims so that God's will might be channeled toward them.

The legacy of Massignon, the particular theological proclivities of Pope Paul VI, the acknowledged need for interreligious dialogue in the years after the Second World War, and the growing conflict in the Middle East all lurked in the background of Vatican II. And all would leave their indelible mark on those documents that dealt specifically with the Church's relationship to other religions. Although we will encounter in these documents the invocation of Abraham, the "seed of Abraham" and other such phrases, it is still largely invoked in the spirit of Massignon. That is, while Judaism and Islam may well make certain claims to be the true descendants of Abraham, the final arbiter in matters of the spirit and salvation is, for obvious reasons, the Church, whose claim to Abraham and the Abrahamic covenant is considered to be eternal and absolute.

Nostra Aetate (In Our Age), also referred to as the Declaration on the Relationship of the Church to Non-Christian Religions, is perhaps the best known and most discussed of the documents dealing with interfaith relations that came out of Vatican II.[31] It is not without its fair share of behind-the-scenes controversy, however. In 1961, just prior to the Council, the Secretariat produced a draft document detailing the Church's relationship to the Jews entitled *Decretum Iudaeis* (Decree on the Jews). This document was passed on to the Central Commission which was responsible for ultimately deciding whether or not to bring it forth to the Council. It never made it, however, on account of increasing pressure from Arab countries, many of whom feared the Vatican was on the verge of diplomatically recognizing the State of Israel. A subsequent draft of the document— now entitled *De Catholicorum habitudine ad non-christianos et maxime ad Iudaeos* (The Attitude of Catholicism to non-Christians and especially to the Jews)—denounced the idea that the Jews were guilty collectively of dei- cide and recommended "mutual understanding and appreciation" among Christians and Jews. Again, however, this never made it to the Council because Pope Paul VI wanted to avoid controversy before his pilgrimage to the Holy Land which was to occur at the beginning of 1964, since many of the Holy Sites were then under the control of the Arabs.

A new draft of the document appeared on September 25, 1964, entitled *De Iudaeos et de non-christianis* (On Jews and Non-Christians). Whereas previous drafts had primarily been devoted to Jews, this new document, to the surprise of many, introduced paragraphs devoted to other religions, especially Islam. It is impossible to know if this was the result of Pope Paul VI, who was, as we saw, part of Massignon's Badaliya movement and, as such, open to Christian–Muslim dialogue. Moreover, some of the earlier language that denounced the accusations of Jews as a "gens dei- cida" was dropped. "This neutralization of themes concerning Jews and the mention of the Muslims," according to Risto Jukko, a historian of the documents, "can be interpreted as a concession to the political pressures applied by the Arab states."[32] Once again the document was revised, rewrit- ten, and resubmitted under the title *De Ecclesiae habitudine ad religiones non-christianas* (The Relation of the Church to non-Christian Religions). Voting took place on the document between the fourteenth and fifteenth of October, 1965. In the final vote 1,763 were for accepting the document, 250 against, and 10 declared invalid; compared to other votes, the num- ber of dissenting voices was quite high. At any rate, on October 28 of that same year Pope Paul VI promulgated the document, whose opening words were "*Nostra Aetate.*"

The document is quick to make a connection between Muslims and the patriarch Abraham. For example, in paragraph 3 we read:

The Church regards with esteem also the Moslems. They adore the one God, living and subsisting in Himself; merciful and all- powerful, the Creator of heaven and earth, who has spoken to men; they take pains to submit wholeheartedly to even His inscrutable decrees, just as Abraham, with whom the faith of Islam takes pleasure in linking itself, submitted to God. Though they do not acknowledge Jesus as God, they revere Him as a prophet. They also honor Mary, His virgin Mother; at times they even call on her with devotion. In addition, they await the day of judgment when God will render their desserts to all those who have been raised up from the dead. Finally, they value the moral life and worship God especially through prayer, almsgiving and fasting.

Since in the course of centuries not a few quarrels and hostilities have arisen between Christians and Moslems, this sacred synod urges all to forget the past and to work sincerely for mutual understanding and to preserve as well as to promote together for the benefit of all mankind social justice and moral welfare, as well as peace and freedom.[33]

In this passage we encounter a number of important features that have direct bearing on the concept "Abrahamic." First, there is the recognition of a common historical heritage: Muslims and Christians have the same God, they both await the Day of Judgment, and so on. Second, Abraham is broached as a possible link between the two religions. This concept of the "Abrahamic" heritage is something that John Paul II (d. 2005), probably the Pope most interested in interfaith dialogue, seized upon and used frequently in his speeches and other documents.[34] Third, there is the attempt to find doctrinal similarities between the Church and Islam that could facilitate dialogue. Both Islam and Christianity, despite their historical quarrels, strive after "social justice and moral welfare, as well as peace and freedom."

It is nevertheless important to note some of the tensions or, at best, inconsistencies that emerge from the document. First, the "Abrahamic" heritage is something to which Muslims "take pleasure linking" themselves; it is not a connection, in other words, that the Church necessarily wants to make for them. In addition, there is no mention in the above paragraph of anything that characterizes Islam as a distinctive religious tradition: no mention, for instance, of Muhammad, of the Quran, or of any of the practices and/or beliefs that put Muslims and Christians potentially at odds with one another.

Lest it be mistaken that Muslims are the only ones who "take pleasure" in linking themselves to Abraham, the paragraph immediately following the aforementioned reminds us to remember "the bond that spiritually ties the people of the New Covenant to Abraham's stock."[35] With this statement—one that incidentally implies that it is the Church that represents the true Abrahamic inheritance—functioning as a bridge, *Nostra Aetate* subsequently goes on to mention Jews and Judaism:

> Although the Church is the new people of God, the Jews should not be presented as rejected or accursed by God, as if this followed from the Holy Scriptures. All should see to it, then, that in catechetical work or in the preaching of the word of God they do not teach anything that does not conform to the truth of the Gospel and the spirit of Christ.
>
> Furthermore, in her rejection of every persecution against any man, the Church, mindful of the patrimony she shares with the Jews and moved not by political reasons but by the Gospel's spiritual love, decries hatred, persecutions, displays of anti-Semitism, directed against Jews at any time and by anyone.[36]

This paragraph, on one level, recycles the trope encountered in the previous chapter that the Jews represent the Old Covenant, one that has been superseded by the New. However, it stops there and instead of engaging in further polemics makes the positive point that Jews should neither be seen as rejected or accursed. Interestingly, there is no mention of the connection between the Jews and Abraham. Either this is to be taken for granted or, even more interestingly, perhaps it is Jewish denials of Jesus and Mary, two individuals whom Muslims acknowledge, that removes them from some sort of perceived "Abrahamic" bond, defined by the Church, that both Muslims and Christians are perceived to share. This latter position would certainly not be out of line with the Badaliya movement, to which Pope Paul VI belonged.

About a month later—on November 21, 1964—Pope Paul VI promulgated another document, entitled *Lumen Gentium* (Light of the Nations), part of which also concerns the Church's relation to non-Christian religions. Despite the "Abrahamic" status granted to Muslims in *Nostra Aetate*, this document is slightly more hesitant. The latter's hesitancy becomes even more interesting when we focus on the history of one of its sentences. In the draft document this sentence read:

> The sons of Ishmael, who acknowledging Abraham as their father also believe in the God of Abraham, are not total strangers to the revelation made to the Patriarchs.[37]

Of the 530 proposals for improving the seventy-four-page document roughly half focused on this one particular sentence. Many were bothered that the Muslims were referred to as the "sons of Ishmael" and that Islam somehow possessed the authentic revelation of Abraham and the other patriarchs. In the final version of *Lumen Gentium*, the sentence was replaced with the following:

> But the plan of salvation also includes those who acknowledge the Creator. In the first place amongst these there are the Mohammedans, who, professing to hold the faith of Abraham, along with us adore the one and merciful God, who on the last day will judge mankind.[38]

Note that in the new version of this sentence all references to Muslims as the "sons of Ishmael" have been removed and that they are now described as "Mohammedan" (not "Abrahamic"), and as only *professing* to hold the faith of Abraham (that is, not actually holding it). The struggle over who constitutes the true descendants of Abraham, while certainly different from that encountered in the previous chapter, nonetheless continues to live on in these Vatican II documents.

The political and ideological wranglings behind *Nostra Aetate* and *Lumen Gentium* are fascinating stories in and of themselves. However, I have mentioned them within the context of the present chapter because they add several important layers to our understanding of the term "Abrahamic." Primary is the fact that the term, following the lead of Massignon, is slowly becoming more positive. No longer is the invocation of Abraham confined solely to the realm of interreligious polemics, in particular who represents the true heirs of Abraham and thus which religion is the most authentically "Abrahamic" in the sense of being the purest or most pristine. We now begin to see the term shed some (but certainly not all) of its exclusivity and take on a more inclusive tone. This metamorphosis is directly connected to increased European, but especially French, colonialism of the 1930s, 1940s, and 1950s, primarily within the context of North Africa and the Middle East.

It is also important to emphasize that use of the term "Abrahamic" was largely employed, at least at the beginning, by scholars of Islam. However, its deployment, from what I can tell, seems not to be used in their scholarly writings, but primarily in their theological reflections. "Abrahamic," for example, never appears, again as far as I am aware, in Massignon's massive scholarly study of al-Hallaj. It is certainly worth qualifying this statement, however, with the observation that, for some of these scholars, the line separating academic and theological/personal reflection was fine and they most certainly were informed by their endeavors as scholars. "Abrahamic religions," in short, is quickly ceasing to function, if it ever did, as a scholarly term and in the process is becoming a vague theological referent. It was reimagined and subsequently invoked, as we have seen throughout this chapter, during times of crises and as a way to negotiate beyond it.

"Abrahamic" as the New "Judeo-Christian"

In the decades after Vatican II, the term "Abrahamic" slowly begins to be used by some as a possible replacement for the term "Judeo-Christian." The latter term had come into vogue in the 1940s to refer to a set of ethical interests that Jews and Christians were believed to hold in common. "Judeo-Christian" was largely propagated by the National Conference of Christians and Jews whose mandate was to fight anti-Semitism and in the process create a more tolerant and inclusive idea of America and American values rather than just reproduce Christian or Protestant ones.[39] Not insignificantly for the story being recounted here, the National Conference of Christians and Jews changed its name in the 1990s to the National Conference for Community and Justice "to better reflect the breadth and depth of its mission, the growing diversity of our country and our need to be more inclusive."[40] "Judeo-Christian," in other words, was a term that many increasingly regarded as too exclusive to reflect adequately the reality of a set of perceived qualities believed to be shared by a larger group than just Jews and Christians. "Abrahamic" could at least be used to include Muslims.

As early as 1952, for example, President Dwight Eisenhower could say that "Our sense of government has no sense unless it is founded in a deeply religious faith, and I don't care what it is. With us of course it is the Judeo-Christian concept, but it must be a religion that all men are created equal."[41] In recent years, as more Muslims became a part of the fabric of American life there has arisen the need to open up the "Judeo-Christian" values shared by Jews and Christians to Islam. As a monotheistic religion that worships the same God and shares many of the prophets with Jews and Christians, we increasingly encounter the invocation of "Abrahamic" values and traditions to refer to this new reality. This process of inclusion was no doubt facilitated by the discourses of inclusion ushered in by documents such as those produced by Vatican II.

One of the earliest uses of "Abrahamic" in this regard occurred in America in 1979 at the American Academy of Religion (AAR) annual meeting in New York City. The organizer of the Islamic Studies Group of the AAR, Ismail al-Faruqi, writes that the

> Islamic Studies Committee entertained the vision of bringing together members of the Jewish, Christian and Muslim academic communities in the United States to dialogue with one another on the subject of their own faiths. This was a novel undertaking unprecedented in AAR history; the Islāmic Studies Committee sought and obtained the assistance of the Inter-Religious Peace Colloquium (later called The Muslim–Jewish–Christian Conference—MJCC), the only western body with any experience in the matter.[42]

This meeting of the Islamic Studies group at the AAR is important for several reasons. First, it again gives evidence that in the post–Vatican II era it is primarily Muslims or scholars of Islam who are trying to force change to the traditional, but equally invented, category of "Judeo-Christian" by opening it up to Islam and Muslims under the new rubric "Abrahamic." Second, it is occurring within the context of the AAR, an organization, as we shall see in the following chapter, which has a lot invested in using and disseminating the term "Abrahamic" in the contemporary period. Third, and relatedly, "Abrahamic," by being used at a conference devoted to the *academic* study of religion, is implied to be a historical reality that can be elucidated academically. It is also worth noting that the third edition of this little volume was published in 1991, in the immediate aftermath of the first Gulf War "that left the world with the clear understanding that in order to achieve a lasting peace the members of the three Abrahamic faith communities will have to learn to come to terms with one another."[43]

In his keynote address, "The Catholic Church and the Jewish and Muslim Faiths: Trialogue of the Three Abrahamic Faiths," the late Cardinal Sergio Pignedoli from the Vatican Secretariat for Non-Christians upholds the need for the faith of Abraham in the modern world because "even if it has been enriched with many exterior values . . . [it] has nevertheless become spiritually impoverished to a disturbing degree."[44] He begins his address by acknowledging the work of earlier scholars, most notably Louis Massignon, who "have shown us the road we should walk."[45] This poverty in modern thinking, recalling Cardinal Tisserant's fear of "neo-pagan materialism" almost twenty-five years earlier, requires an antidote, which the Cardinal locates in the figure of Abraham and his tripartite heritage:

> The faith of Abraham, who is rightly considered by our three religions as "the father of our faith," will be the subject of my reflections, I shall remain within the limits of its essential values and not enter into a consideration of the differences of these religions, united as they are in the acceptance of Abrahamic faith and in their considering it to be a source of inspiration and a guide for human life, capable of giving a satisfactory response to the essential problem of man.[46]

A number of telling features emerge from this passage. Why is it "rightly considered" that Abraham is the father of these three religions? There is no historical proof for this claim. It is a claim, moreover, that when this passage was originally written in 1979, was only a few decades old and by no means self-evident. As is fairly typical of this genre, there are passing references to theological concepts such as "belief" and "faith adherence" that are followed by a selection of biblical, Quranic, and rabbinic verses that give evidence to the concepts that he has already chosen to highlight. There is, however, no appeal to the historical record to show how, why, or even if such concepts have been invoked in the past.[47] Also telling is the interest in the "essential values" that the three religions share. Terms such as "covenantal obligation" and "ethics" are mentioned, but no attention is paid to how they have been historically constructed and contested by various groups within and among the three traditions. Instead what we are presented with, and this is probably the defining hallmark of the "Abrahamic religions" discourse, is a series of essential qualities that all three of these religions are believed to share with one another. What happens to those groups within the three larger religions that either do not share such qualities or contest them? No mention is ever made of those individuals and groups that question such qualities. If and when they are mentioned, especially in the post-9/11 world, it is usually to say that they have "misunderstood" or, better, "hijacked" some tradition believed to be normative.[48]

Note that Cardinal Pignedoli's plea is also written well before the year 2001—before September 11, before the first Gulf War, before the second Gulf War, before the "War on Terror," before the invasion of

Afghanistan—before the entire "clash of civilizations" rhetoric. Cardinal Pignedoli's interest in the term "trialogue of the three Abrahamic faiths" is not directed at explaining how rogue elements (read "terrorists") in each religion are outliers who misunderstand the true faith of Abraham. Nor does he give the conflict in the Middle East much thought. His goal is to show how the faith of Abraham gives "a satisfactory response to the essential problems of man."

It is only in the years after this little AAR-sponsored volume was produced that "Abrahamic" would be invoked as a response to religious militancy and internecine strife. Even though the papers were both written and presented in 1979, presumably at the height of the Iranian Revolution and the subsequent Iran hostage crisis (November 4, 1979 to January 20, 1981), very little mention is made of such events.[49] Instead, and telling of this term's history, "Abrahamic" here and in so much of what we have witnessed in this chapter, is held up as a response to irreligion—to materialism, to atheism, and to the spiritual absence of life removed from Abrahamic faith.

Skipping ahead a few decades we witness another attempt to stress the common heritage of Islam and Christianity. In his articulate and well-argued *The Case for Islamo-Christian Culture*, Richard W. Bulliet, perhaps not surprisingly also an Islamicist, argues that these two religions have tremendous common roots and history—as much as, or perhaps even more than, Christianity and Judaism. Writing post-9/11, he argues that the conflation of "Judeo-Christian civilization" with "Western civilization" is based on the desire to include Jews in American and European political discourse in the aftermath of the Nazi atrocities associated with the Second World War. We now use "Judeo-Christian," Bulliet correctly observes, "almost reflexively in our schoolbooks, our political rhetoric, and our presentation of ourselves to others around the world."[50] Rather than exclude Muslims with such concepts, Bulliet argues that we need to acknowledge the shared heritage of the three religions and, thereby, bypass the blanket term "Judeo-Christian":

> Yet the scriptural and doctrinal linkages between Judaism and Christianity are no closer than those between Judaism and Islam, or between Christianity and Islam; and historians are well aware of the enormous contributions of Muslim thinkers to the pool of late medieval philosophical and scientific thought that the European Christians and Jews later drew upon to create the modern West. Despite periods

of warfare, European merchants for centuries carried on a lively commerce with the Muslims on the southern and eastern shores of the Mediterranean; and the European imagination has long teemed with stories of the Moors, Saracens, and oriental fantasy.[51]

Unlike many other examples in this genre, however, Bulliet makes appeals to the historical record to try to show precisely how such commonalities have played out and the ramifications they have on the present. Indeed, perhaps because of this he nowhere uses the term "Abrahamic" and, as such, avoids the blanket essentialisms of so many of those who do. However, what Bulliet does share with many of those examined in this chapter is the fact that he is someone trained in the academic study of Islam and—like Massignon, Kritzeck, and others—he uses his impressive knowledge of this tradition to make appeals to a category—for them "Abrahamic," for him "Islamo-Christian"—that is hopeful and interfaith.

A much less historical account and much more politically motivated attempt to replace "Judeo-Christian" with "Abrahamic" may be found in Imam Feisal Abdul Rauf's post-2001 *What's Right with Islam*. In one stunning passage, he observes that we ought to replace the Christian emphases of the American Constitution with "Abrahamic":

> The intentions of America's founders matched the Islamic idea, namely, a nation "under God." The authors of the Declaration and the Constitution focused especially on the social aspects of the Abrahamic ethic, the rights and liberties of individuals and their freedom to practice their religion, or practice no religion at all, as their consciences dictated, unimpaired by the state. These rights flow from the Abrahamic ethic, from the second commandment to treat one's fellow human beings the way one wants to be treated. But the founders believed in one God, God, the Creator of everything, thus of nature, their concept of such a God was very much the Abrahamic concept, the one all-powerful providential Creator, a concept of God that can be accepted by all Abrahamic religions.[52]

Conclusions

If President Eisenhower introduced the term "Judeo-Christian" into American political rhetoric in the 1950s, President Obama did the same for "Abrahamic" in the year 2009. In his so-called speech to the Muslim world delivered in Cairo on June 4 of that year, he remarked that:

> Too many tears have flowed. Too much blood has been shed. All of us have a responsibility to work for the day when the mothers of Israelis and Palestinians can see their children grow up without fear; when the Holy Land of three great faiths is the place of peace that God intended it to be; when Jerusalem is a secure and lasting home for Jews and Christians and Muslims, and a place for all of the children of Abraham to mingle peacefully together as in the story of Isra, when Moses, Jesus, and Mohammed (peace be upon them) joined in prayer.[53]

Here President Obama makes appeals to the shared heritage of Jews, Christians, and Muslims by invoking what is now becoming a well-worn trope: "the children of Abraham." As neither a historian nor a critical theorist of religion, he invokes this term, as so many do today, as a sign of hope in a world of increasing religious violence. He is not interested, again like many others, in whether or not "Abrahamic" points to or names some sort of independent reality outside of a liberal theological hope for interreligious coexistence.

The goal of this chapter has been to explore how we got from the supersessionist arguments of the previous chapter to its contemporary usage. This journey has seen "Abraham" and "Abrahamic religions" slowly emerge as a response to mid-twentieth-century conflicts associated with the end of World War II, European colonialism, and the formation of the State of Israel. Picked up by the Catholic Church as a trope to find commonality with other traditions, especially Islam, "Abrahamic" increasingly was invoked as a more inclusive category than "Judeo-Christian." Finally, at the end of this chapter, we begin to get a glimpse of its modern usage: "Abraham" and "Abrahamic religions" now function as interfaith terms that proffer a lifeline to a troubled present and future.

It is this modern usage that I now examine in greater detail.

4

Modern Usage

IN HIS *The Divine Programme of the World's History* (1888), the Irish Protestant Christian preacher and key figure in the Ulster Revival of 1859, H. Grattan Guinness, DD, divided humanity into two distinct spheres. His major criterion for classification was the perceived relationship to "the seed of Abraham." He writes,

> But what of the blessedness of this half of humanity compared with that of the larger half which has not yet come under the influence of Abraham and his seed? By blessedness we at present mean only the evident outward manifestations of happiness, prosperity, and hopeful prospects for the future; the mental illumination and physical well-being which we include in the one comprehensive expression, *progressive civilization*. Which of the two halves of humanity is in these senses the most "blessed"? In the monotheist or Abrahamic group we should have the English, Scotch and Irish, the Norwegians, Swedes and Danes, the Dutch, Belgian and French, the Spaniards, Portuguese and Italians, the Swiss, Austrians and Greeks, the Germans, Poles and Russians; the hundred millions of similar races in America, Africa and Australian, and seven millions of Christianized negroes in the United States and those in the West Indies, the eight millions of Jews scattered throughout the world; the Eastern Christians of the Armenian, Nestorian, Marionite and Coptic churches of Syria and Egypt, and in addition to these the entire Mohammedan world numbering 170 millions, and including Arabs, Sikhs, Persians, Turks, Egyptian, Moors and Berbers, extending from India and Arabia to the Atlantic; together with all the converts from heathenism, gathered in of late years through missionary activity.

> In the other group, the non-Abrahamic or polytheistic group, we should have such families and nations as the Japanese and Chinese, including the black hairy Ainos of the former, and the wild Shan and Miautse tribes of the latter; the dark Buddhist Mongols, Thibetians, and Tartars, the wild and cruel Calmucs and Kurds, the superstitious and caste-ridden Tamils, Telegus and Bengalis, the Singhalese, Burmnas and Siamese, the wretched and degraded Gonds, Bhils and Santhals of India; the Malays and Papuans, the blood-thirsty Dyaks of Borneo and the animal-like native Australians; the (heathen) Malagasy, the fierce Zulus and naked Kaffirs, the warlike Griquas and Matabele, the Hottentots and Namaquas, the monkey-like Bushmen of the Kalihari desert, who have lost almost the semblance of humanity....[1]

After having divided humanity into two distinct spheres, Guinness asks rhetorically, "Can any one hesitate for a single moment in deciding as to which of these two groups of the nations of the earth is the 'blessed' or happy one?"[2] Not content to leave matters alone, he subsequently distinguishes between those of the "Abrahamic" variety. Islam, according to him, "though monotheistic," lacks the true blessing of Abraham. And the Israelites, as is the custom in this literature, refused to see that the covenant of Abraham was spiritual and not temporal or fleshly.[3] It is, perhaps not surprisingly, Christianity that represents the true spiritual fulfillment of the covenant between God and Abraham and that guarantees the salvation of mankind. Guinness, however, goes even further and subsequently connects Abraham to race and the various forms of Christianity:

> The Christian nations take the lead this day in the world, and especially those which hold the purest forms of Christianity. Foremost among all the races of the human family stand the Protestant Saxons, German and English, the two mightiest nations of Europe, and the latter, with its American representative, the dominant power of the Western world.[4]

Such attempts to classify the religions of the world based on criteria preselected as critical or essential by the interpreter is certainly not unique to H. Grattan Guinness.[5] What rings clearly in the passages quoted above, however, is his desire to use the imagined category "Abrahamic" as the sole criterion for classification. Once this has been carried out, other differentia can be neatly employed (e.g., race, purity) to create further similarities and differences between the various classes.[6] Instead of such an essential view of classification—namely, the belief that our classification systems accurately reflect the natural world—it is necessary to regard such classificatory systems for what they really are: cultural inventions that arise to provide those doing the classifying with the tools necessary to achieve the specific outcomes that they deem important.[7]

The present chapter seeks to explore some of the ways that the term "Abrahamic religions" has been employed to name a set of Western traditions and subsequently differentiate them from other religions. "Abrahamic religions," as imprecise as the term is, has now been co-opted to name a set of perceived essences (e.g., faith, monotheism, covenant) that are imagined to reside at the heart of Judaism, Christianity, and Islam. These three religions are, in turn, seen as qualitatively different from other religions that are also believed to be in possession of their own unique, yet equally amorphous, essences. "Abrahamic religions" can now be differentiated from and compared with "Eastern religions," "non-Abrahamic religions," the "great Asian cosmic religions," or the "axial religions of Asia and China."

After exploring some of the essential characteristics believed to reside at the common heart of these three religions, I proceed to examine the modern uses to which the category has been put in the years following 2001. No longer perceived in a supersessionist manner (as seen in chapter 2) or as a moral antidote to a contemporary malaise (as in chapter 3), we now clearly see the origins of what I have labeled the "Abrahamic religions" discourse begin to emerge. Now it is used specifically to delineate a set of qualities in the quest for interfaith understanding. Like its predecessors, however, the term is still ahistorical and essential.

"Abrahamic" and Others

"Abrahamic religions" are increasingly used to define a set of traits believed to be common to Judaism, Christianity, and Islam. These traits are then reified and juxtaposed against similarly reified traits perceived to exist in so-called "non-Abrahamic" religions. The end result of this process is that "Abrahamic religions" no longer simply denote a belief in Abrahamic ancestry, but a distinct way of being. Leonard Swidler, the American doyen of interfaith dialogue, for example, writes that

> The three Abrahamic faiths have many more things in common, such as the importance of covenant, of law and faith, and of the

community (witness in the three traditions the central role of the terms *people, church,* and *ummah,* respectively). But just looking at the list of commonalities already briefly spelled out will provide us with an initial set of fundamental reasons why it is imperative to engage in serious, ongoing dialogue with Muslims.[8]

These traits, for Swidler, structure the mentality of believers, thereby differentiating them from the believers of other traditions. This not only creates a set of essences between so-called "Abrahamic" and "non-Abrahamic religions," it provides—as we shall see later in the chapter—the groundwork for believing that if the three "Abrahamic religions" could only realize their common spiritual heritage, they could all somehow get along with one another.

This formation of a second order, generic category that we call "Abrahamic" is, like all such generic categories, largely of our own making. It is, to invoke J. Z. Smith, not a native term, but an imposition on our data for the sake of our higher comparative projects.[9] As witnessed in the previous chapter, there is nothing natural about "Abrahamic religions"; rather, Abraham was only regarded as a common denominator of the three traditions in the early twentieth century, and "Abrahamic religions" was only coined in the 1980s and 1990s to invoke a set of similarities that paradoxically each of the three religions had spent the previous millennia trying to disprove. The category, thus, forces an artificial order on three radically different traditions that are frequently made, as seen in Swidler's remarks above, for the sake of interfaith dialogue.

Perhaps nowhere is this taxonomic use of the term more clear than in a rather obscure book published in 1993, by Ronald Werner, with the title *Transcultural Healing: The Whole Human: Healing Systems under the Influence of Abrahamic Religions, Eastern Religions and Beliefs, Paganism, New Religions, and Mixed Religious Forms.*[10] Without worrying about the contents of the monograph, it is certainly worth noting that Werner's taxonomic division—one that is certainly not uncommon—structures his subsequent understanding of his topic of study, in this case "transcultural healing." In the title we see clearly how "Abrahamic religions" are assumed to consist of a set of essential characteristics that can be juxtaposed with other religions, be they "Eastern," "pagan," "new," or "mixed." Too often, as we shall witness in the pages that follow, such convenient labels are put on all sorts of complex sociocultural formations as way to impose a perceived order on messiness or chaos. However, rather than provide order, they actually tend to obscure our understanding of the data in question by leveling complexity.

A brief survey of some of the uses to which "Abrahamic" has been put in this taxonomic sense is telling. Many of these instances are used to illumine some deep, essential, or necessary trait that somehow makes them unique from all other ("non-Abrahamic") religions. For example, Jürgen Moltmann argues that

> Every comparison with the great Asian cosmic religions shows the unique character of the Abrahamic religions: the future is something new; it is not the return of the past. The world is not held in the great equilibrium of the cosmos and its harmony. As God's creation, it is aligned towards the future of his eternal kingdom and hence is temporal.[11]

Such ahistorical vagaries are one of the hallmarks of this genre. Commonalities are perceived in abstract theological categories, not historical specifics. Ori Z. Soltes, in another example, finds the following set of similarities to be indicative of this shared heritage:

> All three Abrahamic faiths further their exploration of the relationship between *sacer* and *profanus* with deep and wide oceans of interpretive literature directed to the material that they regarded as divinely revealed. Thus, the early Jewish rabbinic literature, the Midrash and the Talmud, will continue as a wealth of medieval and postmedieval commentary; the Christian patristic literatures, East and West, will continue as a rich body of medieval scholastic and postmedieval commentary; the Shi'ite and Sunni branches of Islam will each yield major schools of theological perspective that carry from the medieval toward the modern world.[12]

Such statements are essentially meaningless. Once again we witness how they attempt to draw historical effects from ahistorical causes. The results are extremely general and vague.

The term "Abrahamic" has had such widespread appeal in the last few years in academic and nonacademic works that it is now being employed in rather strange and contorted ways in other disciplines. J. Lorand Matory, an anthropologist, can make the claim: "I have little respect for the sexual Puritanism and homophobia of the Abrahamic religions, and my respect for non-Abrahamic religious traditions could never hinge upon either."[13] Or Prasenjit Duara, a historian of development and international relations, can write that, unlike China, Abrahamic religions "developed a deep tension between transcendence and human effort to realize it."[14]

Such comments further make "Abrahamic religions" into the stuff of imagination and desire. As in previous chapters, some aspect of one particular tradition or even sub-tradition (e.g., homophobia) is magnified and allowed to become a, if not the, defining element of the three religions. In the following passage, for example, Judy Carter and Gordon S. Smith have no problem neatly differentiating the bellicosity of "Abrahamic religions" with the inherent passivity of "Asian religions":

> In contrast to the Abrahamic faiths, religious traditions originating in Asia tend, in their teachings, to be more inclusive and tolerant. Confucianism, Hinduism, and Buddhism offer lessons on how religion and governance can be juxtaposed and how beliefs can inform policy and action. Confucianism, Hinduism, and Buddhism contrast with the Abrahamic faiths in that they tend to encourage an inward focus and discourage proselytization. Instead of trying to persuade others to their beliefs and win new converts, adherents to Eastern faiths tend to focus on making themselves and their fellow believers better people.[15]

All of these examples, while certainly differing from the goal that H. Grattan Guinness set for himself at the beginning of this chapter, nonetheless share certain similarities. For one, all construct "Abrahamic" in their own image. Whether superior or inferior, bellicose or spiritual, homophobic or egalitarian, all take a vague or imprecise term, rearrange it to fit their intellectual or theological agendas, and then raise it to the level of a category. Moreover, all create a system predicated on similarity and difference that requires explanation by making appeals to older comparative and theological claims. Such claims, as witnessed in previous chapters, are based on apologetics and, in the present, they succeed in creating a category with very little room for nuance or variation to compare with or against equally problematic categories.

"Abrahamic Religions" in Interfaith Dialogue

Although for most of its history the term "Abrahamic" has been used primarily in an exclusionary manner, the second half of the twentieth century witnessed, as we saw in the previous chapter, a sea change. In the 1990s, the term became increasingly used to propagate "trialogue" among Judaism, Christianity, and Islam. This trialogue is predicated, for those involved in it, on the desire to acknowledge the perceived shared heritage of the three monotheistic religions. In their coauthored *Faith, Religion and Theology*, Brennan R. Hill, Paul Knitter, and William Madges make this explicit when they inform us, for example, that trialogue between the three is necessary and must be predicated on the notion that "all three claim their origins in Abraham."[16]

In the same year that their book appeared, the aforementioned Leonard Swidler published his *After the Absolute*. The goal of this volume, as the author makes clear in his introduction, is to help create "a common language, an 'ecumenical Esperanto,' [that] must be developed to supplement, though not supplant, the various religious and ideological languages."[17] In the course of the work, he devotes a chapter to "Jewish–Christian–Muslim Trialogue," which is necessary because, according to him, all three of these religions "come from the same Hebraic roots and claim Abraham as their originating ancestor; the historical, cultural, and religious traditions all flow out of one original source, an *Urquelle*."[18] Such a claim, of course, is difficult to maintain except in an abstract theological way. What is this "original source"? Can all "historical, cultural, and religious traditions" really be reduced to flowing from such a source?

The goal of this interfaith literature is not about various identity formations, their appeals to ideology, which take place in distinct temporal and geographic contexts. The goal, on the contrary, is to find essential commonalities. The easiest way to do this is not to confront the present which is the heart of the conflict between the three traditions, but to return to a murky past where such commonalities can be imagined. To quote Swidler, quoting Hans Küng, another key figure in the interfaith dialogue effort, "*the criterion for being a Christian* is not the later developed doctrine of the Trinity, but the belief in the one and only God, the practical following of Jesus in trust in the power of the Spirit of God.... *Back to the origins*. At the origins we Jews, Christian and Muslims are closer to each other."[19]

Perhaps not coincidentally the year 1993 also witnessed the reconstitution of the Parliament of the World's Religions to mark the centenary of the original Parliament in 1893. Convening in the Palmer House Hotel in Chicago, this Parliament witnessed over 8,000 delegates from all over the world, representing the planet's diverse religious traditions.[20] Their collective goal was to celebrate, discuss, and explore how the world's religious traditions could work together on a number of critical issues. Most notable was the issue of interfaith dialogue, particularly how different religions could talk to one another in such a manner that they might solve some of the pressing problems of the day.[21]

In 1995 Karl-Josef Kuschel, a student of Hans Küng, published a hefty volume entitled *Streit um Abraham: Was Juden, Christen und Muslime trennt—und was sie eint* and translated into English as *Abraham: Sign of Hope for Jews, Christian and Muslims.*[22] Kuschel's motivation behind writing the book is to make others aware that, at the origin of all three religions, there "lies a source of peace which time and again has been and still is obscured on all sides by fanaticism and exclusiveness."[23] He locates this origin, not surprisingly, in the patriarch Abraham. Carrying the myth further than we have seen by others, Kuschel argues that even though Abraham's two children, Isaac and Ishmael, were rivals, they nevertheless were blood relatives. From this primal history located in biblical myth, Kuschel reads the ongoing tensions between kindred peoples—Jews, Christians, and Muslims.

To try and solve the contemporary impasse between these three religious traditions, Kuschel proposes establishing an "Abrahamic ecumene." While not wanting to ignore differences between the three religions, his goal is to make it possible for Jews, Christians, and Muslims to recognize "the presence of the primal father and primal mother in each other's brothers and sisters within the Abrahamic family."[24] Reflecting on this shared heritage, moving toward an inclusive as opposed to an exclusive understanding of Abraham is what permits the establishment of this "ecumene." Kuschel argues that

> Those who think ecumenically, as brothers and sisters, in the spirit of Abraham, Hagar, and Sarah, have parted company with any exclusivism and thus resolved the paradox of the commandeering of Abraham. They have recognized in gratitude how fruitful the tribe of these ancestors has been all down the centuries, they no longer feel jealousy or exclusion, but only joy at how many different children spring from the one stem and how much substance of faith, energy for hope and power of love have come and still come from the one root. They have drawn a line under a theology which reclaims the blessing of the parent only for its own branch.[25]

Once again, from a liberal theological or interfaith perspective, this desire to find commonality between three discrete traditions in order to get certain constituencies within each to talk to one another is certainly a noble endeavor. Surely, it is better to have Jews, Christians, and Muslims talking to one another about Abraham than killing in his name. However, my objections to Kushel, like so many others discussed in this chapter, is that they have largely transcribed a theological category into a historical one with very dubious results. Kushel, for example, implies that the three religious traditions have been aware of their "Abrahamic bond" for "centuries." As I have tried to argue throughout this study, they most certainly have not. This acknowledgment of an Abrahamic bond, and the formation of an "Abrahamic religions" discourse that manufactures such a bond, is a very modern phenomenon that dates to the period immediately after World War Two.

Also telling of Kuschel's theological desire is his unwillingness to look at history or the historical record. His three-hundred-plus-page book is devoted to a theological elucidation in Jewish, Christian, and Muslim scriptures and theological writings. He makes no mention of how these three religions have actually put into praxis their perceived Abrahamic heritage. I certainly do not have a problem with this, because the likes of Kuschel, Swidler, Küng and others are, for the most part, honest about what they are doing and not doing: they are writing liberal interfaith theology and not history. Although they sometimes have strange ideas about history and what is an "authentic" expression of religion,[26] they all, for the most part, seem to be aware that they are writing as theologians.

When "Abrahamic religions" is used today within the academic study of religions, this type of ecumenicism is usually lurking in the background. Only now the intentions of those who employ the term are not nearly as clear and transparent. In the section that follows I examine some of the uses to which the category has been put in the years after the attacks of September 11, 2001. Therein we will see how the interfaith desires of the present section have been further exploited and elaborated. The difference between this section and the next, however, is that whereas in this section the "Abrahamic religions" discourse discussed has been used by theologians writing works of theology, in the next section we will see that it is often adopted by scholars of religion.

"Abrahamic Religions" Post-9/11

Hans-Josef Kuschel, writing in the conclusion to his 1995 work, prayed that the year 2000, the beginning of Christianity's third millennium, "would provide a unique opportunity for a demonstration of Abrahamic hospitality and brotherhood and sisterhood worldwide."[27] Instead, a year into the start of the third millennium, the world witnessed planes fly into the twin towers of the World Trade Center in New York City, and the subsequent "War on Terror" world in which we all now live. This war, framed by many as a "clash of civilizations," was regarded as pitting Islam against the West or, phrased in the language of many, of Ishmael against Isaac.

Recall that "Abrahamic religions" only became a Subject Heading at the Library of Congress in 1995. Since that time thirty-nine volumes have used this heading, all but two of which were published before 2001. Although it is worth noting that not every book published on the topic of Jewish–Christian–Muslim relations chooses to use this heading,[28] the great majority of the volumes that fall under the "Abrahamic religions" rubric are devoted to interfaith and ecumenical examinations of the topic.

Much of the literature published after 2001 is not surprisingly devoted to the topic of trying to show filiations between the three traditions. Exemplary is a small work published by the United States Institute of Peace[29] in 2007 with the title *Unity in Diversity: Interfaith Dialogue in the Middle East*. The authors of the book—Mohammed Abu-Nimer, Amal Khoury, and Emily Welty—inform us that

> Jews, Muslims, and Christians share and identify as fellow pilgrims on a path—a path all three faiths understand to be profoundly rooted in concepts of truth and peace. Adherents of the Abrahamic faiths believe that right conduct is essential and that sacred texts hold instructions about how to live an ethical, just life that is pleasing to God. Jews, Christians, and Muslims share the belief that God wants them to live a life full of respect for justice, peace, and human relationships. All three believe in the validity of revelation as a sign from God and struggle to maintain unity in spite of splits in their populations (Reform/Orthodox, Shiite/Sunni, Protestant/Catholic).[30]

Once again we see appeals to a vague notion of "Abrahamic religions" to show a set of commonalities that all three religions *essentially* possess. They are described here as "fellow pilgrims" on the way; they all share common notions of truth and peace that are rooted in their respective scriptures. After such generalities, there is a halfhearted appeal to history. Although the three religions "struggle to maintain unity," we are informed that each religion split into various denominations (i.e., Reform/Orthodox in Judaism; Shi'ite/Sunni in Islam; and Protestant/Catholic in Christianity). All three of these "splits" are presented here as if they are identical to one another. The reasons for the "split" between Reform and Orthodox Judaism in nineteenth-century Germany, for example, are assumed to be similar to the factors that led to the "split" between Shi'i and Sunni Islam in ninth-century Baghdad. Historically, however, these represent two very different schisms and rather than address such difference, they are instead swept under the carpet in favor of making an ecumenical point. See, the authors imply, these three "Abrahamic religions" are essentially the same; they even have "splits" within them based on similar theological differences.

Many of these works seek to offer a scholarly alternative to the so-called "clash of civilizations." Samuel Huntington, it will be recalled, argued that future conflicts will take place between adjacent civilizations with differing sets of core values. He is quick to point to the notion that conflicts are "particularly prevalent between Muslims and non-Muslims," and labels as "bloody" the borders between Islamic and non-Islamic civilizations.[31] To correct this assumption, Richard Bulliet, as we saw in the previous chapter, published *The Case for Islamo-Christian Civilization*. Therein he attempts to show in great detail and with appeals to the historical record the nature and scope of Islam's interactions with the so-called West. Perhaps because of this, as I tried to suggest, Bulliet does not employ the theological category "Abrahamic religions," and is instead content to focus on particular examples of Christian-Muslims relations. Less interested in the specifics of such historical interactions, however, many others opposed to Huntington's thesis invoke the language and spirit of Abraham. In their editors' introduction to the *Heirs of Abraham: The Future of Muslim, Jewish, and Christian Relations*, Bradford E. Hinze and Irfan A. Omar write that

> Some, with Harvard political theoriest [sic] Samuel Huntington, believe that we are witnessing a new era defined in terms of the clash of civilizations. This book seeks to offer an alternative to those who see only a future of ongoing contestation between members of these three faith traditions. Instead, we wish to advance mutual respect and appreciation, even friendship, and most importantly, collaboration among the heirs of Abraham, building on the long history of such effort and achievements.[32]

As is fairly common in this literature, the editors speak of facilitating "mutual respect and appreciation" among the three religions. The way they go about this, according to this passage, is to demonstrate the "long history" of collaboration among the three, although the authors rarely, if ever, make appeals to this "long history." Instead we are presented with living representatives from the three different "Abrahamic" traditions—Mahmoud Ayoub (Islam), Reuven Firestone (Judaism), and Archbishop Michael Fitzgerald (Christianity)—offering their takes on Abraham. Each account, however, is largely based on scripture and scriptural theology as opposed to history. The result is, as the editors themselves make clear in their preface, "a significant example of the kinds of interfaith work under way in communities in the United States and around the world."[33]

This use of Abraham and "Abrahamic religions" is common in interfaith work, and it is this use that largely drives the employment of what is now, for all intents and purposes, an academic discourse. In his editorial introduction to *The Meeting of Civilizations: Muslim, Christian, and Jewish*, Moshe Ma'oz also emphasizes the importance of stressing the common Abrahamic bond of Judaism, Christianity, and Islam as a way of "denying the recently propagated concept of 'clash of civilizations.'"[34] In a section devoted to the topic "Contemporary Relations and Challenges," several contributors to Ma'oz's volume further articulate a trope that we have seen throughout this chapter: if the three religions would just become aware of their common heritage they would be in a position to resolve real and potential tensions. According to Nathan C. Funk and Meena Sharify Funk, for example,

> Nevertheless, it is to be hoped—and we do not have the luxury of giving up on hope—that the children of Abraham may now be on the threshold of finding within themselves the magnanimity required to appreciate one another on deeper levels. The fact that they have not achieved this in the past may have much less to do with inherent deficiencies within the faiths than with the psychology of fear and adversarialism that has developed in the shadow of political conflict.[35]

The authors here hope that the three religions can realize their shared heritage and, invoking the sibling metaphor that is a common feature of this literature,[36] their emotional attachment to one another. The reason for the current malaise, they argue, may have nothing to do with the religions themselves, but with what they call the "psychology of fear" that emerges not from religious sentiment, but political conflict.[37] The key to co-existence is to return to the spiritual aspects of religion, seeking common ground in the search for respect of both self and other. They write,

> Given the extent to which Abrahamic religions have been coopted by religious nationalism and drawn into contemporary geopolitical conflict, building Abrahamic solidarity will require sustained efforts to challenge the legitimacy of religious as well as secular militancy, and to transform the role of religion in conflict by providing positive options.[38]

As vessels of peace, religions do good in the world. When they do not or are invoked for a variety of nefarious purposes, this is the result of religion being hijacked or distorted for political ends. In such arguments, there are no analyses of historical interactions of the religions in question other than vague invocations of, for example, Muslim Spain or the fact that Muslims transmitted Greek philosophy to the West.[39] In such literature, facts can be distorted if they get in the way of a good story. In this latter sense, another contributor to the volume, Azyumardi Azra, writes that

> Seen from an Islamic perspective, the three religions—Judaism, Christianity and Islam—have their shared origin in the personage of Abraham (Arabic, Ibrahim). The original religion of Abraham was called in the Qur'an *millah Ibrahim*, Abrahamic "way of life," or rather, religion. According to the teaching of Islam, Muslims should recognize not only the prophecy of Abraham, but also the relations of Islam with Judaism and Christianity, the followers of which are called *ahl al-kitab*, people of the (revealed) Books.[40]

In this paragraph, Azra stresses both the universal and the particular dimension of "Abrahamic religions." From the "Islamic perspective"— although which one, he never specifies—all three religions have a shared origin. He argues that this origin stems from the *millat Ibrāhīm*. However, he nowhere mentions the claim that, according to both the Quran and subsequent normative Islamic theology, Abraham's religion was Islam and was subsequently corrupted or bastardized by later generations of Jews and Christians. This plays a large role, as we witnessed in chapter

2, in Muslim supersessionist arguments. Azra then goes on to claim that Islam's respect for the other two monotheisms became systematized under the legal rubric "People of the Book." This is only partly true, however. This rubric was primarily promulgated, many years after the Quran, as a way to levy taxes among those who had not converted to Islam. It is a legal term, not an interfaith one.

For Azra, as for so many others writing about "Abrahamic religions" at the present moment, actual textual citations and historical uses of terms are unimportant. What is important is that a reified and sanitized "Abrahamic religions" be held up as a beacon for peace in a world of conflict. Azra, like the Funks in the same volume, blames not religion, but rogue elements, for conflict:

> Therefore, we may suggest that religions are one of the sources of harmony and peace; but we have to admit that at the same time the Abrahamic religions, as any other religion, have been and could be used by certain individuals or groups of believers as a justification of conflict, violence and even war. In recent times, the use and abuse of religions for political purposes steadily increased.[41]

So if one of the major uses of "Abrahamic religions" in the contemporary period is to imagine a shared heritage in the face of the "clash of civilizations," another major usage is that it now becomes a metaphor for a pure, peaceful, and uncorrupted (and incorruptible) monotheism. This monotheism, the inheritance bequeathed by Abraham to his siblings, must be guarded and protected lest it be corrupted for political purposes. Practitioners of "Abrahamic religion" must, according to Karen Armstrong, another staunch proponent of Abrahamic coexistence, "reclaim their traditions from murderous sectarianism and return to the compassion that is the core of their faith."[42]

More academic than many of the aforementioned books, Fordham University Press, in the aftermath of 9/11, created The Abrahamic Dialogue Series. The first volume in its series is entitled *Beyond Violence: Religious Sources of Social Transformation in Judaism, Christianity, and Islam.* Its editor, James L. Heft, S.M., writes that

> Serious interreligious dialogue is, historically speaking, only in its infancy. The purpose of interreligious dialogue is not always clear. Is it conversion? Better mutual understanding? Collaboration

without any effort at conversion? Is the point for a Christian, for example, to help a Muslim become a better Muslim or a Jew a better Jew?...Answers to these questions vary and at times contradict each other. Two things are certain: people of different religions mix with each other now more than ever before, and respect for people of other religions is better than violence.[43]

Despite the tone of the volume, including essays by the likes of Charles Taylor, we again see "Abrahamic religions" used and invoked in the sense of interfaith dialogue. This, to reiterate, is the overwhelming manner in which it has been deployed since the 1990s, and especially since 2001. Abraham, appealed to as the original source of all three religions, becomes—as we have seen time and again in this chapter—the figure that can heal old wounds and encourage coexistence in the modern era.

The results are extremely mixed. From an interfaith and liberal theological point of view, "Abrahamic religions" function as a meeting place, a locus of hope, in which members of different religions can talk with one another and discuss their perceived commonalities. If the category can get such individuals and groups to talk to one another, it certainly fulfills its ecumenical role. This is certainly not my quarrel with the term. My problem is that the term has increasingly been invoked and used in academic sources as if it were a valid analytical tool. Thus we are told that "Abrahamic" myths and themes can be distinguished from others because they have a different set of emphases. They are driven by faith in the divine, a promise of future greatness, of moral and ethical responsibility, and the like. These traits or qualities can then be neatly juxtaposed and compared with other religions, so-called "Eastern," "non-Abrahamic," or "non-prophetic" ones.

Certainly, on some levels, comparison of religious forms involves a degree of caricature. Features can be and are grouped together for the sake of examining something in counterpoint to others and appreciating difference. The comparative enterprise is predicated on distortion and, for this reason, as J. Z. Smith notes, "in comparison a magic dwells."[44] Yet this distortion, and this is my concern in this study, threatens to impede understanding. Caricatures risk becoming fixed as clichés or as natural (as opposed to scholarly) objects of study. The constant repetition of clichés, such as shared heritages, common origins in faith, and the like, or invocations and references to what "*the* Abrahamic religions" believe create the impression of a generalized historical or religious unity for which there is very little evidence and against which there is a great deal.

Institutions

Before I leave this examination of contemporary invocations of "Abrahamic religions," let me examine some of its other non-academic or quasi-academic usages.[45] Within this context, there exist many foundations and conferences that use the term "Abrahamic" in them. A brief survey provides another discursive site to explore the uses to which "Abrahamic religions" are put.

Perhaps the earliest of such institutions is the Fraternité d'Abraham, which was founded in 1967, in the aftermath of the Second Vatican Council, as a response to the new initiatives toward Jews and Muslims, and which is still active to this day.[46] It is comprised of the chief rabbi of France, the Chancellor of the Great Mosque in Paris, in addition to numerous high-level Catholic, Protestant, and Orthodox leaders in France and abroad. In 2000, for example, the late Pope John Paul II was named President of the Fraternity. From its original charter in 1967, we read that "Abraham, constitutes the common spiritual and cultural inheritance [of Jews, Christians, and Muslims]" and that they must "work together to reconcile the descent from Abraham in order to release the world from the clutch of hatred, fanatic violence, racial pride by revealing the authentic and divine sources of a fraternal humanism."[47]

In order to realize the bond of Abrahamic fraternity, the organization sponsors annual conferences, with titles such as "Convergence des trois monothéismes dans l'amour de Dieu et des hommes" ("The Convergence of the Three Monotheism on the Love of God and Humans) and "Les Ecritures dans les religions abrahamiques: rôle et lectures" ("Scripture in the Abrahamic Religions: Their Role and Readings"). From this a variety of other interfaith meetings have taken place in France, such as the three-day conference in 1982 on the topic "Faith in Abraham" that took place in Chantilly, or the 1986 conference on "The Search for God" that took place in Toulouse.

In Britain, the Maimonides Foundation was founded in the 1990s with the aim of promoting coexistence between Jews, Christians, and Muslims in the United Kingdom. According to its web page, the foundation works

to enhance and further dialogue between the three communities through a series of innovative and progressive programmes.
The Foundation continues to initiate new activities with a greater
degree of cooperation between Jews, Christians and Muslims; by

involving prominent leaders and individual members of all three communities in the hope of furthering a peaceful and meaningful co-existence for the Children of Abraham.[48]

The foundation uses the name of the great twelfth-century Jewish philosopher and legalist Moses Maimonides (1135–1204). Their Web site describes him as "a symbol of the best of our common past and of human kind's ability to transcend and overcome intolerance, hatred, bigotry, and ignorance. He was the product of an era of enlightened religious tolerance and cultural co-existence between Jews and Muslims, these are the ideals which we in the Maimonides Foundation try to emulate."[49]

In the United States the "Trialogue of the Abrahamic Faiths" began in 1978, sponsored by the Kennedy Institute of Ethics at Georgetown University.[50] The trialogue was organized and directed by Sargent Shriver, Eugene Fisher, and Leonard Swidler. The trialogue was composed of twenty Jewish, Christian, and Muslim scholars who met for three days twice a year between 1978 and 1982. This gave way in 1989 to the International Scholars' Annual Trialogue (ISAT)[51] run by Leonard Swidler of Temple University and sponsored by the *Journal of Ecumenical Studies.*[52] The purpose of the conferences that emerge from these trialogues, as their Web site makes clear, is to involve academics in interfaith dialogue:

> These conferences bring together leading scholars from each of the Abrahamic faiths in regions where interreligious understanding is crucial to promoting stability and peace. Through intensive dialogue, academics and regional leaders use religious diplomacy to address communities in crisis.[53]

These are not Jewish, Christian, and Muslim professors of mathematics or physics, but scholars of religion. Once again we witness a certain slippage between theological and academic work that, in my opinion, has negative consequences on our ability to understand the dynamics of these three religions and their historical interactions. Subsequent post-9/11 American interfaith initiatives include "Abraham's vision"[54] and "The Abrahamic Alliance."[55] The advisory board of both organizations is made up of academics, many of whom specialize in religion and/or Near Eastern Studies.

Other "Abrahamic" institutions based in academic settings include the Henry Luce Forum in Abrahamic Religion—which was co-sponsored by the Greenberg Center of Judaic Studies at the University of Hartford and the Hartford Seminary's center for the study of Islam and Christian–Muslim relations—which ran from 1996 to 2002. The goal of this forum was to advance scholarship and public understanding concerning the interfaith interconnections between American Jews, Christians, and Muslims. The forum sponsored conferences, invited visiting scholars to campus, and was the subject of a public television film, *The Road to Morocco: Journey to Understanding*, which documented American Jews, Christians, and Muslims in trialogue with one another.

A Chair in the Study of the Abrahamic Religions at Oxford University was established in 2008. It was announced to the media in the following terms:

> Relations between Judaism, Christianity, and Islam often hit the world's headlines because of violent conflict. But research at Oxford University reveals stories of fruitful co-existence that point towards creative possibilities for future relations.[56]

I am uncertain as to the type of research that was conducted in the famed laboratories at Oxford, but "coexistence" only tells one side of the complicated relationships between these three complex and multi-faceted social formations. The news briefing even goes so far as to define what the study of "Abrahamic religions" consists of:

> The term "Abrahamic Religions" is increasingly used to refer to the three religions of Judaism, Christianity and Islam—all of which refer to the teachings of Abraham and his descendants. As an academic subject, Abrahamic Religions focuses especially on relations between the three religions. Research in the Abrahamic Religions involves studying the founding texts of each religion, through a range of philosophical, historical, artistic and political topics. Its field stretches in time from the ancient world through to the present and spreads out from the Middle Eastern origins of the three religions to span the globe.[57]

According to this passage "Abrahamic religions" are to be studied in a manner that focuses on their "relations." Note that it nowhere specifies what these relations consist of. Are they historical relations? Theological? Sociological? Following this, we learn that research should be based on a study of the "founding texts" of each of the three religions. Is this study to be literary, philological, source-based, or a combination of the three? We are then informed that the texts in question are to be examined through a range of "philosophical, historical, artistic and political topics." Yet we know that these three religions interacted not just scripturally, but also legally, economically, materially, and so on, often in ways that had nothing to do with their "founding texts."[58] Although Oxford would ultimately appoint an excellent scholar of late antiquity, Guy G. Stroumsa, in the press release announcing his hire, Paul Joyce, the Chairman of the Theology Faculty Board, was reduced to the clichés that we have seen time and again this chapter: "Jews, Christians, and Muslims all refer to Abraham as a friend of God, and I hope that the establishment of this important post will contribute to deepening friendship among these three great religions focused especially on relations between the three religions."[59]

Moving from Oxford to Merrimack College in North Andover, Massachusetts, we witness the establishment of the Goldziher Prize named for the famed Jewish scholar of Islam, Ignác Goldziher (1850–1921). At Merrimack, the Goldziher Prize, sponsored by the Center for Jewish–Christian–Muslim Relations, is awarded "for work that contributes significantly to reverence, understanding and collaboration in common moral purposes between Jews and Muslims."[60] It is uncertain to what "reverence" and "common moral purposes" might refer, or even to how an adjudicating committee might quantify or judge it. "Reverence," to quote Bruce Lincoln, "is a religious, and not a scholarly virtue. When good manners and good conscience cannot be reconciled, the demands of the latter ought to prevail."[61] Reverence, in other words, is associated with political correctness and a refusal to engage in certain kinds of analyses because they might prove insensitive to certain individuals or groups.

Recent years have witnessed a rise in various conferences and colloquia devoted to the subject of "Abrahamic religions." In 2007, for example, the Harvard Divinity School and the Weatherhead Center for International Affairs jointly sponsored a conference entitled "Children of Abraham: Trialogue of Civilizations."[62] The goal of the conference was to "discuss theological and historical relations among Christians, Jews, and Muslims: commonalities and divergence, as well as cooperation and strife, during both medieval and modern eras. It will also highlight the issues of education, interfaith activities, and Jerusalem as foci of dispute and 'trialogue.'" Once again we witness the tensions between the so-called historical and the theological. Is a theological presentation of these three religions the same thing as a historical one? Do they complement or contradict one another?

In 2004 Marquette University hosted an Interfaith Symposium on Peace Service in the Abrahamic Traditions. "The two chief aims of the symposium were to highlight the need for collaboration among diverse groups in working toward peace, and to take concrete steps toward developing the notion of peace service in the Abrahamic tradition."[63] In like manner, the Center for Christian–Jewish Understanding at Sacred Heart University, in Fairfield, Connecticut, hosted another symposium in April 2003, again with the goal of aiding interfaith understanding and thus coexistence. According to the symposium's web page, "The purpose of the conference was for leaders and scholars in the Jewish, Christian and Muslim religions to identify those teachings and values in each tradition that promote peace, the failures of each tradition to live up to their ideals, and ways to improve the teachings and practices to achieve peace."[64] Again we see the conflation of religious leaders and scholars of religion. Yet these are not one and the same thing.[65]

I could go on and list other such interfaith organizations and ecumenical quasi-academic conferences. However, I think I have already established my point that the term "Abrahamic religions" as conceived and utilized in the contemporary period is one that is highly theological and largely based upon interfaith dialogue. Its sole purpose is to facilitate coexistence and cooperation, not to engage in historical analysis.

"Abrahamic" and Its Discontents

In the midst of all this interfaith dialogue in the name of Abraham, there exist numerous outliers. Many, as witnessed at the end of chapter 2, seem to come from those conservative theologians and seminarians who still want to argue, in good supersessionist fashion, that Christianity is the true heir to the Abrahamic covenant as established in the book of Genesis. Invoking arguments of old, such individuals argue that Jesus, as the spiritual heir of Abraham's seed, makes possible the true fulfillment of God's covenant.[66]

Yet another iteration of this may be found among those who wish to deny Islam's claim to be an "Abrahamic religion." This argument is a fairly common one among neoconservatives, many of whom wish to return to the "Judeo-Christian" values of old and often have an ideological ax to grind with what they perceive the "real" Islam to be.[67] Such critics are notoriously hostile toward Islam and what they perceive as "Islamist," "Wahhabi," or "jihadist" attempts to undermine the American Constitution and replace it with some vague form of "Sharia law."[68]

In a somewhat different twist, Michael Knowles—a self-described "freelance student of theology"[69]—attempts to argue that Islam cannot be Abrahamic because of its tenuous relationship to Jesus. Judaism is an "Abrahamic religion," according to him, because Jews can claim "physical descent" from Abraham. Christianity, of course, transcends this because even "God's promises were made to Abraham and were realised in the person of Christ, not for a single nation however but for all mankind."[70] Because Judaism led to Jesus, according to Knowles's estimation, it is permitted to be called "Abrahamic," but because Islam does not, it cannot be part of the "Abrahamic family." "The assertion that Islam does match what we have to say about Judaism," according to him, "is not compatible with God's saving plan."[71] Knowles looks to Paul's letter to the Galatians and argues that Paul's anger in the letter was motivated by his concern that "his Galatian Christians might be turned from the true 'good news' of what Jesus Christ was to a false gospel."[72] These are harsh words indeed and their implications are both severe and would seem to take us back to a different era.[73]

Conclusions

With Knowles's article we return to the Pauline epistles, the place from whence we set out on our genealogical survey at the beginning of chapter 2. There we saw how both Christian and Muslim thinkers invoked "Abraham" as a way to discredit the claims of rival monotheisms. For many Christian theologians, Abraham represented the true covenant with God, one that was not based on the strict legalism of the Law, but upon faith, the virtue that defined every true believer of Jesus. For Muslims, on the contrary, the religion of Abraham represented the most authentic and pristine form of monotheism, the one that Muhammad restored on the Arabian Peninsula in the seventh century of the common era; the one that was meant to remove all of the imperfections that generations of Jews and Christians had introduced into their own scriptures and traditions.

Chapter 3, however, introduced us to the sea change in the use of the term "Abrahamic religions." Beginning in the 1950s—in the aftermath of both the Second World War and the Holocaust, and at the beginnings of the formation of the State of Israel and colonial unrest—Abraham suddenly appeared as a common source of what had hitherto been three rival monotheisms. Especially in Catholic circles, Abraham became the sign of hope in a world that was threatened with anomie and chaos. Against the chilly winds of history, Abraham provided a cloak of dignity and security. Increasingly, many began to see this inclusive use of Abraham as a replacement for the equally invented "Judeo-Christian."

It was but a short step from here to its employment as an interfaith term in the contemporary period. Now "Abrahamic religions," especially in the aftermath of 9/11, became a symbol of peaceful coexistence and of peace-building. Time and again in this chapter we have seen appeals to this ahistorical construct as the seeds of hope for global harmony and a future in which Jews, Christians, and Muslims will finally—after centuries of hostility—recognize their shared patrimony.

These three chapters have attempted to demonstrate that the term "Abrahamic religions" has always been invoked and employed ideologically and theologically. Whether to exclude or include, "Abrahamic religions" performs very little analytical or historical work. Used heuristically, the term flattens and levels numerous and important differences between not just three discrete religions, but also all of the variations that take place— geographically and temporally—*within* these three traditions. This is certainly not to say that there are no striking similarities or patterns among them or subsets within these three traditions, no features that justify the creation of common categories or terms with which to group or label them. Rather, my argument is that the category "Abrahamic religions" is not the answer to organizing this complexity.

5

On Words

THE PREVIOUS THREE chapters have explored the genealogical heritage responsible for imagining and subsequently creating the modern category "Abrahamic religions." As a concept, Abraham has been used in many ways and for a variety of purposes over the centuries. Common to all such usages, however, is an appeal to theological and quasi-theological interests. Recent years, as recounted in the previous chapter, have witnessed "Abrahamic religions" becoming largely intertwined with a religious and political agenda that stresses interfaith dialogue based on perceived common origins and a shared religious heritage. Rarely do we encounter the term grounded in the historical record, even though many assume the category to be a historical one. It may surprise us that when historians, such as S. D. Goitein or Richard W. Bulliet, look at the specifics of Jewish, Christian, and Muslim interactions, they actually eschew employing the term and instead tend to focus on more localized social, economic, and intellectual interactions among the three religions.

If the previous chapters have sought to show numerous ways that "Abrahamic religions" have been imagined, the remaining chapters of this study now attempt to undermine the category with an eye toward its ultimate dismantling. The primary way to do this is to avoid the type of broad generalizations and essentializations that have been and continue to be indicative of so much of the "Abrahamic religions" discourse. The present chapter does this by focusing on the semantic and taxonomical problems associated with the words scholars of religion use. The following chapter subsequently turns to the historical record and argues that this record is the best antidote available for countering such generalist and essentialist arguments. In so doing, I now use "Abrahamic religions" as my own datum to think through some issues that are relevant to the field more generally.

***

The present chapter, the most theoretical of my study, begins the process of dismantling the category "Abrahamic religions" by turning to the intimate connections that develop between words and disciplinary formation. My basic argument is simple enough: Scholars of religion have to avoid employing words that we think adequately analyze or theorize our data without asking where the words themselves came from. It might well be the case that the histories and prehistories of such words taint our examination by introducing sets of assumptions of which we are largely unaware. Words, as encountered in previous chapters, are not always as innocent or as value-neutral as they may appear at first glance. My concern now is with how words help (or hinder) our ability to understand. What is gained (or lost) from our use of vague terms such as "Abrahamic religions"? Because we put far too much stock in such generic and essentialist terms, we risk losing sight of the variations subsumed under them.

As the basic building blocks of human communication, words structure and classify the manifold worlds we inhabit. Yet locking the world into fixed meanings, words also have the potential to undermine communication precisely as they facilitate it. Since we create names for various physical, intellectual, and emotional phenomena, there exists the tendency to mistake the word for the reality that it seeks to name. Unless reflected upon and nuanced, words calcify and harden, thereby presenting a monochromatic world that exists solely according to our liking and existing primarily for our own consumption.

The tensions endemic to words, and the taxonomies which they produce, are clearly on display in the academic study of religion. As the putative cross-cultural study of religious phenomena, Religious Studies sets as its primary goal the examination of the world's religions. However, it undertakes this activity using terminology and categories that Western scholars have largely invented based primarily on their own understanding of (Protestant) Christianity.[1] While this is certainly not unlike other disciplines in the humanities, it demands special reflection when the discipline in question prides itself on cross-cultural analysis. Perhaps there is no better example of this than the very word "religion," which marks out a sphere of Western life, at least as envisaged since the eighteenth century.

Scholars of religion subsequently project this category, and all the baggage that it carries with it, onto earlier eras and other cultures.[2] Because the West has "religion" and a "religious" sphere that is both differentiated and draws its power from a so-called "secular" one, it is then assumed that other cultures must also possess such spheres. Although these other cultures may well lack autochthonous names or categories for them, scholars of religion have no hesitation forcing others to use our words and categories. Through this process, the so-called "world religions" discourse was invented and, with it, a set of terms, structures, and categories.[3]

Religious Studies and Its Words

There is an unfortunate tendency to assume that words have fixed meanings that are believed to transcend cultural particulars. In all of these musings signifier and signified are perceived to be inseparable from one another, two sides of the same linguistic coin.[4] Such a relationship, however, risks perpetuating the status quo since it maintains various cultural and epistemic assumptions that function as the primary tools for imagining and constructing the world. What is dear to us must not or cannot be unique, but must be part of the natural order. Our terms and vocabularies, to invoke Michel Foucault, provide a set of techniques and procedures that are responsible for the manufacture of truth claims—the values that we invent and which we ultimately seek to uphold by, among other things, discovering them in other cultures.[5]

Yet words do emerge from historical contexts. They are not timeless entities with predetermined meanings. It is then incumbent upon us to be cognizant of the histories and secret lives that words possess. Where do they come from? How do we employ them? What do we expect them to do? And how has their usage changed over time? This is not simply an idle dispute over the words we invoke to describe real things in the world (e.g., religion, faith, experience).[6] Neither is it to assume that we can never adequately describe the objects of our study. Instead, it should and must function as an imperative that we interrogate our first principles, and be aware of the classificatory systems that they produce.[7]

On the Word "Abrahamic"

"Abrahamic" or "Abrahamic religions" is certainly one of these words. In fact much of the proceeding analysis has used this term as a case study that examines how we create words and then pretend that they name real historical concepts. We have increasingly employed "Abrahamic religions" to refer to a common source (spiritual? historical? structural?) that is perceived to undergird Judaism, Christianity, and Islam. Why do we insist on collectively using this term even though, as the previous chapters have demonstrated, it is both distortive and inaccurate? Do we use it because we are unaware of its genealogy? Or do we do so because we implicitly want to believe in some sort of ontological bond among three religions that are increasingly at odds with one another in the modern world? And, perhaps most importantly, is our use of this term any different from our use of other terms or categories in the academic study of religion?

Terms such as "Abrahamic religions" take us to the heart of the problems associated with the academic study of religion. As humans we engage—especially in disciplines such as Religious Studies—in the creation of meaning, a large part of which concerns the need to arrange and make sense of the world we inhabit. In terms of our scholarly reproductions, this means that we tend to project our own beliefs onto stories, whether historical or philosophical, and use narrative to create or uphold certain myths we either believe or want to believe. Bruce Lincoln has appropriately labeled this scholarly ethic as "mythology with footnotes."[8] As mythmakers ourselves, scholars—and especially scholars of religion—ultimately revalorize the terms and categories of those we study and often try to reinforce, whether consciously or unconsciously, those values we deem worthy.

We tend to study phenomena in Religious Studies because they matter to us. There are, in other words, sincere and well-intentioned reasons why people continue to write books on the so-called "Abrahamic religions." Such authors presumably would not speak of "Abrahamic religions" if they did not earnestly believe in some form of shared conversation or coexistence among the three religions. However, we must necessarily be aware of the motivations, methods, and cultural baggage that we bring to our study. It may well be that often our motivations and methods are so invested in personal circumstance and potentially so self-contradictory as to render the entire analysis of something such as "Abrahamic religions" illegitimate from the perspective of scholarship.[9]

This is not to imply that we all become robotic and approach our data from the cold and disinterested distance afforded by some ill-defined sense of scientific objectivity. Should such a distance exist, its utility in the human sciences would surely be of limited viability. On the contrary, what we can do as scholars of religion is to avoid personal preference, ecumenical desire, transcendence, or vague concepts (e.g., faith, experience) that others cannot access. For those who wish to persist in the use of "Abrahamic religions" as a scholarly term that invokes some sort of familial resemblance between Judaism, Christianity, and Islam, it is necessary to reflect upon and be honest about the type of intellectual work that such a term can and cannot perform. We could certainly make the case, as we have seen so far in this study, that the term serves an interfaith agenda much more than it does a scholarly one.

In his groundbreaking *Imagining Religion*, Jonathan Z. Smith reminds us that the craft of Religious Studies demands self-reflection and self-consciousness on the part of those who engage in it. Our ability both to articulate why we have chosen particular exempla or data as opposed to others and to analyze how such exempla or data relate to larger issues, Smith argues, represents the professional religionist's "primary skill."[10] He writes, in a now well-known statement, that

> Religion is solely the creation of the scholar's study. It is created for the scholar's analytic purposes by his imaginative acts of comparison and generalization. Religion has no independent existence apart from the academy. For this reason, the student of religion, and most particularly the historian of religion, must be relentlessly self-conscious. Indeed, this self-consciousness constitutes his primary expertise, his foremost object of study.[11]

It is the scholar of religion, according to Smith, who is responsible for making the intellectual incisions that remove religion from cognate cultural and sociological phenomena and who thereby treats it as a distinct object of scholarly study. This very act of removal, however, carries with it innumerable permutations of slippage and potential for distortion.

Folk Taxa and the Quest for Scientific Objectivity

It is perhaps natural to believe that there is a certain scientific objectivity to the terms we employ to describe and analyze the data we construct as religious.[12] Despite this desire, however, we must ultimately confront the reality that many of the terms and categories that we are fond of employing are little more than untheorized folk taxa (e.g., religion, the "sacred"). These taxa are then made to correspond to what we consider to be actual aspects of reality that can be readily quantifiable and analyzable. Certainly all cultures (not to mention subcultures and sub-subcultures, etc.) are in the possession of complex taxonomic systems that they employ to classify the worlds they inhabit; however, unlike our own classification systems, we do not develop a scientific study for each of these systems in such a way that they are believed to have universal and cross-cultural properties.[13]

A case in point is the very term religion. Although this term emerges from a particular civic context in the late antique period of the West, we have subsequently used it and related terms to describe every culture of the globe and forced these cultures to define themselves using its assumptions. *Religio*, the Latin word originally employed to denote some sort of civic responsibility, was subsequently picked up by early Christian thinkers and reframed to refer to some sort of bond between humans and God. Even Augustine (354–430) writes that

> The word "religion" might seem to express more definitely the worship due to God alone, and therefore Latin translators have used this word to represent *thresekeia* [worship]; yet, as not only the uneducated, but also the best instructed, use the word religion to express human ties, relationships, and affinities; *it would inevitably produce ambiguity to use this word in discussing the worship of God*, unable as we are to say that religion is nothing else than the worship of God, without contradicting the common usage which applies this work to the observance of social relationships.[14]

Here we witness Augustine's ambiguity concerning the term "religion," especially the fact that its initial civic sense is now being used to connote another type of relationship. Neither time nor space permits a discussion of this transference of meaning; suffice it to say, however, that an initial, very specific, folk term has now become a universal phenomenon that we now claim to study objectively and cross-culturally.

On this issue of folk taxa, Russell McCutcheon asks us to engage in a thought experiment. Imagine a contemporary Polynesian author— one whose intellectual, religious, and social life has been steeped in the autochthonous religion of the Polynesian Islands—arguing that mana is a natural part of pan-human cognition and not simply a local term that is merely of ethnographic curiosity to us.[15] Such a study would inevitably explain the mana-like experiences that Europeans have, despite the fact that the word does not appear in European dialects, which would be assumed to have limited vocabularies. This, McCutcheon argues, is precisely what Western scholars have done in their insistence upon using "religion" and all that it implies to name an aspect of their social world as if this word names a stable, cross-cultural reality.

Words employed in the academic study of religion—generic terms such as "religion," "liturgy," or "prayer," a list to which we could append "Abrahamic religions"—are potentially lazy signifiers. Although we employ them academically and heuristically, they are often little more than reified versions of ourselves or, as McCutcheon claims, universal projections of our own folk taxa. We have thus largely taken the terms and categories that define our own understanding of the world, ones that let us arrange it in meaningful ways, and assumed them to be stable markers in an often distorted historical record. All of this will have major repercussions for the rather generic term "Abrahamic Religions." A folk taxon that has emerged from various supersessionist and ecumenical conversations is now largely perceived to function in the academic study of religion as a historically meaningful entity. We now use the term to conflate three unruly religious traditions, each of which consists of its own set of equally unruly subtraditions.

The Imperialism of Words

The meanings of words, according to Ludwig Wittgenstein, emerge from the cultures in which they appear.[16] These "forms of life" are social products, and to see how language works, we have to see how it functions in specific social situations. Despite the fact that our social and linguistic environments provide limitations on our cognitive and experiential abilities, scholars of religion have no qualms taking words and terms that define the intellectual attributions of the West and applying them to what they regard as similar phenomena throughout the various cultures of the globe.

In many ways this, as others have well demonstrated, makes the academic study of religion complicit in defining—and thus controlling—other cultures.[17] Religion, returning briefly to J. Z. Smith, is the "creation of the scholar's study."[18] That is, the scholar is the one responsible for ultimately creating the modes of analysis, the very terms used to define the practices of others. These modes of analysis, as David Chidester well reminds us, were born not just in the scholar's workshop, but also on the frontier zones as colonial subjects were divided and conquered.[19] The very discipline in which we ply our trade is not simply an innocent endeavor, but, one could argue, the end product of a lengthy and violent history of colonial conquest and domination.

Words distort. It is absolutely crucial, therefore, that we think about how and for what purposes we deploy them in the present. "We need only remember," according to Daniel Dubuisson, "that the selection and recognition of the facts identified as religious have always depended on criteria borrowed from our indigenous tradition."[20] Distinctions that we make—for example between the "sacred" and the "profane," the "religious" and the "secular," the "soul" and the "body," or the "spiritual" and the "political"—are often not made in other cultures.[21] Yet our choice of words, the reification of our own vocabulary and desire to give it a transcendental quality, demands that we transfer these words to other cultures and make them appear as universal signifiers.

The danger in such a formulation is that our own conceptions of truth and meaning, ones that we have largely made to conform to our own images of ourselves, become universal traits thought to exist naturally in the world. The result of this process is not to throw up our hands in frustration and bemoan the impossibility of understanding various cultures of the globe, but to be highly critical and self-conscious of the words, terms, and categories that we deploy. Dubuisson, for example, argues that we should no longer use the word "religion" and instead replace it with "cosmographic formation."[22] Fair enough. However, a change of term will not replace a change of attitude. So rather than replace all of our traditional terms, thereby removing ourselves from established speech, it seems to me that it is much better to understand the terms we use: their malleability, their genealogies, and their traditional investiture in ideology. Only then will it be possible to reconstruct the field of Religious Studies.

Words and the Problems of Definition

There is a tendency in the academic study of religion, as indeed there is in many cognate disciplines, to locate in words that which does not exist in the observable world. Many of the terms and categories that define our field, from the introductory classroom to more specialized monographs, are given an essential core that are then perceived and studied as moving effortlessly through the historical record. Classifying the phenomena we encounter with generic words—such as "myth," "ritual," or, as here, "Abrahamic"—risks nuance at the expense of convenience. Even the very religions we purport to study—"Judaism," "Islam," "Christianity," "Buddhism," and so forth—are all assumed to be valid markers and vessels or containers of some sort of stable identity. The universal properties that such words and categories are assumed to contain make analysis difficult and often prevent us from looking at the various ways that the concepts that such words purport to name often intersect with one another and related phenomena, sharing certain traits and defining themselves both with and against variously constructed others.

Defining anything, let alone something as gargantuan and complex as *a* "religion," is neither an easy nor a straightforward matter. As J. Z. Smith argues, using early Judaism as his *exemplum*, even the act of simply or categorically defining something such as ancient Judaism demands a complex or polythetic system of classification.[23] Given the available historical evidence of something we now call "ancient Judaism," in addition to the methodological problems inherent to definition and classification, Smith argues that there can exist no one "differential quality" that marks Jews from non-Jews. However, the persistence remains to define ancient Judaism and its distinction from other religions of late antiquity in monothetic terms. These efforts, writes Smith, "have not been convincing; they have failed to achieve a consensus. They have been poorly formulated and violate the ordinary canons of definition. But this is less disturbing than the fact that the presuppositions of the monothetic enterprise have been deliberately tampered with for apologetic reasons."[24] This deliberate tampering emerges from the desire, both scholarly and non-scholarly, to construct our data as somehow unique.

As a result, the pursuit for a "normative Judaism" (or a "normative" anything) tends to ignore all those data sets (historical evidence, material remains, and so one) that fly in the face of such a constructed normativity. This is not just about diversity within religious traditions; it gets to the very heart of the conceptual difficulties inherent to the act of defining. Employing a polythetic mode of taxonomy to define an ancient Jew, for example, need not be dependent upon any single marker of belief or practice (e.g., circumcision or synagogue attendance). On the contrary, all an ancient Jew need do is adhere, more than a non-Jew, to some of the defining features of so-called "Jewish identity." An ancient Jew, then, might speak Greek, be uncircumcised, and be uninterested in attending a synagogue, yet still identify as a Jew. Defining this ancient Jew (or anyone else) tells us very little, at least a priori, about which taxonomic indices define such an individual.

Yet many of us continue to ignore Smith's warning even though it has become in vogue to invoke his name in various discourses that pass for theory in the field. Take as an example the term "Islam" or "Muslim." In his discussion of the defining features of "Muslimness," John Esposito writes that

> For Muslims throughout the centuries, the message of the Quran and the example of the Prophet Muhammad have constituted the formative and enduring foundation of faith and belief. They have served as the basic sources of Islamic law and the reference point for daily life. Muslims today, as in the past, continue to affirm that the Quran is the literal word of God, the Creator's immutable guidance for an otherwise transient world. This transhistorical significance is rooted in belief that the Book and the Prophet provide eternal principles and norms on which Muslim life, both individual and collective, is to be patterned. The challenge for each generation of believers has been the continued formulation, appropriation, and implementation of Islam in history.[25]

Keeping in mind Smith's warnings above, Esposito goes out of his way to establish a kernel of stability that grounds the vagaries and instabilities of various historical, social, and cultural forms that we can, in hindsight, neatly characterize as "Islam" or "Islamic." The perceived stability of Islam is based on an essential characteristic that, later in the book, Esposito defines as "epitomized by a common profession of faith and acceptance of the Shari'a, Islamic law."[26]

Such essentialist pronouncements, defining Islam by slogans such as "Islam is peace" ("The very word 'Islam' means 'peace and submission to God'"[27]), do little to provide any nuance to Islam as a multifaceted historical phenomenon. Esposito defines Islam as an essence and this enables him to decide who the good (and bad) Muslims are. He is not interested in the manifold ways that Islam has been contested because his hermeneutic dictates that those who contest what he has constructed as the essential Islam are not really Muslims.[28] For example, he writes that

> Religion plays a multidimensional role for those engaging in acts of global terrorism. Some terrorists truly believe and are religiously observant, if distorted in their vision and tactics. Others are less observant, cultural Muslims, who see being Muslim as part of their nationalist or social/cultural identity but may retreat to their

religious tradition when under siege or faced with death. Still others appeal to religion primarily as a tactic to legitimate their struggle and mobilize popular support.[29]

None of these individuals, according to Esposito, are using religion properly. Many of the "bad" Muslims are "less observant" than presumably "good" Muslims are. But what does Esposito's taxonomy do with "good" Muslims who are not observant or "bad" ones who are? Similarly, Esposito argues that many who commit violence in the name of Islam are only "cultural" Muslims. This good/bad, proper/improper, religious/cultural dichotomy puts Esposito in the uncomfortable position of articulating what gets to count as authentic Islamic expression. So what does Esposito do with those Muslims who do not accept sharia law? He matter-of-factly claims that they are not *real* Muslims:

> Research indicates that 69.4 percent of the men who committed honor killings in Jordan did not perform their daily prayers, and 55 percent did not fast. That these men fail to observe the most obligatory rituals of Islam suggests that their act of murder is not motivated by religious zeal or devotion.[30]

Esposito, based on his false dichotomy between "religion" and "culture," here acts as the arbiter of what gets to count as an authentically "religious" act and what does not. Because these "Muslim" men who kill their daughters or sisters do not pray on a daily basis or fast during Ramadan, they are, according to him, not really Muslims.[31] Esposito—and as I have argued elsewhere his comments here are indicative of a particular discourse in the academic study of Islam[32]—uses the word "Islam" to denote a liberal essence that he, and many like him, connotes as the essence of Islam. This Islam is then upheld as the arbiter by which other, less savory, Islams can be compared.

Such essentializations, however, are not the sole provenance of Islamic Studies. Take as another example a recent book entitled *Judaism: A Way of Being* written by David Gelernter. In the book's opening, he argues that "unless the essence of Judaism is written down plainly as can be, the loosening grip most American Jews maintain on the religion of their ancestors will fail completely, and the community will plummet into the anonymous depths of history."[33] What might this essence consist of? For Gelernter it coincides, as he makes clear on the book's first page, with "normative," that is, "Orthodox" Judaism.[34] Orthodox Judaism's teachings about Jewish chosenness, gender relations, and the answers it supplies to "the great questions of human existence" are the only ones that the author finds worthy of consideration.[35] Orthodoxy, for the author, represents "Judaism at full strength, straight up; no water, no soda, aged in oak for three thousand years."[36] Rival Judaisms—Reform, Conservative, egalitarian, secular, and the like—are, in comparison to the manner in which he has constructed Orthodoxy, implied to somehow be watered down.[37] Not only has Gelernter defined Judaism's essence as that which corresponds to Orthodoxy, he goes on to make its essence the spiritual core of Western civilization. In an appendix entitled "What Makes Judaism the Most Important Intellectual Development in Western History?" he writes that Judaism

> Has given moral and spiritual direction to Jewish, Christian, and Muslim society, and indirectly to the modern and postmodern worlds. But not only that. Judaism formed our idea of God and man, of sanctity, justice, and love: love of God, family, nation, and mankind. But not only that. Judaism created the ideal of congregational worship that made the church and the mosque possible. But not only that. Much of the modern liberal state grew out of Judaism by way of American Puritans, neo-Puritans, and quasi-Puritans who revered the Hebrew Bible and pondered it constantly.[38]

This essence of Judaism, moving effortlessly throughout human history, is the origin of virtually everything that we are supposed to hold dear in the modern world. No mention is made that such ideas took shape through a synergy of so-called "Jewish" and "non-Jewish" ideas—indeed to such an extent that it is probably impossible to pull them apart and decipher which is which.[39] Many of the pieties and platitudes that we find in works such as Gelernter's are more appropriate for the synagogue than the academy. For it is ultimately in the former that matters such as identity creation and maintenance are never questioned, but assumed as given, something handed down from generation to generation.

Any attempt to get at the essence of Judaism, of Christianity, of Islam, or of any religion, is bound to fail for the simple reason that religions—contrary to the likes of Esposito and Gelernter—are not reified essences. They are, on the contrary, large canopies under which coexist manifold, complex, and often contradictory elements. It is oftentimes difficult enough to appreciate this for a religion, but when numerous religions are subsequently put under another taxonomic canopy, such as "Abrahamic religions," our task of appreciating difference and complexity becomes extremely difficult if not impossible.

Words, Definitions, and the Creation of False Essences

Implicit in words is the need, the desire, to define. Definitions seek to provide order to what is otherwise a discrete set of concepts and subsets that we project as related to one another. This imposition of order on chaos is reflected in the very act of defining something: we must first isolate that which is to be defined, the *definiendum*, from its immediate contexts, subsequently dislodge it by removing all that had hitherto connected it to these contexts, and then analyze it by comparing and contrasting it to other *definienda*. Such analysis can either signal an object's uniqueness or attempt to point out the resemblances, familial or otherwise, with other phenomena that have been ascertained using similar methods. Definition, like so many of our academic activities, is a fragile, highly fractured, and ultimately artificial process.

In using words to define any object, there is always a problem of data selection. What counts as valid data, or invalid? Who decides on the parameters of inclusion and exclusion? This activity, as witnessed for instance in Esposito's attempt to define the "real" Islam or Gelernter's attempt to do the same for Judaism, is a politically and ideologically motivated activity, wherein something is imposed, both retroactively and from the outside, on a complex and often unwieldy set of data. That which fits the definition is accepted; that which makes us uncomfortable or does not somehow fit with our own understanding, is marginalized and completely ignored at best or written off as somehow "inauthentic" at worst.

As we have seen so often in this study, we tend to use terms such as "Judaism," "Christianity," and "Islam" as if they were words that denoted univocal, timeless, and stable entities. It is often assumed—both by individual actors and those engaging in scholarly analysis—that to be an adherent of one of these religions is an objective reality, when in point of fact "Jewish," "Christian," or "Muslim" identity, like any identity, is a state of consciousness that is constructed based on a host of temporal, spatial, cultural, and ideological forces. Any of these identities is as fictive and ultimately as empty as any other identity formation.[40] Yet we persist in our belief that "Jewishness," "Christianness," and Muslimness" names some objective and value-neutral reality in the world.

Obviously without definitions we would have chaos and even more uncertainty. I do not present this, as Plato did in his *Seventh Letter*,[41] in such a manner that the only true contemplation is one that takes place outside of the narrow bonds of language. In fact, my point is the opposite: that there is no reality outside of language; it creates, structures, and ultimately distorts the world we inhabit. All I want to do here is call attention to the fact that what makes defining anything possible and necessary also makes it problematic. If we lock the world and all of the phenomena within it into a series of rigid categories and terms of our own invention, we risk seeing the world monochromatically. Defining a religion univocally comes at a cost—a cost of distortion, a cost of exclusion, a cost of misrepresentation—unless we keep our sense of definition and our task of defining open.

Definitions seek to understand their *definienda*—claiming, for example, that it is "a" and "b" as opposed to "c" and "d"—both as real phenomena and as analytical categories. This slippage between naming and analysis is particularly acute, I have argued hitherto, in the academic study of religion wherein terms such as "religion," specific religions (e.g., Islam, Judaism), and even groups of religions, such as "Abrahamic," are largely untheorized terms that are assumed to carry much analytical weight. Primarily interested in locating and ascertaining essence, such definitions rarely want to tell us about the permutations their objects undergo historically in relation to a series of other such objects. How can a pithy few sentences define, describe, analyze, and celebrate at the same time? They cannot and this difficulty is exacerbated whenever we attempt to make definitions, as we inevitably do, a central component of imposing order, deciding what is in and what is out, to unwieldy traditions that span centuries and diverse geographical areas.

David Chidester, someone whose work I invoked earlier, has argued that the modern study of religion works on an "apartheid" model. According to him, we are determined to "identify and reify the many languages, cultures, peoples, and religions of the world as if they were separate and distinct regions."[42] This enables us to compare and contrast religions as if they were stable entities that move unchanged throughout history and in all those places—temporally and geographically—in which they have existed and continue to do so. Definition plays a key role in this activity, which perpetuates both the imagination and the formation of hermetically sealed containers that conveniently allows us to compare and contrast various human beings and ideologies (including religion). This is a model that we still largely buy into in classrooms, in textbooks, and very often in writings about religion. This approach, again to quote Chidester, is responsible for organizing "human diversity into rigid, static categories [as] one strategy for simplifying, and thereby achieving some sort of cognitive control over, the bewildering complexity of a frontier zone."[43]

Even though we are habituated to essentialisms, we should avoid speaking of religions as if they were a series of discrete traditions existing within hermetically sealed borders. In the same manner, it is highly problematic to move up another level and speak of "families" of religions wherein diverse traditions are made to cohabit. Instead of this, as the following chapter will argue using concrete examples, we need to be aware of the myriad of specific and localized contexts wherein specific "religions" have been contested, interpreted and reinterpreted, and configured and reconfigured. These specific contexts often witness not what we have been accustomed to call discrete "religions" interacting with one another, but various subgroups within these religions overlapping with one another around certain shared cultural and intellectual semantics in ways that often appear indistinct from one another. Often this is done to such an extent that the evocation of specific religious adjectives—for example, "Jewish," "Muslim"—is unhelpful if not distortive.

Our goal, then, ought to be to understand how various individuals—living in different times and places—have successively labeled and defined something as "Jewish" or "Muslim" or "Christian." Our goal is decidedly not to cover over all these particulars with generic names such as "Abrahamic religions." It is important, in other words, to understand how such categories have been subsequently deployed in ways that seek to make sense of a series of overlapping human beliefs, behaviors, practices, and institutions.[44] This permits a nuance that omnibus and overly general terms like "Abrahamic religions," not to mention the invocation of specific religions, does not. It is necessary both to show and understand the paradoxes, the contradictions, and the confusions that emerge when such terms have been, often all too neatly, differentiated from a variety of cognate beliefs, behaviors, and institutions within manifold cultural contexts.

Instead of invoking reified claims to monotheism, ethics, or transcendence—something that the term "Abrahamic religions" seeks to do—it is important not to overlook the porous boundaries that have historically separated the three religions that make up this term, boundaries that are rarely airtight and often breached.[45] Once we do this, we recognize the inherent artificiality of defining something like "Abrahamic religions." A naïve understanding of definition risks leading us to the assumption that because there exists a single word then there must also exist some essence that the word itself signifies. This nominalist view of language, to quote Tim Murphy, effaces history because it assumes that there exists an "unchanging, constant meaning to the *definiendum* which is there, regardless of context, time or place."[46] We need to be cautious that our categories are little more than a series of attempts to fit or, perhaps better, force the world we encounter into a set of conceptual boxes that we have created for it. In so doing, we establish what will count as facts and subsequently the disciplinary fields in which these facts become objects of analysis.

On the Adjective "Abrahamic"

The employment of the term "Abrahamic" to account for Judaism, Christianity, and Islam is a modern attempt to dismantle boundaries among the three religions for the sake of some ecumenical coexistence in the modern period. Yet, as I have intimated above and for reasons I shall articulate in the following chapter, a focus on boundaries, not essences, decenters the entire enterprise that neatly separates phenomena. A shift toward boundaries, toward the ideal that real action is at the margins and not the center, destabilizes our notions or attachments to identity, whether collective or otherwise. Attachments to some positive projection of a *sui generis* core of group identity are often precisely that, a projection. For example, how is it possible to think about borderlines separating "Christians" from "Jews" in the third century or "Muslims" from "Jews" in the seventh? We often do so from the vantage point of today where the lines separating such identities are now often firmly entrenched. How does the current impasse between Jew and Arab, or Jew and Muslim, in the Middle East refract the ways in which we think about premodern boundaries between the two? Are we forced to inscribe modern notions of religious and ethnic identity—for example, "Jewishness," "Arabness," or "Muslimness"—onto an earlier period?

This talk of shared boundaries, as I will suggest in the following chapter, might be a more insightful manner of showing similarities among the three traditions as they have grown with, thought with, defined themselves against, and struggled against one another. But before I entertain this idea, it might be useful to summarize the above discussion and ascertain how exactly it illumines our understanding of "Abrahamic Religions." The term "Abrahamic religions" attempts to impose a structural order on three traditions by claiming common ancestry with a mythical Middle Eastern individual. Owing to this common ancestry, various "similarities" are perceived to run through the three traditions that are presumed to be historical as opposed to phenomenological. In a recent edited collection entitled *Abraham's Children: Jews, Christians, and Muslims in Conversation*, a title that clearly reveals the scope of the volume, the editors—Norman Solomon, Richard Harries, and Tim Winter—write of Abraham:

> [He] is a person of faith, one who believes in the one true God. His faith is a tested faith, as Judaism brings out in its Midrash of ten tests. It is a surrendering, obedient faith, as Islam emphasizes. It involves going out into the unknown as Hebrews 11 stresses, drawing on the story of how Abraham was exiled from his home country into unknown lands, a story also central to the Qur'ān.[47]

Abraham is here presented as faith personified and although these three religions may provide different perspectives of what ideal faith consists of, they are all in firm agreement that this attribute is tantamount to the essence of all three religions.

Faith, then, is one of the major words used to characterize "Abrahamic religions." Other words that come to mind from examining those who write about the commonalities of these three religions include loyalty, obedience, and submission. While I have no doubt that such words figure highly, both in the premodern and modern worlds, in various elaborations of these religions, they are primarily theological attributes. Secondly, none of these words imply any sort of interfaith connections. Each specific religion perceives itself to be the sole possessor of these virtues, and that the practitioners of rival religions firmly reject them.[48]

Despite this, many still engage in the project of ignoring the historical record and replacing it with one of potential cooperation, of trialogue, in the contemporary world. Solomon, Harries, and Winter, for example, end their discussion of the figure of Abraham by stating that he "can set the tone for dialogue between Jews, Christians and Muslims by offering the premise that we treat each other on an equal footing."[49] Or, John Esposito who writes in the conclusion to his *The Future of Islam* that

Jews and Christians have come to affirm that beyond their distinctive beliefs and past conflicts, they have a shared Judeo-Christian heritage.... Few until recently have possessed the broader Abrahamic vision that recognizes the integral place of the descendents of Abraham, Hagar, and Ismail, Muslims who are co-equal citizens and believers in the West.... The future of Islam and Muslims is inextricably linked to all of humanity. All of our futures will depend on working together for good governance, for freedom of religion, speech, and assembly, and for economic and educational advancement. Together we can contain and eliminate our preachers of hate and terrorists who threaten the safety, security, and prosperity of our families and societies.[50]

I have quoted this passage at length because it seems to me that it is emblematic of so much of the literature that is the subject matter of this study. If Solomon, Harries, and Winter are interested in various aspects of faith that can unite Jews, Christians, and Muslims in the present, Esposito here wants to dismantle in the name of exclusivity the older "Judeo-Christian" and replace it with the more inclusive "Abrahamic." Both of these positions, however, emerge from political expediency. Both are ideologically motivated and neither makes appeals, except in the broadest possible terms, to historical specifics in the relations among the three religions.

It would seem more accurate to claim that, at various points in their historical development and intersection, these three "religions" that we construct as monotheistic shared numerous taxic indicators and defined themselves vis-à-vis one another. These indicators are not generic, but specific to particular times and places. Instead of such nuance, so much of the literature devoted to "Abrahamic religions" assumes that three reified religions sit together monothetically. "Abrahamic religions," with all of its theological and ahistorical baggage, distorts, as opposed to supports, the historical record. Many who use it, as we have witnessed throughout this study, are highly selective in their use of words and adjectives to describe this perceived coexistence. As this chapter has tried to demonstrate in detail, our use of words, especially when it comes to the academic study of religion, is never value-neutral. Rather there is a tendency to create terms, definitions, and essence that create the type of reality that we want to see. In the case of "Abrahamic religions," many of the terms employed even today in academic study derive their meanings and potencies from interfaith circles. "Unity," "dialogue," "shared," "commonalities" all come to mind and they are subsequently and retroactively fitted onto the historical record. One of the better known cases of this is the so-called "interfaith utopia" of al-Andalus or Muslim Spain, which will be the subject matter of following chapter.

Conclusions

Too often scholars working in the area of Religious Studies fall into the trap of writing as though communities constitute themselves through a simple recuperation of a true essence, thereby ignoring the task of communal invention and reinvention, and the multiform challenges posed by enforcing the bounds of community. Communities, as Benedict Anderson reminds us, are, after all, imagined and,[51] as such, we should focus our attention more on the contents and ideologies associated with such imaginings. I have tried to demonstrate in this chapter that this overly tidy concept of simple recuperation of group essence and existence tends to inform both the way we imagine specific religions and, increasingly in both the popular and scholar communities, in the very construction of some ill-defined and highly idealized concept of "Abrahamic religions."

The following chapter will take the theoretical insights of the present chapter and examine in detail several particular instances of Jewish–Christian–Muslim interaction. Not the least of these is the so-called "golden age" or "interfaith utopia" of medieval Spain that is usually held up as a high point in "Abrahamic" coexistence.

6

On History

ONE OF THE most disturbing characteristics that plagues much comparative work, to quote Jonathan Z. Smith, is that its first principles, often the very reasons for engaging in the comparative act in the first place, "have been deliberately tampered with for apologetic reasons."[1] In terms of "Abrahamic religions," as previous chapters have argued, this means appealing to a perceived and manufactured essence for the sake of various theological agendas. This occurs whether the agenda is supersessionist, in which case there is a desire to argue and demonstrate that only one of these religions represents Abraham authentically and to the exclusion of others, or it can be ecumenical, in which case a set of inclusive commonalities among the three religions is discovered. Implicit in the "Abrahamic religions" discourse, in other words, is comparison. And the way in which this comparison has been and indeed still is ostensibly carried out is through vague appeals to history.

Because we have no evidence for the existence of Abraham or his progeny and because "Abrahamic religions" now largely functions as an interfaith category—albeit one that is increasingly employed in academic study—it becomes difficult if not impossible to map historically. Yet partisans of the discourse persist. We see invocations, for example, of the Late Antique period or especially in recent years of al-Andalus or "Muslim Spain" as times or eras when these three religions coexisted. History, in other words, is appealed to as the backdrop against which various contemporary theological constructions can be imagined. The historical record provides both the justification and the legitimation for the comparative enterprise. In earlier centuries, and indeed in some circles to this day, this may mean appealing to either the Bible or the Quran as if they were historical documents that recount the way things really were as opposed to the way they should be. Salvation history, in these discourses, is often mistaken for history. For a devout Christian to say that Jesus is the true fulfillment of the Abrahamic covenant or for a pious Muslim to make the point that Muhammad reinstituted the original religion of Abraham is *not* a historical argument, it is a theological claim. Unfortunately these theological arguments, defanged of their overly exclusivist claims, remain in the background of current discourses.

Religions, however, are much more complicated and unwieldy phenomena than the essence and manifestation assumptions behind so much of what passes for "Abrahamic religions" discourse. Rather than witness three essentially discrete traditions interacting with one another, we need to begin the process of rethinking and redressing how religions intersect with one another, including the various ways in which they exchange and interchange ideas, identities, and the like. It is usually assumed that Judaism, Christianity, and Islam simply bumped up alongside one another and exchanged ideas.[2] Far less attention, however, is given to the dynamics of how, why, when, and by whom such interactions occurred.

Yet closer examination of the three generic religions that comprise the even more generic category "Abrahamic religions" reveals porous boundaries and much greater complexity than originally meets the eye or at least the eye accustomed to seeing three discrete "religions" interacting with one another. Rather than imagine "Jews," "Christians," and "Muslims" working with or against one another, we need to examine specific, localized encounters that involve shared cultural vocabularies or semantics around which various subcultures within each of the so-called religions define themselves. Some of these subcultures may well exhibit greater similarities with subcultures of the other two "religions" than they do with those we often think of as their own.[3] Many subgroups, whether assimilating to or fighting against such shared cultural semantics, ultimately define group identity in similar ways. This messiness and overlap, however, has often been neatly dismissed, even in academic circles associated with Religious Studies, using the "orthodox/heterodox" binary. Yet such binaries are usually constructed much later and only imposed retroactively. When we say that this is what "Judaism" looked like in Late Antiquity or what "Islam" looked like in the eighth century, and so on, we have to ask: for whom and for what purposes? The problem with "Abrahamic religions" is it adds yet another order of monovocality, further homogenizing or leveling our view of what is going on.

It is these complex sets of similarities, what theorists of yesteryear used to call family resemblances, that most interests me here. Yet I am not interested in these resemblances in a phenomenological or ahistorical manner. On the contrary, we need to focus on how subgroups from different religious traditions can often share more similarities among them than they do with other subgroups within their own religion. In fact the very term "religion," and all of the baggage that it carries in its wake, is probably not even the best term to use. Like so many of our "analytical" terms, as argued in the previous chapter, it has the propensity to force square pegs into round holes for the sake of order.

The "Abrahamic religions" discourse, however, rarely if ever takes such historical and conceptual complexity seriously. Rather, in such discourses, identities are never queried and the dialectical relationship between centers and margins, insiders and outsiders, is frequently overlooked. To examine these themes in more detail, this chapter uses two case studies. One is usually held up as a shining *exemplum* of the peaceful coexistence and interfaith relations of the three Abrahamic religions, the so-called "Golden Age" of Muslim Spain. The other, with which I shall begin, is the highly complex, almost to the point of unfathomability, set of interactions that emerges at the origin of Islam in seventh-century Arabia.

In the first example, that of Islam's formation in the sixth- and seventh-century Arabian Peninsula, there is an assumption that "Islam" borrows from preexistent monotheisms—"Judaism" and "Christianity"—in the region. Even those who resist such a model as the rantings of an outmoded Orientalism, which it most certainly is, rarely offer an alternative model. Rather, there is a tendency among such critics of Orientalism to take the episodes of Muhammad's life, many of which we have knowledge only from later sources when Islam was almost fully developed, as if they were historical facts as opposed to creative mythopoeia.[4] Far too many Islamicists, with a handful of exceptions, prefer to see salvation history as if it were real history.[5] I use this example to illustrate the argument that the contours among these three "monotheisms" at this particular time and in this particular area are anything but clearly defined. In fact, they are so vague and obscure that it is impossible, on multiple levels, to differentiate among them. This is the case not only because "Islam" does not exist at the time of Muhammad, but because it is impossible to ascertain with any degree of clarity what "Judaism" and "Christianity" looked like on the Arabian Peninsula at the time in question. This historical complexity, I submit, makes a mockery of terms such as "Abrahamic religions."

The second example, "Muslim Spain," raises a different set of issues. Muslim Spain, or more accurately the shifting borders of al-Andalus between the tenth and eleventh centuries, is frequently held up as a "Golden Age" of interfaith tolerance and ecumenical coexistence. Certainly by the tenth and eleventh centuries the borders of the three religions are more stable and certainly more clearly delineated than they were in the seventh century. However, it is still difficult to maintain that these borders are hermetically sealed, and there is indeed a great deal of movement across them. My concern now is that even the terms used to describe this period—such as "tolerance" and "coexistence"—need to be nuanced in ways the secondary literature that both points out and upholds these virtues rarely does. "Tolerance" and "coexistence" did not mean in the eleventh century what they do today. But, as I shall show, such historical distinctions are rarely important in this secondary literature because the interest is not in the past, but the present and the future. The past that is appealed to is one that has been retrofitted with the concerns of the present. The result, as in the previous example, is the conflation of mythic and real histories.

Taken as a whole, the aim of the present chapter is to show that those who make appeals to history for interfaith reasons do so based primarily on a set of impressions created in a contemporary context.[6] This context, rarely invested in nuanced analysis and disinterested observation, subsequently attempts to read these impressions or virtues back onto the historical record. None of these impressions, however, are sustainable for long. In fact both reveal to what extent "Abrahamic religions" cannot be used as a term meant to perform comparative or historical work.

Example One: Muhammad's Arabia

The emergence of Islam within the Arabian Peninsula in the sixth and seventh centuries c.e. provides a scenic window onto the complexities of religio-social formation. In so doing, it provides an important argument for the need to relinquish vague qualifiers, such as "Abrahamic." Such words—as the previous chapter explored—afford little or no clarity and they ultimately represent the crossover of untheorized theological taxa into the domain of social, cultural, and historical analysis. Instead of using such terms and categories we need to replace them with ones that communicate greater complexity and multivocality, and that better reflect the multiform interactions and negotiations that take place "on the ground." For it is "on the ground" that various social groups interact with one another, often in ways that make it impossible to differentiate neatly and in ways that militate against the use of essentialist terms such as "Judaism," "Christianity," and "Islam." What is needed is a change in the way we both think about and describe the contours of religious interaction and exchange.

The Arabian Peninsula into which Muhammad (570–632) was born provides an initial segue into this complexity. First of all, it reveals clearly the dangers of assuming the existence of discrete religious traditions. In sixth-century Arabia, for example, there is little historical or textual evidence that terms such as "Jew," "Christian," or "Muslim" (or even "Arab") were mutually exclusive markers of identity. As a result, we should be cautious of projecting later sectarian notions—such as "Arabness" or "Jewishness" onto the period in question. Adding to this complexity, it is important to realize that the so-called Jewish tribes of Arabia were not necessarily "Jewish" in the way that we use this term today, but Jewish-Arab tribes, and the Christian ones were Christian-Arab tribes. Moreover, we know very little when it comes to the belief structures and religious contours of these groups. Most likely modern Jews or Christians would recognize very little of the practices and liturgy of such tribal groups if they were transported back in time to the seventh-century Arabian Peninsula. All of this instructs us that we should avoid assuming that race, religion, and ethnicity—largely modern constructs—functioned in the periods before, during, and even immediately after the formative period of Muhammad's movement. "Arab" and other "religious" identities, in other words, were anything but stable or uniform.

If we wish to get a clearer sense of the ways religious groups define themselves in relationship to others, including the many constituent parts that make this possible, we owe it to ourselves both to appreciate and attempt to bring some order to this complexity. Within this context I certainly do not deny that many of the religions that others have labeled as "Abrahamic" share a number of traits and family resemblances. My goal in examining Muhammad's Arabia is not to deny this, but to theorize such resemblances by showing how they are neither arbitrary nor reducible to a common ancestor, but the result of complex interactions between fluid traditions with porous borders. An attention to this porosity of social formations and the liquidity of socio-religious identities can ideally allow us to see the rise of Islam in ways that glossing over these processes by employing the generic term "Abrahamic" cannot.

According to the traditional narrative, as recounted by both Muslims and most introductory textbooks,[7] in Mecca—an oasis on the western

Arabian Peninsula (referred to as the Hijaz)—there lived an illiterate businessman by the name of Abu al-Qasim Muhammad ibn Abdallah. Not satisfied with worldly and material pleasures, he became increasingly attuned to matters of the spirit and was accustomed to traveling in the hills around Mecca. On one of these journeys, he encountered Jibril (Gabriel), who told him to "Recite in the name of your Lord!" These revelations would continue to be transmitted to Muhammad from God on a regular basis over the following twenty-three years until Muhammad's eventual death in 632, whereupon they were eventually collected and codified as the Quran.[8]

Upon returning home from his initial encounter with Gabriel, Muhammad began preaching a general monotheistic and apocalyptic message to the inhabitants of Mecca. Owing to its call to renounce the idolatrous polytheism of the town, many perceived his message as a critique of their habituated life and customs and as an affront to the socioreligious status quo. The ensuing persecutions forced Muhammad and his followers to migrate to another oasis called Yathrib (later to be named *medinat al-nabi* ["the City of the Prophet"] or, simply, Medina), which had invited him to function as an arbitrator between various feuding factions there. In addition to his new role as statesman in Medina, there also existed a large Jewish population, not to mention the presence of Christian merchants in the region. As Muhammad began to state-build, it became increasingly clear to him that most of the Arabian Jews and Christians would never follow his message. This gave impetus, so this master narrative goes, to the creation of a new religion, Islam, which quickly spread beyond the Arabian Peninsula to become one of the so-called "world religions."[9]

This narrative is predicated on numerous assumptions. First is the assumption that there existed two stable religious traditions (i.e., Judaism and Christianity) that, depending upon the model in question, either functioned as the catalyst for Muhammad's message or the backdrop against which Muhammad gradually articulated Islam. Both models work on the classic essentializing model: Judaism and Christianity (and eventually Islam) possess an essence or a spirit that moves throughout history and that manifests itself in various temporal eras and geographic locales. Space is rarely accorded to the contest and conflict that contributes to the construction of perceived normativities. Or, if they are acknowledged, such normativities are often projected from a later age onto the period in question. In sixth- and seventh-century Arabia, however, we have very little indication what "Judaism" and "Christianity" looked like, other than that later Muslim sources used these (religious?) designations for various tribes. If they did exist, assuming that these later sources do not have an ideological ax to grind (which they all do), we most certainly could not label them using the politically loaded term "normative."

This essentialist model, which is responsible for positing the existence of discrete and monolithic religious traditions, is further undermined by the fact that there is no evidence that these "Judaisms" and "Christianities," or parts thereof, were not absorbed into Muhammad's developing framework. Rather than simply call this framework "Islam," it might be more appropriate to use terms that account for the complexity such as "a shared Judaizing Muhammad message." What would eventually become Islam, for example, might well have been a set of beliefs, customs, and practices that represented various local "Jewish" and/or "Christian" traditions and only at a later date, in the eighth century, as the architects of Islam (e.g., hadith collectors, legal experts, historians) began to crystallize their own tradition, was it neatly excised from a Judaism and a Christianity that were then regarded as normative and as existing side-by-side with Muhammad's Islam. An all too tidy example that is used to show these discrete traditions interacting with one another is the claim that whereas the Jews prayed facing Jerusalem, Muhammad, early in his stay at Medina, had his followers turn and pray facing Mecca, the birthplace of his message. When he did this—obviously a story with much symbolic meaning for later generations—there most certainly would have been "Jews" who joined him, although they were not "converts" in the way we use the term today because they literally had nothing to "convert" to.

A second assumption is that we have very little evidence that Muhammad set himself the express goal of founding a new religion. Although Islam would be worked out, both theologically and legally, in the centuries after his death, none of these later elements were present at the beginning. As many have shown, Muhammad—especially during the early years in Mecca—preached an inclusive monotheistic message that warned the unbelievers that the Day of Judgment was near. He most decidedly did not preach an exclusive and highly developed teaching that we now recognize as Islam.[10] The journey from his original message to the rise of Islam is a very difficult and convoluted one and it is still by no means clear how it occurred.[11] However, we must be cautious of using a conceptual model, unfortunately one that is all too common, which asserts that Muhammad simply preached the Islam of later generations.

A third assumption is that we have absolutely no idea what the modern term "religion" would have meant in sixth- and seventh-century Arabia. One thing that we can be certain of is that the term, for which there is no equivalent in Arabic, would not mean what we take it to mean today, where it is primarily used to denote some sort of inner or spiritual feeling that is regarded as immune from a variety of cultural, political, social, and ideological forces.[12] As many theorists of religion have demonstrated, "religion" is a term specific to the West, particularly a modern West that has developed a category of the "secular" that gives "religion" shape and generates its articulation.[13] Many languages, as we have seen, do not even possess the term "religion." Within this context, it is worth noting that two of the three religions that we take to be "Abrahamic" do not have a native term that corresponds exactly to "religion." Neither Arabic nor Hebrew, by extension, possess a native term or category of "Abrahamic religions,"[14] something that has largely been imposed on them from the outside.

These three assumptions begin with the wrong premise—namely that "religion" meant in sixth-century Arabia what it does today and that, as such, the three religions we now refer to as "Abrahamic" were discrete traditions at that time. As mentioned, the existence of "Abrahamic religions" as a natural category not only leads to problematic conclusions, it obscures rather than clarifies the complex interactions among the three religions. Rather than ask what the contours of religious, ethnic, and social identities were in the period in question, the "Abrahamic religions" discourse assumes that all three of the traditions that comprise it are somehow stable or essential constructs.

Any discussion of the collisions, overlaps, and interactions of these three "religions" or, better, social movements, must recognize—especially in earlier periods—their inner fluidity and the instability of boundaries among them. What, for example, do the varieties of Judaisms and Christianities look like in sixth- and seventh-century Arabia? Are they discrete religious traditions in the way that we think of each of these traditions today? Is Judaism an ethnic or a cultural marker in the sixth century as it is, say, in a post-1948 world? Is Christological speculation in sixth-century Arabia simply a reflection of what was then emerging as "orthodox" in the either the Byzantine or Roman churches? Even the term "Islam" is implicated in this conceptual difficulty. At what point, for instance, does Islam emerge as the "five-pillared" and theologically worked out tradition of later centuries?

The three so-called "Abrahamic religions" then are not related by means of a common mythical ancestor. They are not siblings with the same father. They are, on the contrary, historically symbiotic in that many subgroups within and among these three religions derive their identities and historical formations from manifold and complex interactions in distinct temporal and geographic eras. What started out as a "Jewish" tribe, for example, on the eve of Muhammad's preaching might well have ended up as "Muslim" in the century or so after his death. The crossing of this boundary has nothing to do with conversion, but with a shifting set of ideas and social practices that were in flux and that only became stable at a later date. "Abrahamic religions" provides a false sense of security by promoting a "theoretical" model predicated upon essential sameness and similarities (that occasionally manifest themselves as conflict).[15] Rather than simplicity, we need to account for complexity, and opposed to a retroactively imposed clarity, we need to be aware of the distortion that our categories introduce. Rather than regard Judaism, Christianity, and Islam as three discrete traditions in the early seventh century, it might be more helpful and productive to envisage them, using the language of J. Z. Smith encountered in the previous chapter, polythetically. That is, rather than employing a schema wherein a religion (e.g., Islam) and all of its subgroups share a common essence that neatly differentiates it from the essences of other religions (e.g., Judaism or Christianity), it might make more sense to conceive of a set of taxa (e.g., apocalypticism, messianism, prophecy) that various subgroups of all three traditions share and contest with one another.[16]

This model has the distinct advantage of showing the overlap among the three groups as opposed to positing well-defined distinctions, many of which are based on slogans or polemics of later centuries.

***

Returning to the Red Sea Basin, of which the Arabian Peninsula is a part, we have to be cautious of simply using the essentialist terms of later generations. Instead we witness a series of social groups that possess overlapping traits or taxic indicators. In this sense, various subgroups of what will later be called Jews, Christians and Muslims may well appear indistinct from one another when it comes to certain of these taxic indicators. Certainly some of these subgroups will eventually become or become associated with the normative traditions of later centuries, but my concern now is with those that do not. In this respect we must necessarily attune ourselves to the fact that manifold interactions and negotiations that take place "on the ground" are often far removed from later theological legitimations.

What, for instance, *might* the Red Sea Basin in general and the Arabian Peninsula in particular have looked like socially, culturally, economically, and religiously at the time of Muhammad? It is important to be aware that neither of these geographic areas was monolithic in terms of its cultural, religious, and material practices. The Arabian Peninsula, for example, consisted of distinct geographical regions, each of which was settled by various peoples with their own cultural and religious traditions. Scholars who study pre-Islamic Arabia tend to divide the region into three cultural regions: East Arabia (comprised of modern-day Kuwait, Bahrain, Qatar, the East Coast of Saudi Arabia, the Emirates, and Oman); South Arabia (roughly corresponding to modern-day Yemen); and North and Central Arabia (modern-day Saudi Arabia minus the east coast, the Sinai and Negev deserts, and parts of modern Jordan, Syria, and Iraq).[17] Each one of these regions possessed its own autochthonous traditions. The earliest written sources from East Arabia date to roughly 2500 BCE and those from the other regions to roughly 900 BCE. The Arabs made up but one group in this area, even though they would become the most successful, eventually absorbing all of the other groups in the region.

Casting our gaze a little wider, we know that the pre-Islamic Red Sea Basin occupied a distinctive geographic location that, in many ways, functioned as a conduit between civilizations and continents. It witnessed the emergence of several civilizations, the relics of which are still evident today. One such civilization was that of the Nabateans, who created the city of Petra (in modern-day Jordan), one of the seven wonders of the ancient world. Other Arabian civilizations prior to the fifth century C.E. include the Lakhmid kingdom in the North around the Euphrates River, and the Himyar kingdom in the Southwest near Yemen.

The Arabian Peninsula was surrounded by three major agricultural centers: Iraq, Syria, and Yemen. Each of these three lands was connected to what one historian calls "political hinterlands."[18] That is, if one traveled east, north, or south, one would soon come upon one of the major civilizations of Late Antiquity. In Iraq, for example, there existed the Sassanian Empire; just beyond Syria lay the Greek-speaking Byzantine Empire; and in Yemen there existed the Abyssinian Empire. Subsequent Islamic myths of isolation and separation to the contrary, Arabs seem to have been active participants in the various social, economic, cultural, and religious features of these diverse imperial powers.

As in those worlds, the major form of religious expression was polytheism, the belief in many gods and/or goddesses.[19] We know many of the names of the Arabs' tribal deities, since the most common aim of inscriptions was to invoke them, praise them, or give thanks to them. Yet as Robert Hoyland, a specialist in pre-Islamic Arabia, remarks, "names do not tell us much, and the brevity of most of these texts makes it difficult for us to understand the nature and function of the gods or to comprehend what they meant to their worshippers."[20] The main god, based on surviving inscriptions, was Athtar, who seems to have been related to the Ishtar cult in the northern part of Arabia. The cult of Athtar also appears to have been widespread throughout the region, albeit with various manifestations as attested by inscriptions in local shrines. One inscription has an individual thanking another god for "interceding on his behalf with Athtar."[21]

If Athtar was a remote deity, there were also many other gods and goddesses who were of significance to particular tribes. The popularity of these gods and goddesses seems to have been determined by both the tribe and the particular period in question.[22] From the Quran (e.g., 71:23) we are able to glean the existence of a number of other gods and goddesses, including Al-Qaum (the god of war and of night), Wadd (the god of love and friendship), Nasr (the god of time), and Nuha (the sun goddess). Based on inscriptions from South Arabia we also know that some of these gods functioned as patron deities to particular tribes: Wadd, for example, was the patron of the Mineans, Amm of the Qatabanians, and Sayin of the Hadramites.

Increasingly in the fourth century C.E. a number of South Arabian inscriptions begin to speak of a monotheistic cult of a deity known as Rahmanan—the "Merciful One"—whose subtitle is "the Lord of heaven and earth." Scholars are unsure if this high god is related to the earlier polytheistic structure or a new development, perhaps connected to the increased prestige or importance of Jewish-Arab and Christian-Arab tribes within the Peninsula. It is also difficult to determine whether Rahmanan is related to Allah, which is literally the Arabic word for "the God."[23]

Given both the importance of the trade routes to Arabia and the fact that larger geopolitical forces surrounded Arabia, it is certainly unlikely, as we have already seen, that the Peninsula existed in some sort of religious vacuum or was untouched by the existence of other imperial powers and their monotheisms. Not only were all of the political hinterlands mentioned above connected to monotheistic civilizations, there is evidence for the existence of Jews, Christians, and even Zoroastrians in Arabia well before the time of Muhammad. Rather than asking whether or not other monotheisms existed in the area, the more accurate and pressing question is: what were the contours and contents of these monotheisms? And, perhaps equally important, given the fluid ethnic and religious contexts of sixth- and seventh-century Arabia, is it even possible to assume that these monotheisms represent distinct markers of identity and difference?

The case of Jews in the Arabian Peninsula provides a remarkable example of this fluidity. Just because later Arabo-Islamic sources call them by this name does not necessarily mean that they were "Jewish" in the sense that later generations use this term. Rather than assume that they were halakhic Jews, for which we possess very little evidence, it is perhaps better to think of them as Arab tribes with some knowledge of what they considered to be Jewish custom and belief. The existence of these tribes, for instance, predated the Babylonian Talmud, one of the main documents of rabbinic Judaism, which was codified around 500 CE. Although this codification occurred in the rabbinical academies of Babylonia, which were in relative close proximity to the area, it is unclear how much jurisdiction such academies would have had among Jews in Arabia.

Would these Jewish-Arab tribes have been considered "heterodox" from what was emerging as an "orthodox" (i.e., rabbinic) sense of Judaism? Of course, it is certainly important not to assume an orthodoxy of fixed and ascertainable Jewish identity and practice based upon the rabbinic academies of Babylonia and then use this as the standard against which to judge the "authenticity" of Arabian Jewishness. Indeed, if anything, the Talmud, as a product of Late Antiquity, further reveals the fluid and evolving nature of Judaism in this period.

The monotheistic beliefs of those Jewish-Arabian tribes and the monotheistic message of Muhammad were probably indistinguishable. This fluidity is underlined by the fact that the Constitution of Medina—a text attributed to Muhammad when he established a polity in Medina/Yathrib—names no less than seven Arab tribes of Jews. Other passing references to a house of study (*bayt al-midrash*) also exist there.[24] How did Muhammad envisage himself and his message in relation to these tribes? What happened to them? Were they subsumed into the nascent Islamic polity? Or was this fledgling polity subsumed into the monotheistic structures of such tribes—the end product of which would eventually emerge as Islam?

The same kinds of questions arise for the existence of Christianities in the area. If the period just before the rise of Muhammad was one in which rabbinic Judaism was being formulated in Babylonian academies, it was also a period in which the Church was defining itself and working out what would become "orthodox" belief and doctrine by weeding out what would subsequently become labeled "heretical" movements. Interestingly, all of the main forms of Christianity in Arabia seem to have been forms of the religion that the Church in Western Europe would deem more heterodox.[25]

Monophysite Christianity appears to have been one of the more dominant strains of Christianity in the area. Monophysitism adopted the Christological position that Jesus has only one nature (*mono* = one, *phusis* = nature) as opposed to what would emerge as the orthodox position adopted at the Council of Chalcedon (451 CE) that Jesus possesses two natures, one divine and one human. This might well account for the fact that the Quran mentions that Jesus was not crucified on the Cross, but that only a likeness was. The other major form of Christianity in the area was Nestorianism, which held that Jesus existed as two separate persons—the man Jesus and the divine Son of God, or Logos—rather than as a unified person.

The existence of Christian Arabs at the time before Muhammad raises all sorts of interesting questions regarding identity. What, for example, did it mean to be a Christian Arab at this time? Although these tribes may have identified and even allied with larger Christian empires in the region, the perceived "heterodox" and even heretical teachings that dominated in Arabia would certainly have limited such identification. Or again, as we saw in the possible existence of Judaisms in the area, perhaps some form of Arab Christianity—along with other forms of (Arab-)Judaism and (Arab-)Zoroastrianism, in addition to other local cults, represented the fluidity of loyalties and practices out of which Muhammad's social movement emerged.[26] And, perhaps unlike those who sought to impose upon them orthodoxies, orthopraxies, and exclusive loyalties to one community or another, Muhammad's movement succeeded because it both appealed to and encouraged—at least in its formative stages –a variety of beliefs and practices.

As can be seen from the above, it is unhelpful to describe the complex set of polythetic taxa—the numerous interactions and negotiations—among "Jewish" Arabs, "Christian" Arabs, and what will eventually emerge as "Muslim" Arabs with appeals to unhelpful slogans such as

"Abrahamic religions." There would have existed, as the previous examination has alluded to, numerous overlaps among the three groups: the importance of prophecy; the coming Day of Judgment; a belief in Allah (all the tribes spoke some dialect of Arabic); and that they were monotheists who could neatly be differentiated from nonmonotheists or idolaters. In addition to such features, many of these groups shared a common language and culture.

It is important to avoid positing sharp ethnic, racial, or religious distinctions among "Jews," "Arabs," "Christians," and others in sixth- and seventh-century Arabia. We do know that tribes of "Jewish Arabs" or "Arab Jews" appear to have had ready access to long established local Jewish authorities (in the Yemen and in Yathrib). Perhaps what will eventually emerge as "Islam" in subsequent centuries preserves an amalgam of local Jewish (or other) "orthodoxies" that no longer competed with the Palestinian or Babylonian religio-legal schools for the simple reason that it now became identified with Islam and the Arabian Jews who practiced it were absorbed into the Islamic community.

At any rate we should be cautious of assuming that our modern categories of race and ethnicity were mutually exclusive cultural markers in the periods before, during, and even immediately after the formative period of Muhammad's movement. There is also a danger of imposing our own theological differences—for example, what defines a "Christian," "Jew," "pagan," and "Muslim"—on this period. If we look at all of these terms as fluid and unstable, we might get a different appreciation or understanding of the period in which Islam arose.

The quest for "Abrahamic religions" creates too much distortion here. If we retell the above story, as is customarily done, by claiming that Muslims took over the story of Abraham, but from the perspective of Ishmael as opposed to Isaac, we miss out on the nature of the borders between the traditions and the activity that goes on around them. We see quite quickly that the ecumenical point that the three religions share a common ancestor is not helpful at all, except of course for those wanting to promote peaceful coexistence in the present.

Example Two: Muslim Spain

The other example that I wish to examine is that of the so-called "Golden Age" of Muslim Spain. Unlike the example of Muhammad's Arabia discussed above, we now see the three religions as discrete in the sense that all three have developed distinct legal and theological traditions that clearly demarcate them from one another. Muslim Spain is generally held up as an interfaith utopia, one wherein the three religious traditions got along and not only tolerated, but respected, one another.[27] For Muslims, this is usually regarded as one of the high points of premodern Islamic history, the age of cosmopolitanism, scientific development, and cultural achievement. For Jews it was the age of some of the greatest names of the tradition: Samuel Hanagid (993–ca.1056), Judah Halevi (1075–1151), and Moses Maimonides (1135–1204), as well as the time of important innovations in Hebrew poetry, grammar, science, and philosophy. And while the Christian impact within Muslim Spain tends not be emphasized as much, it was also a time of relative peace for those who lived under Muslim rule. Like Jews, many Christians adopted Arabic as their main language of speech and expression, and Arab customs and manners as their own.

Let me begin my analysis here from the contemporary period and look backward. In a speech commemorating the signing of the 1993 Israeli–Palestinian peace agreement, then-President Clinton remarked,

> Therefore, let us resolve that this new mutual recognition will be a continuing process in which the parties transform the very way they see and understand each other. Let the skeptics of this peace recall what once existed among these people. There was a time when the traffic of ideas and commerce and pilgrims flowed uninterrupted among the cities of the Fertile Crescent. In Spain and the Middle East, Muslims and Jews once worked together to write brilliant chapters in the history of literature and science. All this can come to pass again.[28]

One of the hallmarks of the "interfaith utopia" of Muslim Spain is that of *convivencia* ("coexistence"),[29] a term whose creation and use in the mid-twentieth century mirrors that of "Abrahamic religions." *Convivencia* designates the interplay of cultural ideas among the three religious traditions, especially the idea of religious tolerance. It is certainly in this sense that President Clinton conjures up the period so as to juxtapose it against current strife in the Middle East and to hold it up as the symbol of hope on the signing of the (now failed) peace agreement of 1993. In 2008—after the attacks of 9/11, the War on Terror, and the rising conflict in Israel/Palestine—a conference entitled Convivencia was sponsored by the Bellarmine College of the Liberal Arts at Loyola Marymount

University in Los Angeles. The literature accompanying the conference describes this "golden age" in the following terms:

> the meeting of culture and religion in medieval Spain—a period of several centuries during which Jews, Christians and Muslims managed to live together in comparative peace. Together, they created a bridge culture—la convivencia—which was far more than the sum of its parts. Christian architects used Islamic motifs in their buildings. Muslim and Jewish philosophers kept alive the works of Aristotle in Arabic commentaries and translations. Mosques were used as synagogues on Saturdays and churches on Sundays. Later in history, more troubled times and places would look back on that period as a golden age of understanding and tolerance.[30]

It is a fairly small step from such language to the creation of an interfaith Abrahamic utopia. Much of the literature associated with the "Abrahamic religions" discourse uses Muslim Spain in precisely this manner. An additional example of this use of the *convivencia* trope is the Cordoba Initiative, founded in New York in 2004, which functions as a multinational, multifaith organization dedicated to improving understanding and building trust among people of all cultures and faith traditions.[31] One of its cofounders, Feisal Abdul Rauf, writes in his book *What's Right With Islam* that "many Jewish and Christian artists and intellectuals emigrated to Cordoba during this period to escape the more oppressive regimes that reigned over Europe's Dark and Middle Ages. Great Jewish philosophers such as Maimonides were free to create their historic works within the pluralistic culture of Islam."[32]

Of course much of this romanticism is fueled by contemporary motives. Maimonides, for example, certainly created some of the most important legal and philosophical works in Judaism. However, he did so not in an "interfaith environment," but against the backdrop of Islamic persecution associated with the Almohad (Muslim) conquest of Cordoba in 1148. Many Jews had no option but to flee these conquests, most going north to the Christian part of the peninsula, although some (including Maimonides and his family) went south to North Africa.[33] And although some will claim that the Almohads were foreign "colonizers" from North Africa who threatened the "Andalusian" way of life,[34] the idea of an ecumenical utopia does not emerge from the sources.

If more evidence of this romanticized and imaginatively constructed interfaith utopia of "Muslim Spain" is needed, I also point to an advertisement in the May 2011 edition of *Religious Studies News*, published by the American Academy of Religion (AAR). Therein we see publicized a "documentary" film entitled *Out of Cordoba: Averroes and Maimonides in Their Time and Ours*. The film, directed and produced by Jacob Bender, uses the great Muslim philosopher, Averroes (1126–1198), and the afore-mentioned Maimonides as a window onto modern ecumenicism. The film's synopsis explains that

> *Out of Cordoba* is a feature documentary about Jews, Muslims, and Christians struggling for coexistence and against the hijacking of their respective religions by extremists. The film profiles several contemporary people of faith, who, inspired by two "wise men" from the city of Cordoba in medieval Spain—Averroes the Muslim, and Rabbi Moses Maimonides the Jew—are challenging the propositions that there is an inevitable "clash of civilizations" between the West and the Muslim world, an incompatibility between Islam and democracy, and an unsolvable conflict between Muslims and Jews.
>
>   *Out of Cordoba* is also the story of the film's director, Jacob Bender, an American Jew and peace activist, as he undertakes a journey around the Mediterranean world after the attacks of 9/11—in Spain, Morocco, France, Egypt, Palestine, and Israel—following in the footsteps of these two "wise men of Cordoba" in search of Muslims, Jews, and Christians committed to utilizing their religious traditions as sources of tolerance, democracy, and human rights.[35]

This synopsis again reveals the interfaith possibilities and histori-cal abuses to which the category "Muslim Spain" can be put. From the description it is clear that the director is not interested in history. Averroes and Maimonides, despite the implications in the quotation above, did not know one another. The two most certainly did not engage in "interfaith dialogue" or dwell upon a common "Abrahamic descent" that had been obscured or "hijacked" by "fundamentalists." All of the terms in the pre-vious sentence that have quotations around them are modern constructs and have absolutely no historical precedence in twelfth-century Spain or anywhere else. They are terms that are important to us today and that have been retrofitted onto the historical record. This has been especially the case in the years following 9/11, the attacks that symbolize religious fanaticism and exclusivity.

Maimonides, as we have seen, was forced out of Cordoba and the Iberian Peninsula while still in his early teens. And Averroes, despite a lifetime of commenting on the works of Aristotle and functioning as an important judge in Seville, Cordoba, and North Africa, eventually fell out of favor for the perceived radicalism of his thought. His lot, then, was not a happy one.[36] Neither was interested, as the passage above implies, in dismantling a "clash of civilizations" discourse, if for no other reason that neither had ever heard of such a discourse. And while we may romanticize them for their commitment to reason and Aristotelian philosophy, their views on women, homosexuality, and apostasy would inevitably strike us today as extremely intolerant.

When we make the concerns of the medievals into our own (and vice versa), we have to be cautious of introducing distortion and manipulation. This, however, is rarely the concern of individuals such as Rauf, Bender, or even President Clinton. While I do not think they consciously manipulate the sources for their own purposes, they certainly are not interested in their complexity, including the various social, cultural, economic, intellectual, and religious contexts out of which they emerge. They do, nevertheless, ultimately present misleading accounts that selectively emphasize that which supports their arguments for coexistence and that excise all those elements that might make us uncomfortable. When Chris Lowney writes in his *A Vanished World: Muslims, Christians, and Jews in Medieval Spain* that "they almost built the peaceful, common society that we must learn to build,"[37] we know that historical accuracy is not paramount to this genre.

Another good example of the sacrifice of historical accuracy for the sake of interfaith and political optics is the critically acclaimed *The Ornament of the World* by Yale Professor of Spanish and Portuguese María Rosa Menocal. Also on the advisory board of the film *Out of Cordoba*,[38] Menocal is a firm proponent of Muslim Spain as a utopia for the coexistence of the three faiths that, as she claims, nourished a "complex culture of tolerance."[39] She speaks of an "Andalusian ethic" that made this possible although al-Andalus was anything but a monolith. In fact, after the collapse of the Caliphate in Cordoba in 1039, the Muslim part of the peninsula splintered into a number of independent and often warring kingdoms, known as the *taifa*, or "successor," kingdoms.[40] It was some of these independent kingdoms, not the unified Caliphate per se, that witnessed the rise of various cultural exchanges and cooperation among *certain* Christian, Muslim, and Jewish subgroups. In fact, it was most likely on account of this political uncertainty and impending chaos that these subgroups focused less on turning on one another than on any abiding spirit of "Andalusian tolerance."

Curiously, Menocal begins her study with two unsupportable claims. In the first she creates an artificial binary between the first two dynasties, or caliphates, of Islam. The Umayyad Caliphate, which will be deposed in the East and exist solely in Spain (at least until 1039), is described as "symbol[izing] the original fusion of a culture ... with a revelation," as "cosmopolitan," as "being able to assimilate and even revive the rich gifts of earlier and indigenous cultures."[41] The Abbasid Dynasty, which overthrew the Umayyad in 750 (with the exception of Spain), however, is described as bloodthirsty. They "eradicated"[42] and "massacred"[43] the Umayyads, they "slaughtered"[44] and engaged in a "bloody massacre"[45] of the family of the Caliph. And the capital of the Abbasid Caliphate, Baghdad, is described as "resembling nothing so much as a fortress."[46] It is unclear to me why she does this. Perhaps it is because Muslim Spain will derive its ideological legitimacy from the Umayyads that Menocal feels the need to cast their successors in the East as "bloody" usurpers. She labels another dynasty, the Fatimid, founded in 909 and based in Egypt, as the Abbasid Dynasty was beginning to fragment, as "pretenders," and she even goes so far as to question their legitimacy to rule.[47]

If anything, the early Abbasid Empire was responsible for facilitating many important cultural and intellectual contributions to Islamic and world civilization. Baghdad quickly became the intellectual and artistic center of the Empire, the place where many Islamic and nonreligious sciences (e.g., philosophy, astronomy, mathematics) were developed and studied. Itself often called the "Golden Age,"[48] Muslim scholars encountered the sciences, mathematics, and medicine of antiquity through the works of Aristotle, Plato, Galen, Ptolemy, Euclid, and others.[49] These works, translated into Arabic, and the important commentaries written on them, were the wellsprings of science during the medieval period and beyond. It is also important to note that much scientific, literary, and poetic activity in the Muslim world occurred in the eastern part of the Empire, and was exported from there to other areas, such as al-Andalus. Learning, science, poetic license were confined, on Menocal's reading, solely to Muslim Spain, which is certainly not the case.

In her second major assumption, Menocal tries to argue that most scholarship on Islam has traditionally ignored Muslim Spain. She claims, for example, that "the conventional histories of the Arabic speaking peoples follow the fork in the road taken by the Abbasids."[50] This is untrue. Many important works have been written on the history of Muslim Spain.[51] Yet her notes make no mention of these, perhaps because if they did she would not be able to make such gross assertions. For instance, she mentions in an extremely favorable light the Arab Ibn Hazm (994–1064), a philosopher and litterateur who wrote, among other works, *The Ring of the Dove*, a treatise devoted to the art of love. Indeed, Howard Bloom, who wrote a foreword to Menocal's volume, describes Ibn Hazm as the "hero of the book...a Don Quixote, holding on to an aesthetics, an erotics, and a cultural tradition unrecoverable but unforgettable."[52] However, both completely overlook the fact that Ibn Hazm was a vitriolic critic of other religions,[53] was opposed to the allegorical interpretation of the Quran (something that many philosophers and mystics engaged in), thought that revelation was superior to reason, and focused on the literal injunctions of the Quran and hadith. Indeed, if we were to use modern language to describe Ibn Hazm—as many of these modern commentators do—we could perhaps call him a "Muslim fundamentalist with a poetic streak." He was also extremely critical of Jews who had positions of authority over Muslims. Ibn Hazm is a perfect example of what is wrong with so much of the literature that promotes Muslim Spain as a bastion of intellectual freedom and religious tolerance. Both "freedom" and "tolerance" are modern virtues and we have to be extremely cautious of employing them to earlier times and places, where such virtues were either unknown or not regarded as virtuous.

The collapse of al-Andalus occurred not because of the *Reconquista* of Christian armies from the north, but, on Menocal's reading, from the forces of the "antisecular" and "religiously intolerant" Berber invasion from North Africa.[54] Lacking "the Andalusian experience," these Berbers, whom she defines by their "obtuseness," signaled the end of an "authentic multiculturalism."[55] Such claims, however, are impossible to verify.

Menocal's book was highly successful among both academic and popular audiences. Indicative of its widespread appeal, for example, is the fact that at the end of the book we encounter "A Reading Group Guide" and "A Conversation with María Rosa Menocal." Menocal's book is not based on historical research, but on a romantic wistfulness: Muslim Spain created, for a brief period, a culture of tolerance that was subsequently lost. We, in the present, can and must learn from it.

The Ornament of the World, like so many books devoted to showing the high point of Abrahamic coexistence, is predicated on the contemporary need to find a "historical" precedent. If a time and a place can be located, then interfaith coexistence has been realized and, as such, can happen again, whether in the present or the future. If Menocal locates this spirit of tolerance in the time of the Hebrew poet Samuel Hanagid or Harold Bloom in the time of Ibn Hazm, Chris Lowney catches a glimpse of it during the reign of King Alfonso the Learned (1221–1284):

> Today's Muslim, Jews, and Christians still share Abraham's common patrimony and still are divided by reconcilable doctrinal differences. Our era, suffering from the same schizophrenia that afflicted our ancestors, might heal it by embracing the wisdom that Alfonso and his medieval contemporaries uncovered yet never fully grasped.[56]

The noble lie of overlooking events or actions for a good ecumenical story in the present is one of the hallmarks of various discourses associated with "Abrahamic religions." Much of it claims to find historical evidence for this coexistence, but is then hard-pressed to contextualize it. We thus witness the creation of a series of historical myths. This is the case, it seems to me, because most of those engaged in such activity are neither historians nor in possession of the requisite linguistic skills.

Without wanting to deny completely the existence of some sort of *convivencia* between Jews, Muslims, and Christians, it is important to note that it was marked by what Mark R. Cohen describes as a legally prescribed "regime of discrimination."[57] That is, Jews and Christians had both rights and a legal standing based on their status as dhimmis ("non-Muslim minorities," sometimes also referred to as "People of the Book").[58] Cohen is quick to point out, correctly in my opinion, that we must be cautious of reading into this modern virtues such as tolerance and "our modern, liberal sense of full equality."[59]

Speaking generally, Jews and Christians in Muslim lands enjoyed security in return for the payment of an annual poll tax and adherence to other regulations, including the acknowledgment of Islam's superiority. Violence was not unheard of against dhimmis, but this was usually limited to times when they were perceived to flaunt the laws of their inferiority. One of the most famous events in this regard was the massacre of the Jews of Granada in 1066, an event that gets little or no mention in the interfaith literature. Indeed, as David Nirenberg, a historian who specializes in Muslim Spain, argues, it is important to nuance the notion of a "peaceful *convivencia*" with the more realistic notion that "violence was a central and systemic aspect of the coexistence of majority and minority in medieval Spain, and even suggests that coexistence was in part predicated on such violence."[60]

As in the previous example, that of Muhammad's Arabia, it may even be the case that we are still working with conceptions of religious and ethnic identities that are too modern. If we move, as many in cultural studies want us to, toward the idea that real action occurs at margins and not centers, how does such activity redefine our notions of or attachments to perceived stable religious traditions? It is important to be aware not only of the constructed nature of all identities, whether personal or collective, but also the ongoing construction and constant maintenance that goes on among ethnic, religious, and other collective identities.[61]

We must resist the temptation of assuming that communities simply constitute themselves around an essential core. What did the borders between Jews, Muslims, and Christians look like in eleventh-century al-Andalus? Were there sets of features or traits that absolutely defined who was what? It certainly was neither language nor culture—as all partook of Arabic culture and all were largely Arabophone. Jews and Christians articulated even their religions in Arabic using the categories of that language and all of the implications that it carried.[62] Rather than assume that identities in the premodern world are fixed and inherited in predetermined ways, we ought to be aware of the ways in which they are invented, reinvented, enforced, and patrolled. Jewish, Christian, and Muslim identities in al-Andalus, as indeed in many other historical periods, were always contingent, constantly in need of maintenance, reinvention, and repair.[63]

When Jews, Christians, and Muslims got along in al-Andalus, they did so not based on a perceived sense of "Abrahamic heritage." If we simply assume that these groups constituted themselves as we perceive them to do so today—that is, as holding on to an attachment to a positive projection of some *sui generis* core of group identity—we miss the complex interactions and negotiations that took place among these three groups. Historical myths take the place of real analysis.

Conclusions

This chapter has provided two extended examples to demonstrate, from an academic perspective, the fatal flaws inherent to the "Abrahamic religions" discourse. Implicit in the latter are such outmoded yet seductive essentialisms—not only of "Abrahamic," but of each of the three religions that are imagined to comprise it—that we fail to notice the complexities beneath the surface. In the case of Muhammad's Arabia, this leads to the assumption that the three "religions" existed in seventh-century Arabia in the same manner that they do today. This means that terms we are quite happy employing—such as "religion," "ethnicity," "identity," "multicultural"—are assumed to have existed in the same manner in different times and in different places. I tried to show that this is not the case. Rather, these three modern constructs begin to break down when applied to the Arabian Peninsula on the eve of Islam's rise.

The second example, that of tenth- and eleventh-century al-Andalus, is equally complex, albeit for different reasons. By this time the three "religions" certainly have coalesced in ways that they had not in the previous example. However, we have to be aware of the complex interactions and negotiations that take place among them. Judaisms, Christianities, and Islams all partake of the semantics of the same cultural language. Certain of these subgroups might well perceive and define themselves as radically different from one another. However, among others—especially when it comes to those subgroups that engage in activities such as philosophy or mysticism or poetry and poetics—the features that absolutely define who is a Jew, Christian, or Muslim frequently demonstrate real overlapping and indistinguishable characteristics.

The result is complexity. Real complexity based on sets of shared traits of overlapping subgroups that comprise each "religion." What we decidedly do not possess—whether in sixth-century Arabia or eleventh-century al-Andalus—is three discrete "Abrahamic religions" interacting with one another in some retroactively imagined interfaith utopia.

Conclusions

ORIGINALLY CONCEIVED IN supersessionist drawing rooms as a way to legitimate one's own claim and to denigrate rival claimants, Abraham eventually and paradoxically became the cornerstone of an interfaith agenda. Although employed sporadically in the decades following Vatican II, the years since 9/11 have witnessed the creation of a veritable "Abrahamic religions" discourse. Yet this movement from exclusivity to inclusivity has created a nebulous category within which Judaism, Christianity, and Islam sit, often uncomfortably, with one another. A set of essential features is accepted to keep them there, and we are encouraged to imagine a handful of ecumenical characteristics that somehow justify their cohabitation.

The previous six chapters have attempted to provide both a history and an analysis of how the category "Abrahamic religions" came to be. I trust that I have made the case that the term is, for all intents and purposes, meaningless. If we are going to persist in the endeavor—something that is surely a desideratum—to explain the manifold contacts, exchanges, interchanges, and (re-)configurations among Judaisms, Christianities, and Islams we would be better suited to explore different theoretical and methodological languages. The traditional essence and manifestation model that eschews the particulars of historical interactions in favor of some vaguely constructed interfaith dialogue no longer seems a viable option, except, of course, in the various ecumenical circles associated with liberal theology.

This study has argued just how misleading and inappropriate this kind of picture is as a general description for a set of far-ranging temporal and geographic interactions among various social groups that are often conveniently labeled as "Jewish," Christian," or "Muslim." The clichés and assumptions that are thought to describe shared characteristics within the "Abrahamic religions" discourse do not—despite claims to the contrary—capture something essential about these interactions. Some of the clichés and stereotypes recounted in the preceding pages may well occasionally be appropriate to invoke with this or that particular source. However, to take the next step and argue that such clichés conform to all or most of these interactions is problematic in the extreme. The manifold interactions among these various social groups cannot and must not be sweepingly reduced to a universal strategy or quest for meaning in the present.

Such a reduction flattens these sources. It is this flattening, more than anything, that concerns me about the "Abrahamic religions" discourse. It presents a univocal straightjacket on what are overlapping sets of multivocal and antiphonal utterances that emerge from specific encounters. To make the bold claim that all such encounters conform to some ill-defined "Abrahamic" model is both simplistic and incorrect. It is to force uniformity where none exists. This is not tantamount to saying that we should avoid comparative analyses between certain subgroups of Judaisms, Christianities, and Islams. On the contrary, we should persevere; however, such analysis must involve an appreciation of the historical dynamics that occur at the local level, or "on the ground," as opposed to the macro level. To do this, we must begin with an interrogation of the words and categories that we use.

Having provided such an interrogation here, I think it safe to conclude that "Abrahamic religions" is a category that performs very little or no analytical work. It is predicated on essences—not only for each of the three traditions taken individually, but for all three imagined as a whole. This is tantamount to the creation of an essence from three essences, which is little more than a tautology. The problem with this essentialism, like all essentialisms, is that it creates a set of vague generalizations claiming that certain properties (as opposed to others) are universal traits that exist independent of context. This leads to the position that words have single meanings and that all things can be precisely defined or described by them. Instead of such generalizations, I have suggested in the pages above that it is more productive to explore the social construction of terms and categories, focusing on their dependence on various social groups rather than any inherent quality.

The "Abrahamic religions"—at least as imagined by the likes of Louis Massignon—assumes that each of the three "Abrahamic" religions possesses a common ancestor. Theologically and not historically imagined, this led to the formation of a modern Abraham, the creation of someone who possessed of a set of virtues that many want to see reflected, both individually and collectively, in each of the three monotheisms. This "Abrahamic religions" discourse, then, is about the present, about our desire to see the modern concept of interfaith tolerance reflected in the historical record. If it can be shown that these three religions are actually part of the same "family," it follows that some sort of reconciliation may well be possible. Although politics and history may get in the way of this reconciliation, it can be imagined in the pages of scripture and in the hearts of believers.

This commonality among the three religions—and this is one of the hallmarks of the genre—is not confined to the distant past, although the historical record is often the place where it is vaguely located. Recall the discourses involved in creating the "interfaith utopia" of Muslim Spain recounted in the previous chapter. "Muslim Spain" can be held up as an authentic representation of ecumenical coexistence because it is largely romanticized and its various legal, social, and historical specifics can be safely ignored because such specifics get in the way of a good story, one that is full of meaning for the present.

The "Abrahamic religions" discourse is future-directed. Perceived commensurability in the past—whether in the Genesis narrative, the Quranic narrative, some modern pastiche of the two, or in places like Muslim Spain—produces the seeds of hope for future coexistence. Recent years have seen the expansion of this commensurability to include a host of essences, traits, and characteristics. If previous generations imagined a common ancestor to find meaning after the collapse of Europe in the Second World War, our generation locates in Abraham the antidote to the "clash of civilizations." We now encounter, for example, "Abrahamic" takes on peace, social justice, and ethics, all of which are somehow assumed to be qualitatively different from "non-Abrahamic" (alternatively conceived of as "Eastern") takes on the same themes.

This invocation of a vague set of essential characteristics is done primarily in the name of theological ecumenicism. Political correctness and the need to see both in other centuries and in other cultures the modern virtues of interfaith coexistence trumps research into historical particulars. In this sense the invocation of "Abrahamic religions" to make sense of three unwieldy traditions actually obscures our understanding, functioning as an impediment to how we conceive of the dynamics of religious exchange and interchange.

All of this comes at a real cost. A conceptual model that upholds three monolithic religious traditions interacting with one another based on a

perceived patrimony may well prevent us from examining the dynamics of specific interactions because we have already convinced ourselves
that these three religions are somehow "related" to one another. A priori
assumptions of a shared genetic code here have the potential to threaten
empirical investigations into actual historical relations.

The academic study of religion has to resist the temptation to use
untheorized terms and taxa taken from interfaith circles and then pretend that they name some historical reality. In this respect, the terms,
categories, and the discourses associated with "Abrahamic religions" present a case study of the slippage that can occur between Theology and
Religious Studies. We must resist using the former as if it were a simple
extension of the latter and vice versa. Unless we do so, unwarranted value
judgments potentially enter the analysis. When "Abrahamic religions" is
invoked and used—as it frequently is—in Religious Studies, it conjures
up, whether consciously or unconsciously, a wistful hope for coexistence.
This hope, in turn, implies a set of essential traits that impede further
analysis. Why continue using a term that has no basis in the historical
record and reflects little more than an interfaith agenda?

Yet, as I argued in the final two chapters, the problem is deeper than
simply the term "Abrahamic religions." It is not the choice of terminology
but the category itself that needs rethinking. What is the worth of a category if it is too imprecise and too unclear to establish a consensual agreement on interesting and relevant data? What, for example, do we do with
all those historical formations from the three traditions that do not neatly
fit the characteristics that we have pre-ordained as "Abrahamic"? What is
the worth of a category, moreover, if it encourages intellectual shortcuts
predicated on misleading generalizations?

I have tried to suggest in this study one possible alternative to the
employment of the category "Abrahamic religions." Rather than perceive of
a common ancestor that gives rise to three "children," it is more helpful to
imagine a set of fluid traditions within which certain subgroups—within
and among these traditions—possess a number of shared characteristics.
It then becomes our job to identify such characteristics—when are they
used? by whom? how?—with the aim of mapping and classifying their
manifold configurations. When we employ such a model, as witnessed
for example in the previous chapter with the various social formations
at the time of Muhammad, we begin to see overlapping characteristics
among and between groups that we might otherwise mistake for discrete
"religions," using the language of later centuries.

The result is that the slogans we have largely convinced ourselves of, that to each religion there must be an essence, slowly begin to break down. Terms that we take for granted—for example, religion, ethnicity, identity, and their range of meanings within each religion—become little more than jingoistic signifiers, often with no reflection in the sources themselves. Such slogans hardly convey the range of complexity and messiness that occurs "on the ground," as a variety of social groups interact with one another in their desire to create meaning for themselves. For it is ultimately there, not in the lofty pages of scriptures taken by some to be transcripts of divine revelation, where we witness contest and conflict, and the creation of manifold selves and others.

As I have tried to argue throughout this study, the imposition of super and generic categories such as "Abrahamic religions" both create and lead to further imprecision. Such categories are threatened by the messiness of details because their overarching concern is not nuancing inter- or intrareligious exchanges and polemics in specific temporal or geographic locations, but in establishing the parameters for a broad-based interfaith communication in the present.

We thus need to move beyond words, categories, and models that imply three discrete religious traditions—namely, Judaism, Christianity, and Islam—with a shared essence that interact with one another. In particular, we need to avoid using "family" and related metaphors to describe these interactions. If we want to understand the complexity and diversity of sources produced by various Judaisms, Christianities, and Islams, we need a precise language and not one that has simply been recycled from various supersessionist and interfaith conversations.

Notes

INTRODUCTION

1. An informative analysis of the Goldstein massacre and its roots in religious violence, especially that associated with the Jewish holiday of Purim, may be found in Elliot Horowitz, *Reckless Rites: Purim and the Legacy of Jewish Violence* (Princeton, NJ: Princeton University Press, 2006), esp. 4–10.

2. See Jon D. Levenson, *The Death and Resurrection of the Beloved Son: The Transformation of Child Sacrifice in Judaism and Christianity* (New Haven, CT: Yale University Press, 1993), 68–75.

3. David S. Powers, *Muhammad Is Not the Father of Any of Your Men: The Making of the Last Prophet* (Philadelphia: University of Pennsylvania Press, 2009), 3–10.

4. Although one could quite easily make the case that the origins of the academic study of religion in the eighteenth century emerge precisely from liberal Protestant circles. See, for example, J. Samuel Preus, *Explaining Religion: Criticism and Theory from Bodin to Freud* (New Haven, CT: Yale University Press, 1987), 3–20.

5. Bruce Lincoln, *Theorizing Myth: Narrative, Ideology, and Scholarship* (Chicago: University of Chicago Press, 1999), ix.

6. Arthur McCalla, "When is History not History?" *Historical Reflections* 20.3 (1994): 435–452, at 435.

7. According to Jonathan Z. Smith, for "a student of religion such as myself to accept willingly the designation 'historian of religion' is to submit to a lifelong sentence of ambiguity. I cannot think of two more difficult terms than 'history' and 'religion.' Their conjunction, as may be witnessed by every programmatic statement from this putative discipline that I am familiar with, serves only to further the confusion." See his "In Comparison a Magic Dwells," in his *Imagining Religion: From Babylon to Jonestown* (Chicago: University of Chicago Press, 1982), 20.

8. I am certainly aware of the debates that go on in the subfield of historiography about, for example, what a historical "fact" consists of and how it is constructed. See, in this regard, Hayden White's classic treatment in *Metahistory:*

The Historical Imagination in Nineteenth-Century Europe (Baltimore: Johns Hopkins University Press, 1973), 40–58; idem, *Tropics of Discourse: Essays in Cultural Criticism* (Baltimore: Johns Hopkins University Press, 1978), 120–125. Less philosophical, but equally rewarding, is Georg Iggers, *Historiography in the Twentieth Century: From Scientific Objectivity to the Postmodern Challenge*, with a new epilogue by the author (Middleton, CT: Wesleyan University Press, 2005).

9. As for example in John L. Esposito, "Foreword" to F. E. Peters, *The Children of Abraham: Judaism, Christianity, Islam*, A New Edition (Princeton, NJ: Princeton University Press, 2006), xi. Despite Esposito's foreword, Peters does what few others do in this genre. He is able to present an historical introduction to the three religions that is neither wistful nor romantic, but sound and highly readable. Back to Esposito, who is more representative of the historical vagueness that characterizes this literature, we read in his more recent *The Future of Islam* (New York: Oxford University Press, 2010), 198–199: "Our next step is to acknowledge this 'missing link' to recognize that the Children of Abraham are part of a rich Judeo-Christian-Islamic history and tradition. Despite the rhetoric and actions of Muslim extremists and terrorists, and religious and cultural differences, the people of America, Europe, and the Muslim world have many shared values, dreams, and aspirations.... Together we can contain and eliminate our preachers of hate and terrorists who threaten the safety, security, and prosperity of our families and societies."

10. See, for example, the table of contents in *Abraham's Children: Jews, Christians, and Muslims in Conversation*, edited by Norman Solomon, Richard Harries, and Tim Winter (London: T & T Clark, 2005). Other examples of this "Abrahamic religions" genre, of which there are numerous representatives, will be discussed in the pages that follow, especially in chapter 4.

11. See, for example, Jonathan Z. Smith, *Drudgery Divine: On the Comparison of Early Christianities and the Religions of Late Antiquity* (Chicago: University of Chicago Press, 1990), 52: "Comparison provides the means by which *we* 're-vision' phenomena as *our* data in order to solve *our* theoretical problems."

12. Clifford Geertz, years ago, warned us of moving away from small, real-time events in favor of more grandiose efforts of "discovering the Continent of Meaning and mapping out its bodiless landscape." See his *The Interpretation of Cultures: Selected Essays* (New York: Basic Books, 1973), 20.

13. Although the term was made famous by Samuel Huntington, *The Clash of Civilizations and the Remaking of the World Order* (New York: Simon and Schuster, 1996), he actually borrowed it from an essay by Bernard Lewis, "The Roots of Muslim Rage," *The Atlantic Monthly* (September, 1990): 47–60.

14. Smith, *Imagining Religion*, xi.

15. To give a sense of Smith's notion that our own data illumine larger problems in the field, a work that I draw inspiration from is devoted to Tibetan Buddhism. See Donald S. Lopez, Jr., *Prisoners of Shangri-La: Tibetan Buddhism and the West* (Chicago: University of Chicago Press, 1998).

CHAPTER 1

1. Bruce Feiler, *Abraham: A Journey to the Heart of Three Faiths* (New York: HarperCollins, 2002), 204.
2. Ibid. His italics.
3. http://www.time.com/time/magazine/article/0,9171,1003355–2,00.html.
4. E.g., Feiler, *Abraham*, 226.
5. Although now is neither the time nor place to elucidate this, I tend to sympathize with those who question the utility of the category "religion." See, for example, Jonathan Z. Smith, *Imagining Religion: From Babylon to Jonestown*; Talal Asad, *Genealogies of Religion: Discipline and Reasons of Power in Christianity and Islam* (Baltimore: Johns Hopkins University Press, 1993); Russell T. McCutcheon, *Manufacturing Religion: The Discourse on Sui Generis Religion and the Politics of Nostalgia* (New York: Oxford University Press, 1997); Donald Wiebe, *The Politics of Religious Studies: The Continuing Conflict with Theology in the Academy* (New York: Palgrave Macmillan, 1999); Timothy Fitzgerald, *The Ideology of Religious Studies* (New York: Oxford University Press, 2000); Bruce Lincoln, *Holy Terrors: Thinking About Religion After September 11* (Chicago: University of Chicago Press, 2003).
6. Jonathan Z. Smith, "Connections," *Journal of the American Academy of Religion* 58.1 (1990): 5.
7. On the various ways that they have been put together, see the masterful study by F. E. Peters, *The Children of Abraham*, new ed. (Princeton, NJ: Princeton University Press, 2006); and his subsequent two-volume *The Monotheists: Jews, Christians, and Muslims in Conflict and Competition* (Princeton, NJ: Princeton University Press, 2003).
8. Esposito, "Preface," to F. E. Peters, *The Children of Abraham*, new ed. (Princeton, NJ: Princeton University Press, 2006), xii. See also, e.g., Reuven Firestone, *Children of Abraham: An Introduction to Judaism for Muslims* (New York: Ktav, 2001), xxiii–xxiv; Leonard Swidler, "Preface: Beyond Violence through Dialogue and Cooperation," in *Beyond Violence: Religious Sources of Social Transformation in Judaism, Christianity, and Islam*, edited by James L. Heft (New York: Fordham University Press, 2004), ix–x; William Stacy Johnson and Peter Ochs, "Introduction: Crisis, Call, and Leadership in the Abrahamic Traditions," in *Crisis, Call, and Leadership in the Abrahamic Traditions*, edited by Peter Ochs and William Stacy Johnson (New York: Palgrave Macmillan, 2009), 2–3.
9. Irfan A. Omer, "Submitting to the Will of God: Jews, Christians, and Muslims Learning from Each Other," in *Heirs of Abraham: The Future of Muslim, Jewish, and Christian Relations*, edited by Bradford E. Hinze and Irfan A. Omer (Maryknoll, NY: Orbis Books, 2005), 136–137.
10. Peters, *The Monotheists*, vol. 1, xvi.
11. This certainly does not claim to be an exhaustive account of this. For an in-depth study of the roles and uses to which Abraham was put in the world of

antiquity and late antiquity, see the various essays collected in *Abraham, the Nations, and the Hagarites: Jewish, Christian, and Islamic Perspectives on Kinship with Abraham*, edited by Martin Goodman, George H. van Kooten, and Jacques T.A.G.M. van Ruiten (Leiden: Brill, 2010).

12. Translation from *Tanakh: The Holy Scriptures* (Philadelphia: Jewish Publication Society of America, 1985), 18.

13. The topic of an ecumenical "Abrahamic religions" has been queried by certain feminist theologians/scholars of religion. Yet rather than try to dismantle the category, they seek to shift it onto Sarah and Hagar. See the collection of essays in *Hagar, Sarah, and Their Children: Jewish, Christian, and Muslim Perspectives*, edited by Phyllis Trible and Letty M. Russell (Louisville, KY: Westminster John Knox Press, 2006). Although they stress Sarah and Hagar as opposed to Abraham, and the matriarchs as opposed to the patriarchs, their ecumenical desire is ultimately no different from that of their male counterparts. In their Introduction, for example, the editors write that the contributors to the volume

> believe that understanding problems and opportunities of the past and present among Jews, Christians, and Muslims, as well as envisioning a different future, resides more in studying the women Hagar and Sarah than in stressing the putative unity located in Abraham. Further, they believe that to the myriad children of Hagar and Sarah, now unto the thousandth generation and beyond, comes the responsibility of seeking understanding, doing justice and walking humbly with one another in the diverse families of faith.

See Phyllis Trible and Letty M. Russell, "Unto the Thousandth Generation," in *Hagar, Sarah, and Their Children*, 1–2.

14. On the various permutations that this story underwent, see Reuven Firestone, *Journeys in Holy Lands: The Evolution of the Abraham-Ishmael Legends in Islamic Exegesis* (Albany: State University of New York Press, 1990), 61–103.

15. F. E. Peters, *The Children of Abraham*, 9. See, further, *idem, The Monotheists*, vol. 1, 6–7. According to Peters, one of the earliest connections made between the Arabs and Ishmael was not in later Muslim sources, but in the extra-canonical second-century BCE *Book of Jubilees*. Therein we read that Ishmael settled "between Pharan and the borders of Babylon, in all the land to the East, facing the desert. And these mingled with each other, and they were called Arabs and Ishmaelites" (20:11–13). Certainly there is no historical evidence for any of this and, if anything, what we have here is the mapping of the known world of the ancient Israelites based on the familiar categories of biblical myth.

16. Firestone, *Journeys in Holy Lands*, 76–79.

17. See, for example, the well-known study "Odysseus' Scar" by Erich Auerbach in his *Mimesis: The Representation of Reality in Western Literature*, translated by Willard R. Trask (Princeton: Princeton University Press, 1953), 1–20.

18. See the discussion in Firestone, *Journeys in Holy Lands*, 135–152.

19. *Book of Jubilees* 20:1–5. Translated in *Old Testament Pseudepigrapha*, edited and translated by James H. Charlesworth (Garden City, NY: Doubleday, 1983).

20. In this respect, the stories surrounding Abraham (and so many of the other patriarchs and matriarchs) have been interpreted in numerous ways—from the rationalist to the mystical—over the past two thousand years of Jewish biblical interpretation. My goal here is not to trace these interpretations, but only to give a basic overview as it relates to the topos of this book, "Abrahamic religions."

21. All translations from the New Testament come from the New Revised Standard Version (NRSV).

22. Translations of the Quran come from *The Qur'ān*, translated into English by Alan Jones (London: Gibb Memorial Trust, 2007).

23. See the perceptive comments in Jon D. Levenson, "The Conversion of Abraham to Judaism, Christianity, and Islam," in *The Idea of Biblical Interpretation: Essays in Honor of James L. Kugel*, edited by Hindy Najman and Judith H. Newman (Leiden: Brill, 2004), 3–40.

24. John Esposito, "Foreword" to F. E. Peters, *The Children of Abraham*, xi.

25. See, for example, Timothy Fitzgerald, "Religion, Philosophy and Family Resemblances," *Religion* 26.3 (1996): 215–236.

26. Ludwig Wittgenstein, *Philosophical Investigations*, edited by G. E. M. Anscombe and R. Rhees, translated by G. E. M. Anscombe (Oxford: Blackwell, 1953), 66.

27. Again, this criticism may be found in Fitzgerald, "Religion, Philosophy and Family Resemblances"; and more fully in *idem, The Ideology of Religious Studies* (New York: Oxford University Press, 2000), 3–32.

28. As I have argued elsewhere, Esposito would probably justify his familial metaphor by claiming that religion has no place in any of these events, and that it was simply evil people using religion to justify their crimes against humanity. See, for example, my *Theorizing Islam: Disciplinary Deconstruction and Reconstruction* (London: Equinox, 2012), chap. 3.

29. Esposito, "Foreword," xi.

30. Perhaps the most famous in this regard is the recently created Chair of Abrahamic Religions at the University of Oxford. The chair's inaugural holder is Prof. Guy Stroumsa, an excellent scholar of Late Antiquity.

31. See, for example, the Lubar Institute for the Study of Abrahamic Religions (http://lisar.lss.wisc.edu/index.html) at the University of Wisconsin at Madison; or the Woolf Institute of Abrahamic Faiths (http://www.woolf.cam.ac.uk) at Cambridge University. For a fuller survey and analysis of such institutes, see chapter 4 below.

32. For example, I recently was part of a conference sponsored by McGill University and held in Istanbul entitled "Philosophy and the Abrahamic Religions: Scriptural Authority and Theories of Knowledge."

33. For example, in the conference mentioned in the previous note, the goal was to interrogate:

the theme of "scriptural authority and theories of knowledge." We propose to explore the varieties of mystical, theological, and philosophical approaches to the interpretation of scripture within these three religious traditions. To what extent do the distinct approaches of Judaism, Christianity, and Islam to the interpretation of the scriptures derive from the methods and epistemology of Hellenic thought?

As can be seen from this description, however, no space or intellectual energy is expended in asking whence the very term "Abrahamic religions" came. See https://secureweb.mcgill.ca/creor/sites/mcgill.ca.creor/files/Istanbul Conference_Dec2010.pdf.

34. See the discussion in McCutcheon, *Manufacturing Religions*, 22.
35. Peter Harrison, *"Religion" and the Religions of the English Enlightenment* (Cambridge: Cambridge University Press, 1990), 12–18.
36. McCutcheon, *Manufacturing Religion*, 13.
37. Feiler, *Abraham*, 204.
38. Examples of the classic publications in the field of phenomenology of religion are Gerardus van der Leeuw, *Religion in Essence and Manifestation*, 2 vols., translated by J. E. Turner (New York: Harper and Row, 1963); Mircea Eliade, *Patterns in Comparative Religion*, translated by Rosemary Sheed (New York: Sheed and Ward, 1958).

CHAPTER 2

1. On a more general comparison between these two reference works, see Donald Wiebe, "The Study of Religion: On the New Encyclopedia of Religion," in his *The Politics of Religious Studies: The Continuing Conflict with Theology in the Academy* (New York: Palgrave, 1999) 197–204. For an interesting exchange, see Neil McMullin, "The Encyclopedia of Religion: A Critique from the Perspective of the History of Japanese Religions," *Method and Theory in the Study of Religion* 1.1 (1989): 80–96; and then the response by Gary L. Ebersole and McMullin's own response in *MTSR* 1.2 (1989): 238–243.
2. Although, as I shall show in the next chapter, it was "invented" in the sense that the Library of Congress brought it into existence taxonomically as a subject heading only in 1995.
3. See, for example, the collection of essays by Donald Wiebe mentioned in the first note to this chapter. Also, see the important work of McCutcheon, *Manufacturing Religion; idem, The Discipline of Religion: Structure, Meaning, Rhetoric* (London: Routledge, 2003).
4. An early biography of Judson, written by the then President of Brown University, has the following to say of Worcester:

In 1809, the Rev. Dr. Worcester delivered the annual sermon before the Massachusetts Missionary Society—a discourse which, for depth of

earnestness and power of appeal, may be advantageously compared with
the most eloquent missionary sermons that have yet appeared.

See Francis Wayland, *A Memoir of Life and Labors of Rev. Adoniram Judson, D.D.*,
2 volumes (Boston: Phillips, Sampson, and Co., 1853), vol. 1, 46.

5. Rev. Dr. Samuel Worcester, *Two Discourses on the Perpetuity and Provision of God's Gracious Covenant with Abraham and His Seed*, 2nd rev. ed. *To which are annexed, Letters to the Rev. Thomas Baldwin, D.D., on his Book, entitled The Baptism of the Believers Only, &c.* (Salem: Printed by Haven Pool, for the Author, 1807), 65.

6. For obvious reasons, my interest in the Pauline letters is not to comment on their purported authenticity or inauthenticity. Rather, it is solely to show how they construct an argument of supersessionism that was subsequently picked up by later Christian theology.

7. Worcester, *Two Discourses on the Perpetuity and Provision of God's Gracious Covenant with Abraham and His Seed*, note to p. 22.

8. Ibid. 27.

9. Powers, *Muhammad Is Not the Father of Any of Your Men*, 119.

10. See, for example, the entry on *tahrīf* in the *Encyclopedia of Islam* (Leiden: Brill, 1960–2005). For a fuller understanding of the Quran and its various contemporaneous contexts, see *The Qur'ân in Its Historical Context*, edited by Gabriel Said Reynolds (New York and London: Routledge, 2008).

11. See Powers, *Muhammad Is Not the Father of Any of Your Men*, 225.

12. On the contested meaning of this term, see Yohanan Friedmann, *Prophecy Continuous: Aspects of Ahmadi Religious Thought and Its Medieval Background* (Berkeley: University of California Press, 1989), 49–82.

13. Firestone, *Journeys in Holy Lands*, 80–93.

14. A modern variation on this theme to explain the origins of Islam may be found in Fred M. Donner, *Muhammad and the Believers: At the Origins of Islam* (Cambridge, MA: Harvard University Press, 2010), 39–89.

15. Text may be found in Daniel J. Sahas, *John of Damascus on Islam: The "Heresy of the Ishmaelites"* (Leiden: Brill, 1972), 133. See also John C. Lamoreaux, "Early Eastern Christian Responses to Islam," in John Victor Tolan, ed., *Medieval Christian Perceptions of Islam: A Book of Essays*, Garland Medieval Case Books, vol. 10 (New York: Garland Press, 1996), 3–31.

16. On a more recent and highly suggestive attempt that argues that the early Muslims claimed legitimacy based upon their relationship to Hagar, see Patricia Crone and Michael Cook, *Hagarism: The Making of the Islamic World* (Cambridge: Cambridge University Press, 1977).

17. Sahas, *John of Damascus on Islam*, 136–137.

18. I base my comments here on Adel-Théodore Khoury, *Les Théologiens byzantins et l'Islam: Textes et auteurs. VIIe-XIIIe s.* (Louvain: Nauwelaerts, 1969), 133–162. Later in life, Khoury has been less interested in documenting the polemics

between religions than in citing their potential coexistence through the figure
of Abraham:

> Rather than being an object of dispute and wrangling between the three
> faiths that claim him, Abraham can become the initiator and the guarantor
> of a serious dialogue between them and of a fruitful cooperation for the good
> of all humanity. (online at http://sedosmission.org/old/eng/khoury.htm).

19. Neither time nor space permits me to go into the history of anti-Muslim medieval polemics here. Excellent treatments may be found in Norman Daniel, *Islam and the West: The Making of an Image* (Edinburgh: Edinburgh University Press, 1960); and more recently John V. Tolan, *Saracens: Islam in the Medieval European Imagination* (New York: Columbia University Press, 2002).

20. Neal Robinson, "Massignon, Vatican II and Islam as an Abrahamic Religion," *Islam and Muslim-Christian Relations* 2.2 (1991), 186.

21. Daniel, *Islam and the West*, 24.

22. Ibid. 29–31, 80. See also Robinson, "Massignon, Vatican II and Islam as an Abrahamic Religion," 187.

23. The classic study remains Ignaz Goldziher, "Über muhammedanische Polemik gegen ahl al-kitāb," *Zeitschrift der Deutschen Morgenländischen Gesellschaft* 32 (1878): 341–387. More recent general studies include David Richard Thomas, "Introduction," *Early Muslim Polemic Against Christianity: Abū 'Īsa al-Warrāq's "Against the Incarnation"* (Cambridge: Cambridge University Press, 2002), 1–10; Martin Accad, "The Gospels in the Muslim Discourse of the Ninth to the Fourteenth Centuries: An Exegetical Inventorial Table," *Islam and Christian-Muslim Relations* 14.1 (2003): 67–91; 14.2 (2003): 205–220; 14.3 (2003): 337–352; 14.4 (2003): 459–479.

24. Abd al-Jabbār, *The Critique of Christian Origins*, edited, translated and annotated by Gabriel Said Reynolds and Samir Khalil Samir (Provo, UT: Brigham Young University Press, 2010).

25. Ibid. 39.

26. Ibid. 96.

27. This negative approach to Islam is documented in Edward Said, *Orientalism* (New York: Vintage, 1978). See also Thierry Hentsch, *Imagining the Middle East*, translated by Fred A. Reed (Montreal: Black Rose Books, 1992).

28. William Muir, *The Life of Mohammad: From Original Sources*, rev. T. H. Weir (Edinburgh: John Grant, 1923), cv–cvi.

29. Ibid. 114.

30. Ibid. 191.

31. For example, the telling title of Abraham Geiger, *Was hat Mohammad aus dem Judenthume aufgenommen* (Bonn: F. Baaden, 1835). Despite the title—literally translated into English as "What Did Muhammad Take From the Jews," though actually given the more sanguine *Judaism and Islam*, translated by F. M. Young (Madras: MDCSPK Press, 1835; repr. New York: Ktav, 1970)— this book actually

is a refreshing change from many of the interpretive strategies that came before it in Orientalist circles. Although he points to the derivative status of Islam, Geiger at least acknowledges it as a valid religion. See Hughes, *Situating Islam: The Past and Future of an Academic Discipline* (London: Equinox, 2007), 16–22.

32. The most famous account is Said, *Orientalism.* For a more nuanced perspective, see Daniel Martin Varisco, *Reading Orientalism: Said and the Unsaid* (Seattle: University of Washington Press, 2007). See also my *Situating Islam,* 9–32.

33. Christiaan Snouck Hurgronje, "La Légende Qoranique d'Abraham et la Politique Religieuse du Prophète Mohammed," translated by G. H. Bousquet, *Revue africaine de Théologie* 95 (1950): 273–288.

34. "Taylor, John," in *Dictionary of National Biography,* 1885–1900, vol. 55, 439–440.

35. "Review of the Covenant of Grace, and Baptism the Token of it, explained upon Scripture principles, by John Taylor, D.D. of Norwich," *The Monthly Review, Or, Literary Journal, By Several Hands,* vol. 17 (1757): 346.

36. D. Dow, *A Dissertation on the Sinaitic and Abrahamic Covenants: Shewing the Former to be Only Temporary, the Latter Everlasting* (Hartford, CT: Peter B. Gleason and Co., 1811).

37. Ibid. 70.

38. Nathaniel E. Johnson, *Household Consecration* (New York: Ezra Collier, 1836), 10.

39. Ibid. 28.

40. Anonymous, "The Covenant of Scripture," *The Danville Quarterly Review,* vol. 2 (1862): 35–57, at 53.

41. Keith H. Essex, "The Abrahamic Covenant," *The Master's Seminary Journal* 10.2 (1999): 191–212, at 191.

42. Online at http://www.tms.edu/AboutInstitutionalPurpose.aspx.

43. *A Debate Between Rev. A. Campbell and Rev. N. L. Rice on the Action, Subject, Design and Administrator of Christian Baptism; Also, on the Character of Spiritual Influence in Conversion and Sanctification, and on the Expediency and Tendency of Ecclesiastic Creeds, as Terms of Union and Communion: Held in Lexington, KY., From the Fifteenth of November to the Second of December, 1843, a Period of Eighteen Days.* Reported by Marcus T. C. Gould, Stenographer, assisted by A. Euclid Drapier, Stenographer and Amanuensis (Lexington, KY: A. T. Skillman and Son, 1844), 275.

44. Ibid. 296.

45. Ibid. 302.

46. Ibid., 305.

47. Jacob Jones Janeway, *Letters Explaining the Abrahamic Covenant: With a View to Establish, on the Broad and Ancient Basis, the Divine Right of Infant Baptism and the Question Relative to the Mode of Administering this Christian Ordinance: Addressed to the Members of the Second Presbyterian Church, in Philadelphia* (Philadelphia: J. Maxwell, 1812).

48. Rev. F. G. Hibbard, *Christian Baptism: In Two Parts. Part First: Infant Baptism* (Part Second = Mode, Obligation, Import and Relative Order) (New York: Carleton and Phillips, 1856), 5.

49. Ibid. 70.

50. Elder Jonas Hartzel, *A Dissertation on the First and Third Abrahamic Covenants, The Covenant at Horeb, and the New Covenant. Their Differential Peculiarities* (New York: T. Holman, 1865), iii–iv.

51. Ibid. 14.

52. Ibid. 14.

53. Ibid. 47–48.

54. Ibid. 54.

CHAPTER 3

1. http://catalog.loc.gov/cgi-bin/Pwebrecon.cgi?hd=1,1&Search%5FArg=abraham ic%20religions&Search%5FCode=SUBJ%40&CNT=100&PID=0plexDYEdII eCJL7h40xLcA-_Wi&HIST=0&SEQ=20120506173953&SID=1 I thank Cheryl Adams, the reference specialist in religion at the Library of Congress, for this information.

2. *Heirs of Abraham: The Future of Muslim, Jewish, and Christian Relations*, edited by Bradford E. Hinze and Irfan A. Omar (Maryknoll, NY: Orbis Books, 2005).

3. Joan Chittester, OSB, Murshod Saadi Shakur Chisti, and Rabbi Arthur Waskow, *The Tent of Abraham: Stories of Hope and Peace for Jews, Christians, and Muslims,* foreword by Karen Armstrong (Boston: Beacon Press, 2006).

4. Norman Solomon, Richard Harries, and Tim Winter, *Abraham's Children: Jews, Christians and Muslims in Conversation* (London: T & T Clark, 2005).

5. This is the title of a special report put out by the United States Institute of Peace (USIP). It may be found online at http://babel.hathitrust.org/cgi/pt?id=mdp.39 015064774204;page=root;view=image;size=100;seq=12.

6. Swinton Lawrie, *An Inquiry, Proving Infant-Baptism to be Untenable, As Well From the Abrahamic Covenant, As From the Scriptures At Large. Containing Also an Investigation of the Principles Which Bind Christians to Unite and Forbear with One Another* (Edinburgh: J. Ritchie, 1810).

7. On the imprecision of "Judeo-Christian," see Arthur A. Cohen, *The Myth of the Judeo-Christian Tradition* (New York: Harper and Row, 1970), ix–xxi.

8. E.g., María Rosa Menocal, *The Ornament of the World: How Muslims, Jews, and Christians Created a Culture of Tolerance in Muslim Spain*, foreword by Howard Bloom (New York: Back Bay Books, 2002); Chris Lowney, *A Vanished World: Muslims, Christians, and Jews in Medieval Spain* (New York: Oxford University Press, 2005).

9. See Mary Louise Gude, *Louis Massignon: The Crucible of Compassion* (Notre Dame, IN: University of Notre Dame Press, 1996), 8–12; other biographical

sources can be found in Herbert Mason, *Memoir of a Friend: Louis Massignon* (Notre Dame, IN: University of Notre Dame Press, 1988); *Louis Massignon*, edited by Jean-François Six (Paris: Éditions de l'Herne, 1970).

10. It is, however, quite easy to show the interrelationship between the academic and religious spheres of his life. His work on al-Hallaj was, for instance, full of Catholic language and entitled *La passion de Husayn Ibn Mansūr al-Hallāj martyr mystique de l'Islam, exécuté à Bagdad le 26 mars 922, etude d'histoire religieuse,* 2nd ed. 4 vols. (Paris: Gallimard, 1975). Translated into English as *The Passion of al-Hallāj: Mystic and Martyr of Islam*, translated with a biographical foreword by Herbert Mason (Princeton, NJ: Princeton University Press, 1982).

11. See, for example, Guy Harpigny, *Islam et Christianisme selon Louis Massignon* (Louvain-la-Neuve: Centre de d'histoire des religions de l'Université Catholique de Louvain-la-Neuve, 1981), 10–12; Pierre Roclave, *Louis Massignon et l'Islam* (Damascus: Institut française de Damas, 1993), 23–31.

12. Robinson, "Massignon, Vatican II and Islam," 191.

13. Mason, *Memoir of a Friend*, 41–43; Gude, *Louis Massignon*, 188–190; Robinson, 191–192.

14. Mason, *Memoir of a Friend*, 41–43.

15. Gude, *Louis Massignon*, 134.

16. Mason, "Foreword to the English Edition," xxxvii; Gude, *Louis Massignon*, 189–190.

17. This is a rare work. Massignon circulated only 300 copies of it. I have not been able to locate a copy and here rely on the analysis of Robinson, "Massignon, Vatican II and Islam," 191–192.

18. According to the Quran and Muslim tradition only a likeness of Jesus—who was transported bodily to heaven—appeared on the Cross.

19. Robinson, "Massignon, Vatican II and Islam," 192.

20. Louis Massignon, "Les trois prières d'Abraham, père di tous les croyants," *Dieu Vivant* 13 (1949): 20–23. Republished in Louis Massignon, *Parole donèe*, 2nd ed. (Paris: Seuil, 1983), 257–272. Translated as "The Three Prayers of Abraham," in *Testimonies and Reflections: Essays of Louis Massignon*, selected and introduced by Herbert Mason (Notre Dame, IN: University of Notre Dame Press, 1989), 3–20. English quotations are from this translation.

21. Massignon, "The Three Prayers of Abraham," 8.

22. *Abraham: Père des croyants* (Paris: Éditions du Cerf, 1952).

23. Son Em. Le Cardinal Tisserant, "Préface," in *Abraham: Père des croyants*, 4 (my translation).

24. On this role of history among Massignon's European contemporaries, see Steven M. Wasserstrom, *Religion after Religion: Gershom Scholem, Mircea Eliade, and Henry Corbin at Eranos* (Princeton, NJ: Princeton University Press, 1999), 85–99.

25. James Kritzeck, *Sons of Abraham: Jews, Christians, and Moslems* (Baltimore: Helicon, 1965), 83.

26. Ibid. 88–89. Although, given my comments in the previous chapter, this comparison to earlier figures may well be unintended.

27. Ibid. 83.

28. Ibid. 95. Again, whether consciously or unconsciously, Kritzeck surprisingly does not mention Ishmael.

29. For historical background and context, consult Raymond F. Bulman, "The Historical Context," in *From Trent to Vatican II: Historical and Theological Investigations*, edited by Raymond F. Bulman and Frederick J. Parrella (New York: Oxford University Press, 2006), 3–18.

30. Robinson, "Massignon, Vatican II and Islam," 194.

31. Pope John Paul II, for example, described it as "the Magna Carta of interreligious dialogue." See the discussion in Risto Jukko, *Trinity in Unity in Christian-Muslim Relations: The Work of the Pontifical Council for Interreligious Dialogue* (Leiden: Brill, 2007), 6–13. The following two paragraphs owe much to Jukko's discussion.

32. Ibid. 8.

33. Online at http://www.vatican.va/archive/hist_councils/ii_vatican_council/documents/vat-ii_decl_19651028_nostra-aetate_en.html.

34. For example, "Among the non-Christian religions, the religion of the followers of Muhamet deserves special attention by reason of its monotheistic character and its link with the faith of Abraham, who Saint Paul described as the "father…of our Christian faith." Quoted in Jukko, *Trinity in Unity in Christian-Muslim Relations*, 127 n. 176.

35. *Nostra Aetate*, paragraph 4.

36. Ibid.

37. Quoted in Robinson, "Massignon, Vatican II and Islam," 195.

38. Online at http://www.vatican.va/archive/hist_councils/ii_vatican_council/documents/vat-ii_const_19641121_lumen-gentium_en.html, paragraph 16.

39. For an analysis of the history of the term, see Mark Silk, "Notes on the Judeo-Christian Tradition in America," *American Quarterly* 36.1 (1984): 65–85.

40. http://www.nccjctwma.org/whoweare/history.html.

41. Dwight D. Eisenhower, "Speech to the Freedoms Foundation in New York," quoted in Silk, "Notes on the Judeo-Christian Tradition in America," 65.

42. Ismail al-Faruqi, "Foreword," in *Trialogue of the Abrahamic Faiths: Papers Presented to the Islamic Studies Group of the American Academy of Religion*, 3rd ed., edited by Ismail Raji al-Faruqi (Alexandria, VA: Al Sadawi Publications, 1991), first page of unnumbered foreword.

43. Taha Jabir al-Alwani, "Introduction to the Third Edition," *Trialogue of the Abrahamic Faiths*.

44. Sergio Pignedoli, "The Catholic Church and the Jewish and Muslim Faiths: Trialogue of the Three Abrahamic Faiths," in *Trialogue of the Abrahamic Faiths*, 7.

45. Ibid. 5.

46. Ibid. 1.

47. Interestingly, al-Faruqi, the editor of the volume, provides an "editor's note" immediately following Cardinal Pignedoli's keynote correcting one of his subsequent claims as historically incorrect. "No Muslim thinker," al-Faruqi writes, "has claimed that any exegesis can or did 'abrogate' any verse of the Qur'ān. The cardinal must have therefore meant the supplanting of one exegesis with another in somebody's mind" (12).

    This "editor's note" is telling in that many who engage in the "Abrahamic religions" discourses—both in the past and especially in the present as the term has become increasingly trendy—tend to speak out of the one "Abrahamic religion" that they know best. This leads to all sorts of potential distortions as there is a tendency to think that one can find parallels or correspondences in other religions if one looks carefully enough.

48. I have already written extensively about this, especially in the academic study of Islam. See, for example, my *Theorizing Islam: Disciplinary Deconstruction and Reconstruction* (London: Equinox, 2012).

49. The one mention of it occurs in the essay by Muhammad Abd al-Rauf, "Judaism and Christianity in the Perspective of Islām," 23.

50. Richard W. Bulliet, *The Case for Islamo-Christian Civilization* (New York: Columbia University Press, 2004), 6.

51. Ibid. 6.

52. Feisal Abdul Rauf, *What's Right With Islam: A New Vision For Muslims and the West*, foreword by Karen Armstrong (San Francisco: HarperCollins, 2004), 105.

53. "Transcript: President Obama Addresses Muslim World in Cairo." Online at http://www.washingtonpost.com/wp-dyn/content/article/2009/06/04/AR2009060401117.html.

CHAPTER 4

1. H. Grattan Guinness, *The Divine Programme of the World's History* (London: Hodder and Stoughton, 1888), 158–159.

2. Ibid. 159.

3. Ibid. 160–161.

4. Ibid. 159.

5. See, for example, the important essay of Jonathan Z. Smith, "Religion, Religions, Religious," in his *Relating Religions: Essays in the Study of Religion* (Chicago: University of Chicago Press, 2004), 179–196. Recently, Guy G. Stroumsa has argued that this desire to taxonomize and create a study of religion dates much earlier than scholars have traditionally thought. In so doing, he dates it to the seventeenth century. See his *A New Science: The Discovery of Religion in the Age of Reason* (Cambridge, MA: Harvard University Press, 2010), 14–38.

6. This process is certainly connected to the aptly titled book of Tomoko Masuzawa, *The Invention of World Religions: Or, How European Universalism was Preserved in the Language of Pluralism* (Chicago: University of Chicago Press, 2005).

7. The classic example of this remains Mary Douglas, *Purity and Danger: An Analysis of the Concepts of Pollution and Taboo* (New York and London: Routledge, 2002 [1966]).

8. Leonard Swidler, *After the Absolute* (Minneapolis: Fortress Press, 1990), 123.

9. Smith, "Religion, Religions, Religious," 193–194.

10. Roland Werner, *Transcultural Healing: The Whole Human: Healing Systems Under the Influence of Abrahamic Religions, Eastern Religions and Beliefs, Paganism, New Religions, and Mixed Religious Forms* (Kuala Lumpur: University of Malaya Press, 1993).

11. Jürgen Moltmann, *God for a Secular Society: The Public Relevance of Theology*, translated by Margaret Kohl (Minneapolis: Fortress Press, 1999), 75. Lest one thinks that such generalizations are simply confined to theological agendas of the 1990s, consider a very recent example:

    The Abrahamic religions of Judaism, Christianity, and Islam tend toward absolutes. The first commandment, that you shall worship no other god, depicts a jealous and exclusive deity that would be unfamiliar to most Asian religions.... In the Abrahamic religions, heaven and hell are final judgments, eternal paradise or never-ending suffering. Paradise and damnation are both present in Chinese religions as well, but they are not final.

    See James Carter, *Heart of Buddha, Heart of China: The Life of Tanxu, a Twentieth-Century Monk* (New York: Oxford University Press, 2011), 75.

12. Ori Z. Soltes, *Mysticism in Judaism, Christianity and Islam: Searching for Oneness* (Lanham, MD: Rowman and Littlefield, 2009), 19.

13. J. Lorand Matory, "Is There Gender in Yorùbá Culture?" in *Òrìsà Devotion as World Religion: The Globalization of Yorùbá Religious Culture*, edited by Jacob K. Olupona and Terry Ray (Madison, WI: University of Wisconsin Press, 2008), 525.

14. Prasenjit Duara. "The Historical Roots and Character of Secularism in China," in *China and International Relations: The Chinese View and the View of Wang Gungwu*, edited by Zheng Yongnian (London: Taylor and Francis, 2010), 59.

15. Judy Carter and Gordon S. Smith, "Religious Peacebuilding: From Potential to Action," in *Religion and Peacebuilding*, edited by Harold G. Coward and Gordon S. Smith (Albany, NY: State University of New York Press, 2004), 279–301, at 286.

16. Brennan R. Hill, Paul Knitter, and William Madges, *Faith, Religion and Theology: A Contemporary Introduction*, revised and expanded (Mystic, CT: Twenty-Third Publications, 1997 [1990]), 238.

17. Swidler, *After the Absolute*, xv–xvi.

18. Ibid. 122.

19. Ibid. 130. The original passage comes from Hans Küng, *Christentum und Weltreligionen* (Munich: Piper 1984), 189–190 (italics in Swidler).

20. On the original Parliament, see Richard Hughes-Seager, *The Parliament of Religions: The East/West Encounter in Chicago, 1893* (Bloomington, IN: Indiana University Press, 1995).

21. The Parliaments continue, with the next one scheduled for Brussels in 2014. The official website of its sponsoring organization, the Council for a Parliament of the World's Religions, describes its mandate in the following terms:

    The Council for a Parliament of the World's Religions was created to cultivate harmony among the world's religious and spiritual communities and foster their engagement with the world and its guiding institutions in order to achieve a just, peaceful and sustainable world.

    http://www.parliamentofreligions.org/index.cfm?n=1&sn=1.

22. Karl-Josef Kuschel. German: *Streit um Abraham: Was Juden, Christen und Muslime trennt—und was sie eint* (Munich: Piper Verlag, 1994). English: *Abraham: Sign of Hope for Jews, Christians and Muslims*, translated by John Bowden (New York: Continuum, 1995). All quotations come from the English translation.

23. Kuschel, *Abraham*, xiv.

24. Ibid. xv.

25. Ibid. 252.

26. Swidler, for example, can write that "the Khomeini distortion of Islam is no more representative of Islam than the Rev. Ian Paisley of Northern Ireland is of Christianity or Richard Nixon was of the pacifist Quaker tradition" (*After the Absolute*, 125). He takes no interest in the political, ideological, or material conditions of such individuals. His only concern is how such interpretations square with what he considers to be "normative" interpretations of these religions.

27. Kuschel, *Abraham*, 253.

28. For example, a natural candidate to employ this subject heading is Francis Peters' two-volume *The Monotheists: Jews, Christians, and Muslims in Conflict and Cooperation*. Instead, however, his book has the following:

    1.Judaism—Relations—Christianity—History. 2. Christianity and other religions—Judaism—History. 3. Judaism—Relations—Islam—History. 4. Islam—Relations—Judaism—History. 5. Islam—Relations—Christianity—History. 6. Christianity and other religions—Islam—History.

29. It might be worth pointing out that, according to its website, the United States Institute of Peace

    is an independent, nonpartisan, national institution established and funded by Congress. Its goals are to help:
    • Prevent and resolve violent international conflicts
    • Promote post-conflict stability and development
    • Increase conflict management capacity, tools, and intellectual capital worldwide

    The Institute does this by empowering others with knowledge, skills, and resources, as well as by directly engaging in peacebuilding efforts around the globe.

    (http://www.usip.org/about-us).

30. Mohammed Abu-Nimer, Amal Khoury and Emily Welty, *Unity in Diversity: Interfaith Dialogue in the Middle East* (Washington, DC: United States Institute of Peace, 2007), 19.

31. Samuel P. Huntington, "The Clash of Civilizations?" *Foreign Affairs* 72.3 (1993): 22–49. Huntington's argument was expanded in his *The Clash of Civilizations and the Remaking of the World Order* (New York: Simon and Schuster, 1996).

32. Bradford E. Hinze and Irfan A. Omar, "Preface," *Heirs of Abraham: The Future of Muslim, Jewish, and Christian Relations*, edited by Bradford E. Hinze and Irfan A. Omar (Maryknoll, NY: Orbis Books, 2005), v.

33. Ibid. x.

34. Moshe Ma'oz, "Introduction," in *The Meeting of Civilizations: Muslim, Christian, and Jewish*, edited by Moshe Ma'oz (Eastbourne, UK: Sussex Academic Press, 2009), 11.

35. Nathan C. Funk and Meena Sharify Funk, "Peacemaking Among the Children of Abraham: Overcoming Obstacles to Co-existence," in *The Meeting of Civilizations: Muslim, Christian, and Jewish*, 204.

36. In their *The Tent of Abraham: Stories of Hope and Peace for Jews, Christians, and Muslims* (Boston: Beacon Press, 2006), Joan Chittister, Murshid Saadi Shakur Chisti, and Arthur Waskow take this metaphor to its most extreme:

    There is an Abrahamic family.

    Like all families, it shares a story. But part of what it shares is that different members of the family tell different versions of the story. They are like people who have lived in the same house, gone to the same schools, traveled the same neighborhood—yet when you ask each family member to tell the family story, you might swear they come from different universes. So it has been for the different religions that trace their genealogical or spiritual lineage to Abraham. (xiii)

37. For a sustained critique of the idea that religions are "irreducible," essentially spiritual, and timeless entities that do not undergo corruption on account of political or cultural reasons, see McCutcheon, *Manufacturing Religions*, 32–50.

38. Nathan C. Funk and Meena Sharify Funk, "Peacemaking Among the Children of Abraham," 214.

39. See, for example, Richard E. Rubenstein, *Aristotle's Children: How Christians, Muslims, and Jews Rediscovered Ancient Wisdom and Illuminated the Middle Ages* (New York: Harcourt, 2003.). Once again, looking at the date of publication, it is no surprise that a volume such as this emerges from the aftermath of 9/11.

40. Azyumardi Azra, "Trialogue of Abrahamic Faiths: Toward an Alliance of Civilizations," in *The Meeting of Civilizations: Muslim, Christian, and Jewish*, 220.

41. Ibid. 224.

42. Karen Armstrong, "Preface," in Chittister, Chisti, and Waskow, *The Tent of Abraham*, x.

43. James L. Heft, S.M., "Introduction," in *Beyond Violence: Religious Sources of Social Transformation in Judaism, Christianity, and Islam*, edited by James L. Heft, S.M., The Abrahamic Dialogue Series, no. 1 (New York: Fordham University Press, 2004), 3.

44. See Jonathan Z. Smith, "In Comparison a Magic Dwells," in his *Imagining Religion*, 19–35.

45. I leave aside all those completely non-academic usages. Just in the last year, for example, I have been invited in the greater Buffalo region alone to "Abrahamic dinners," "Abraham walks," and something called the "tents of Abraham."

46. Its website may be found at http://www.fraternite-dabraham.com/.

47. http://www.fraternite-dabraham.com/Default.asp?ID=110524&IDR=110529.

48. http://www.maimonides-foundation.org/about.html.

49. http://www.maimonides-foundation.org/moses-maimonides.html. Although for the historical problems of this generic narrative of Maimonides' life and times, see my comments in chapter 6 below.

50. For a brief history of the Workshop, see Eugene Fischer, "Kennedy Institute Jewish-Christian-Muslim Trialogue," *Journal of Ecumenical Studies* 19 (1982): 197–200.

51. Although their webpage describes them as the "International Scholars' Abrahamic Trialogue." See http://institute.jesdialogue.org/programs/trialogue/.

52. See Leonard Swidler, "International Scholars' Annual Trialogue," in *Theoria to Praxis: How Jews, Christians, and Muslims Can Move from Theory to Praxis* (Leuven: Peeters, 1998), 30–41.

53. http://institute.jesdialogue.org/programs/trialogue/.

54. According to their mission statement (http://www.abrahamsvision.org/about-us),

> Abraham's Vision is a conflict transformation organization that explores group and individual identities through experiential and political education. Examining social relations within and between the Jewish, Muslim, Israeli, and Palestinian communities, we empower participants to practice just alternatives to the status quo.

55. Their website (http://www.abrahamicalliance.org/about) describes their vision in the following terms:

> We envision a world where children of Abraham unite to save lives; where Jews, Christians and Muslims enjoy peaceful coexistence and mutual appreciation as our faith is deepened by meaningful encounters with each other; where understanding, humility and respect replace ignorance, arrogance, and contempt; where diverse yet faithful worshippers of the God of Abraham move beyond dialog to cooperative action, loving our neighbor together until the hungry are fed, the naked are clothed, the sick receive care, and

the orphan is raised with love, compassion and generosity. We envision a world where God's faithfulness to bless all nations through Abraham's seed is expressed in wonderfully new and creative ways through Jews, Christians and Muslims striving to obey all that the prophets have spoken.

56. http://www.ox.ac.uk/media/news_stories/2008/080708.html.

57. Ibid.

58. Perhaps the best document of this is the magisterial study of S. D. Goitein on the complex interactions between Jews and Muslims in the medieval Mediterranean world. See his *A Mediterranean Society: The Jewish Community of the Arab World as Portrayed in the Documents of the Cairo Geniza*, 5 vols. (Berkeley: University of California Press, 1967).

59. http://www.campaign.ox.ac.uk/news/abrahamic_religions.html.

60. http://warrior.merrimack.edu/academics/JCR/JewishChristianRelations/news_events/Pages/GoldziherPrize2012.aspx.

61. Bruce Lincoln, "Theses on Method," *Method and Theory in the Study of Religion* 8 (1996): 225–227 (thesis number 5).

62. The proceedings of the conference came out in the aforementioned *The Meeting of Civilizations: Muslim, Christian, Jewish*, edited by Moshe Ma'oz.

63. http://www.highbeam.com/doc/1G1-158527196.html. The proceedings from this conference appeared in the aforementioned *Heirs of Abraham*, edited by Bradford E. Hinze and Irfan A. Omar.

64. http://www.sacredheart.edu/pages/1812_2003_conference_pathways_to_peace_in_the_abrahamic_faiths.cfm.

65. Perhaps this difference is best explicated in Russell T. McCutcheon, *Critics Not Caretakers: Redescribing the Public Study of Religion* (Albany, NY: State University of New York Press, 2001).

66. E.g., Keith H. Essex, "The Abrahamic Covenant," *The Master's Seminary Journal* 10.2 (1999): 191–212.

67. These regularly appear on hostile websites such as Islam-watch.org. There we can read statements such as the following:

As such, it is an egregious error to label Islam as an Abrahamic religion as its material values are so far removed from, indeed hostile and diametrically opposed to, both Judaism and Christianity, to the extent that it is unfair and cruel to Jews and Christians to claim that the three religions "share the same values." Islam is simply too far removed from Judaism and Christianity in its perception of the nature of God to ultimately share any material values with the latter.

From "Islam: Abrahamic Religion or Muhammad's Alter-Ego" online at http://www.islam-watch.org/index.php?option=com_content&view=article&id=399:islam-abrahamic-religion-or-muhammads-alter-ego&catid=50:stunich&Itemid=58.

68. See, for example, my analysis of this in *Situating Islam*, 93–110.

69. See his website at http://michael-knowles.co.uk/.

70. Michael Knowles, "The Galatian Test: Is Islam an Abrahamic Religion?" *New Blackfriars* 92.3 (2011): 318.

71. Ibid. 320.

72. Ibid. 320–321.

73. Indeed his conclusion to the article would seem to come directly out of the literature surveyed in chapter 2:

> Like Paul, we must 'speak the truth in Christ' (Rom. 9:1). Ephesians 5:14 advises us how Christians should conduct dialogue and debate, namely: 'Speak the truth in love, so that we may grow unto Christ in all things'. Christ is the promise made to Abraham. Because that is the truth, it devalues no one and nothing. However, it gives us who believe no grounds for boasting, 'Boasting is excluded' (ibid. 3:27) because we have earned nothing. Jesus Christ is the pure gift of the Father. The Spirit has been poured out, not earned. (Knowles, "The Galatian Test," 321)

CHAPTER 5

1. See the discussion in Robert A. Orsi, *Between Heaven and Earth: The Religious Worlds People Make and the Scholars Who Study Them* (Princeton, NJ: Princeton University Press, 2005), 186–194.

2. See, for example, Timothy Fitzgerald, *Discourse on Civility and Barbarity: A Critical History of Religion and Related Categories* (New York: Oxford University Press, 2007), 43–70.

3. See the study of Tomoko Masuzawa, *The Invention of World Religions*, 1–33.

4. This now largely outdated theory of semiotics dates back to Ferdinand de Saussure, *Course in General Linguistics*, edited by Charles Bally and Albert Sechehaye; translated by Roy Harris (LaSalle, IL: Open Court, 1983).

5. E.g., Talal Asad, *Genealogies of Religion: Disciplines and Reasons of Power in Christianity and Islam* (Baltimore: Johns Hopkins University Press, 1993), 1–22; Richard King, *Orientalism and Religion: Post-Colonial Theory, India, and the "Mystic East"* (New York and London: Routledge, 1999), 1–25; Peter van der Veer, *Imperial Encounters: Religion and Modernity in India and Britain* (Princeton, NJ: Princeton University Press, 2001), 1–18. See also Jeremy Carrette, *Foucault and Religion: Spiritual Corporality and Political Spirituality* (London and New York: Routledge, 2000), 7–24.

6. I certainly do not mean to imply here that there exists a stable world apart from the words and names we use to describe it.

7. See Russell T. McCutcheon, *Religion and the Domestication of Dissent: Or, How to Live in a Less than Perfect Nation* (London: Equinox, 2005), 11–14.

8. Bruce Lincoln, *Theorizing Myth: Narrative, Ideology, and Scholarship* (Chicago: University of Chicago Press, 1999), 207–216.

9. Some excellent analyses that show the extent to which "extra-scholarly" baggage informs scholarship may be found in Jonathan Z. Smith, *Drudgery Divine: On*

the Comparison of Early Christianities and the Religions of Late Antiquity* (Chicago: University of Chicago Press, 1990); William Arnal, *The Symbolic Jesus: Historical Scholarship, Judaism, and the Construction of Contemporary Identity* (London: Equinox, 2005). See also my own analysis of this extra-scholarly baggage in Islamic Studies in my *Situating Islam: The Past and Future of an Academic Discipline* (London: Equinox, 2007), 72–92.

10. Jonathan Z. Smith, *Imagining Religion: From Babylon to Jonestown* (Chicago: University of Chicago Press, 1982), xi.

11. Ibid.

12. This is becoming especially true of those working in cognitive science and religion. See for example, Anne Taves, *Religious Experience Reconsidered: A Building-Block Approach to the Study of Religion and Other Special Things* (Princeton, NJ: Princeton University Press, 2009). Similarly, the overwhelming collection of essays in a recent volume devoted to contemporary theories of religion come out of this cognitivist camp. See the essays collected in *Contemporary Theories of Religion: A Critical Companion*, edited by Michael Stausberg (London and New York: Routledge, 2009). For my critique of this approach in general, see Aaron W. Hughes, "Science Envy in Theories of Religion," *Method and Theory in the Study of Religion* 22.2 (2010): 285–296.

13. See the comments in Russell T. McCutcheon, "Will Your Cognitive Anchor Hold in the Storm of Culture?" *Journal of the American Academy of Religion* 78.4 (2010), 1182–1193.

14. Augustine, *City of God*, translated by Marcus Dods (New York: Modern Library, 1950), Book 10, chapter 1 (p. 232).

15. McCutcheon, "Will Your Cognitive Anchor Hold in the Storm of Culture?" 1187.

16. Ludwig Wittgenstein, *Philosophical Investigations*, translated by G. E. M. Anscombe (Oxford: B. Blackwell, 1953), 190.

17. The classic account of the uses to which scholarship can be put in the service of empire-building and -maintenance remains Edward W. Said, *Orientalism* (New York: Vintage, 1978). See also in this regard, David Chidester, *Savage Systems: Colonialism and Comparative Religion in Southern Africa* (Charlottesville, VA: University of Virginia Press, 1996); Dubuisson, *The Western Construction of Religion: Myths, Knowledge, and Ideology*, translated by William Sayers (Baltimore: Johns Hopkins University Press, 2003).

18. Smith, *Imagining Religion*, xi.

19. Chidester, *Savage Systems*, xiii–xiv.

20. Dubuisson, *The Western Construction of Religion*, 42.

21. See, for example, the comments in McCutcheon, *Manufacturing Religion*, 51–73.

22. Dubuisson, *The Western Construction of Religion*, 17–22.

23. Smith, *Imagining Religion*, 1–5.

24. Ibid. 5.

25. John L. Esposito, *Islam: The Straight Path*, rev. 3rd ed. (New York: Oxford University Press, 2005 [1988]), 31.

26. Ibid. 66.

27. John L. Esposito, *The Future of Islam* (New York: Oxford University Press, 2010), 38.

28. I have examined this in significant detail in my *Situating Islam*, e.g., 73–92.

29. Esposito, *The Future of Islam*, 72–73.

30. John L. Esposito and Dalia Mogahed, *Who Speaks for Islam?: What a Billion Muslims Really Think* (New York: Gallup Press, 2007), 123.

31. Lest I am mistaken here, let me be crystal clear: I am certainly not trying to make the case that Islam is inherently more patriarchal than any other religion.

32. See especially my *Theorizing Islam: Disciplinary Decontruction and Reconstruction* (London: Equinox, 2012), 1–9.

33. David Gelernter, *Judaism: A Way of Being* (New Haven, CT: Yale University Press, 2009), 3.

34. Ibid. ix.

35. See the critical review of the book in Elliot R. Wolfson, "That Old-Time Religion," *Azure* 41 (2010): 97–108.

36. Ibid. xi.

37. This argument becomes even more uncomfortable when one reads the acknowledgments and sees Gelernter's relationship to conservative American philanthropist Roger Hertog.

38. Gelernter, *Judaism: A Way of Being*, 198.

39. For a longer discussion of this problem within Jewish Studies, of which Gelernter is but an example, see my forthcoming *The Study of Judaism: Identity, Authenticity, Scholarship*.

40. Jean-François Bayart, *The Illusion of Cultural Identity*, translated by Steven Rendall et al. (Chicago: University of Chicago Press, 2005), 20–25.

41. Plato, "The Seventh Letter," in *Plato: The Collected Dialogues*, edited by Edith Hamilton and Huntington Cairns (Princeton, NJ: Princeton University Press, 1989), 344c–345c.

42. Chidester, *Savage Systems*, 4.

43. Ibid. 22–23.

44. On these key aspects of "religion," see Bruce Lincoln, *Holy Terrors: Thinking about Religion after September 11* (Chicago: University of Chicago Press, 2003), 5–8.

45. See the excellent analysis of this patrolling and breaching of boundaries in the Late Antique period in Daniel Boyarin, *Border Lines: The Partition of Judaeo-Christianity* (Philadelphia: University of Pennsylvania Press, 2006), 1–35.

46. Tim Murphy, *Representing Religion: Essays in History, Theory and Crisis* (London: Equinox, 2007), 5.

47. Norman Solomon, Richard Harries, and Tim Winter, editors, *Abraham's Children: Jews, Christians, and Muslims in Conversation* (London: T & T Clark, 2005), 38.

48. See, for example, Camilla Adang, *Muslim Writers on Judaism and the Hebrew Bible: From Ibn Rabban to Ibn Hazm* (Leiden: Brill, 1996); Theodore Pulcini, *Exegesis As Polemical Discourse: Ibn Hazm on Jewish and Christian Scriptures* (Atlanta: Scholars Press, 1998).

49. Solomon, Harries, and Winter, *Abraham's Children*, 39.

50. John L. Esposito, *The Future of Islam* (New York: Oxford University Press, 2010), 198–199.

51. Benedict Anderson, *Imagined Communities: Reflections on the Origin and Spread of Nationalism*, rev. ed. (London: Verso, 2006), 1–7.

CHAPTER 6

1. Jonathan Z. Smith, "Fences and Neighbors: Some Contours of Early Judaism," in his *Imagining Religion: From Babylon to Jonestown* (Chicago: University of Chicago Press, 1982), 5.

2. One of the most famous examples of this model is that the Arabs and Muslims preserved the philosophical and scientific works of antiquity and subsequently transferred them, with the help of Jewish middlemen/commentators, to Christian Europe.

3. A good example of a work that tries to do this is Steven M. Wasserstrom, *Between Muslim and Jew: The Problem of Symbiosis Under Early Islam* (Princeton, NJ: Princeton University Press, 1995), e.g., 17–46. See also, in this regard, Boyarin, *Border Lines: The Partition of Judaeo-Christianity*.

4. A representative set of examples include Tor Andrae, *Muhammad: The Man and His Faith* (New York: Harper and Row, 1955 [1936]); W. Montgomery Watt, *Muhammad and Mecca* (Oxford: Clarendon Press, 1968); idem, *Muhammad at Medina* (Oxford: Clarendon Press, 1956); Gordon Darnell Newby, *A History of the Jews of Arabia: From Ancient Times to Their Eclipse under Islam* (Columbia, SC: University of South Carolina Press, 1988).

5. Notable exceptions include John Wansbrough, *The Sectarian Milieu: Content and Composition of Islamic Salvation History* (Oxford: Oxford University Press, 1978); Patricia Crone, *Meccan Trade and the Rise of Islam* (Princeton, NJ: Princeton University Press, 1987); Patricia Crone and Michael Cook, *Hagarism: The Making of the Islamic World* (Cambridge: Cambridge University Press, 1977); Thomas Sizgorich, "Narrative and Community in Islamic Late Antiquity," *Past and Present* 185 (2004): 9–42; David Powers, *Muhammad Is Not the Father of Any of Your Men*.

6. Even the term "golden age" of Muslim Spain is a modern invention that largely dates to the nineteenth century. See my "The 'Golden Age' of Muslim Spain: Religious Identity and the Invention of a Tradition in Modern Jewish Studies," in *Historicizing Tradition in the Study of Religion*, edited by Steven Engler and Gregory P. Grieve (Berlin: de Gruyter, 2005), 51–74. In this regard, see also Ivan

G. Marcus, "Beyond the Sephardic Mystique," *Orim: A Jewish Journal at Yale* 1 (1985): 35–53; Paul Mendes-Flohr, "Fin de Siècle Orientalism, the *Ostjuden*, and the Aesthetics of Jewish Self-Affirmation," in his *Divided Passions: Jewish Intellectuals and the Experience of Modernity* (Detroit: Wayne State University Press, 1991), 77–132.

7. For a critique of the introductory textbooks that we use to introduce Islam in university classrooms, see my *Situating Islam*, 81–92. I try to provide an alternative in my *Muslim Identities: An Introduction to Islam* (New York: Columbia University Press, 2013).

8. Standard takes on this narrative can be found in John L. Esposito, *Islam: The Straight Path*, rev. 3rd ed. (New York: Oxford University Press, 2005); Frederick Mathewson Denny, *An Introduction to Islam*, 4th ed. (New York: Macmillan, 2010).

9. On the trope of "world religions" and how Islam came to be designated as one, see Masuzawa, *The Invention of World Religions*, 179–206.

10. E.g., Fred Donner, *Muhammad and the Believers: At the Origins of Islam* (Cambridge, MA: Harvard University Press, 2010). Another example is Powers, *Muhammad Is Not the Father of Any of Your Men*. Although both Donner and Powers agree that the formation of Islam is complicated, it is worth noting that their basic premises are radically different.

11. In Islamic Studies circles, this is known as the "Authenticity Debate." There exist at least three different perspectives in this debate. The first contends that even though the earliest sources of Islam may come from a later period, they nonetheless represent reasonably reliable accounts concerning the matters upon which they comment or describe. Another perspective contends that the Muslim historical record of the first two centuries is historically problematic. The social and political upheavals associated with the rapid spread of Islam fatally compromise, according to such scholars, the earliest sources. These sources, according to this position, are written so much after the fact and with such distinct ideological or political agendas that they provide us with very little that is reliable and with which to recreate the period which they purport to describe. The third perspective acknowledges the problems involved with the early sources, but tries to solve them using form and source criticism, both of which seek to determine the original form and historical context of a particular text.A survey and analysis of these competing positions may be found in Herbert Berg, *The Development of Exegesis in Early Islam: The Authenticity of Muslim Literature from the Formative Period* (London: Curzon, 2000), 6–64.

12. The most forceful critique of this approach to defining "religion" may be found in McCutcheon, *Manufacturing Religion*. See also Fitzgerald, *The Ideology of Religious Studies*.

13. See, for example, Dubuisson, *The Western Construction of Religion*; Fitzgerald, *On Civility and Barbarity*. See also the collection of essays in *Religion and the*

Secular: Historical and Colonial Formations, edited by Timothy Fitzgerald (London: Equinox, 2007).

14. Despite the fact that Jonathan Z. Smith argues that the term "Abrahamic religions" is a term that has been adopted from "Muslim discourse," Muslims only used the term in the singular (religion of Abraham) and not to refer to a shared heritage with Jews and Christians. I can find no evidence to support Smith's claims here. See his "Religion, Religions, Religious," in *Relating Religions*, 187–188.

15. Recall the family feud trope used by the likes of Esposito in chapter 1.

16. The language of this sentence draws on Smith, "Fences and Neighbors: Some Contours of Early Judaism," in his *Imagining Religion*, 3–4.

17. See, e.g., Robert G. Hoyland, *Arabia and the Arabs: From the Bronze Age to the Coming of Islam* (London and New York: Routledge, 2001), 11.

18. Marshall G. S. Hodgson, *The Venture of Islam: Conscience and History in a World Civilization*, vol. 1: *The Classical Age of Islam* (Chicago: University of Chicago Press, 1974), 151.

19. Important scholarship on the existence and contours of religion in pre-Islamic Arabia that I have drawn on include the following: Gerald R. Hawting, *The Idea of Idolatry and the Rise of Islam: From Polemic to History* (Cambridge: Cambridge University Press, 1999), 20–44; Hoyland, *Arabia and the Arabs*, 139–166; Michael Lecker, *Muslims, Jews and Pagans: Studies on Early Islamic Medina* (Leiden: Brill, 1995); and Tilman Seidensticker, "Sources for the History of Pre-Islamic Religion," in *The Qur'ân in Context: Historical and Literary Investigations in the Qur'ânic Milieu*, edited by Angelika Neuwirth, Nicolai Sinai, and Michael Marx (Leiden: Brill, 2010), 293–322. It is also worth pointing out that these scholars are not in agreement when it comes to the "authenticity debate" mentioned in note 11 above.

20. Hoyland, *Arabia and the Arabs*, 139–140.

21. Hoyland, *Arabia and the Arabs*, 140.

22. Joseph Heninger, "Pre-Islamic Bedouin Religion," in *Studies on Islam*, edited by Merlin L. Swartz (New York: Oxford University Press, 1981), 3–22. This study, however, has been surpassed by Hoyland, *Arabia and the Arabs*.

23. See the comments in H. A. R. Gibb, "Pre-Islamic Monotheism in Arabia," and W. Montgomery Watt, "Belief in a 'High God' in Pre-Islamic Mecca," both of which may be found in *The Arabs and Arabia on the Eve of Islam*, edited by F. E. Peters (Aldershot, UK: Variorum, 1999), 295–306, 307–312.

24. See, for example, Nadia Abbot, *Studies in Arabic Literary Papyri*. (Chicago: University of Chicago Press, 1967).

25. See J. Spencer Trimingham, *Christianity among the Arabs in Pre-Islamic Times* (London: Longman, 1979).

26. Gerald R. Hawting, *The Idea of Idolatry and the Rise of Islam: From Polemic to History* (Cambridge: Cambridge University Press, 1999), 20–30.

27. This is nicely captured in the title of María Rosa Menocal, *The Ornament of the World: How Muslims, Jews, and Christians Created a Culture of Tolerance in Medieval Spain* (New York: Back Bay Books, 2002).

28. The transcript may be found online at http://millercenter.org/scripps/archive/speeches/detail/3925.

29. See, for example, *Convivencia: Jews, Muslims, and Christians in Medieval Spain*, edited by Vivian Mann, Thomas Click, and Jerrilynn Dodds (New York: George Braziller, 1992). The essays in this volume are based on an exhibit of the same name at the Jewish Museum in New York City.

30. Amir Hussain and Dorian Llywelyn SJ, "Foreword to Bellarmine Forum." Online at http://bellarmine.lmu.edu/thebellarmineforum/Past_Forums_Archive/2008archive/Foreward_to_2008_Bellarmine_Forum.htm.

31. http://www.cordobainitiative.org/about/.

32. Feisal Abdul Rauf, *What's Right With Islam: A New Vision for Muslims and the West* (San Francisco: HarperCollins, 2004), 2.

33. Recent biographies of Maimonides include Herbert Davidson, *Moses Maimonides: The Man and His Works* (New York: Oxford University Press, 2005), 3–74; Joel L. Kraemer, *Maimonides: The Life and World of One of Civilization's Greatest Minds* (New York, Doubleday, 2008), 83–98.

34. This, for example, is the opinion of Menocal, *The Ornament of the World*, 195–198.

35. http://outofcordoba.com/synopsis-2/.

36. See, for example, Majid Fakhry, *Averroes: His Life, Work, and Influence* (Oxford: Oneworld, 2001), 1–5; Roger Arnaldez, *Averroes: A Rationalist in Islam*, translated by David Streight (Notre Dame, IN: University of Notre Dame Press, 2000), 10–22.

37. Chris Lowney, *A Vanished World: Muslims, Christians, and Jews in Medieval Spain* (Oxford: Oxford University Press, 2005), 3.

38. http://outofcordoba.com/advisory-board/.

39. Menocal, *The Ornament of the World*, 11.

40. See the important study by David Wasserstein, *The Rise and Fall of the Party-Kings: Politics and Society in Islamic Spain 1002–1086* (Princeton, NJ: Princeton University Press, 1985), 1–25.

41. All quotes from Menocal, *Ornament of the World*, 20–21. A richer, more historically accurate portrait of the period in question may be found in Chase Robinson, *Abd al-Malik* (Oxford: Oneworld, 2005).

42. Menocal, *Ornament of the World*, 5.

43. Ibid. 6.

44. Ibid. 8.

45. Ibid. 19.

46. Ibid. 24.

47. Ibid. 31.

48. One could certainly claim that "Golden Age" is such a well-worn trope that it really ceases to have any meaning whatsoever. Every age, to someone or some group, represents a so-called "Golden Age."

49. See, for example, Dimitri Gutas, *Greek Thought, Arabic Culture: The Graeco-Arabic Translation Movement in Baghdad and Early 'Abbāsid Society (2nd–4th/8th–10th Centuries)* (New York and London: Routledge, 1998).

50. Menocal, *Ornament of the World,* 9.

51. Menocal makes no mention, for example, of W. Montgomery Watt, *A History of Islamic Spain* (Edinburgh: Edinburgh University Press, 1977 [1965]); Wasserstein, *The Rise and Fall of the Party Kings; idem, The Caliphate in the West: An Islamic Political Institution in the Iberian Peninsula* (Oxford: Oxford University Press, 1993); Eliyahu Ashtor, *The Jews of Moslem Spain,* 3 vols., translated by Aaron Klein and Jenny Machlowitz Klein (Philadelphia: Jewish Publication Society of America, 1984); Yitzhak Baer, *A History of the Jews of Christian Spain,* 2 vols. (Philadelphia: Jewish Publication Society of America, 1993); L. P. Harvey, *Islamic Spain, 1250–1500* (Chicago: University of Chicago Press, 1992); Mark R. Cohen, *Under Crescent and Cross: The Jews in the Middle Ages* (Princeton, NJ: Princeton University Press, 1994). Hugh Kennedy, *Muslim Spain and Portugal: A Political History of al-Andalus* (London: Longman, 1997).

52. Harold Bloom, "Foreword," *The Ornament of the World,* xiii.

53. See, e.g., Camilla Adang, *Muslim Writers on Judaism and the Hebrew Bible: From Ibn Rabban to Ibn Hazm* (Leiden: E. J. Brill, 1996); Theodore Pulcini, *Exegesis as Polemical Discourse: Ibn Hazm on Jewish and Christian Scriptures* (Atlanta, GA: Scholars Press, 1998).

54. Menocal, *Ornament of the World,* 45.

55. Ibid. 267, 293.

56. Lowney, *A Vanished World,* 225.

57. See the comments in Mark R. Cohen, "The 'Convivencia' of Jews and Muslims in the High Middle Ages," in *The Meeting of Civilizations: Muslim, Christian, and Jewish,* edited by Moshe Ma'oz, 54–65, at 55. See Cohen's larger treatment in *idem, Under Crescent and Cross.*

58. This is a term that has also received a great deal of attention—much of it saturated in contemporary political overtones—in recent years. Menocal, for instance, argues that it was *dhimmi* status that was responsible for "memorable and distinctive interfaith relations" (*Ornament of the World,* 30). Others argue that *dhimmi* status contributed to institutional inferiority for religious minorities and was responsible for their persecution. See, for example, Bat Ye'or, *The Dhimmi: Jews and Christians under Islam,* translated by David Maisel (Rutherford, NJ: Fairleigh Dickinson University Press, 1985). Perhaps not surprisingly this latter position has been picked up by many conservative critics of Islam to argue for, among other things, its anti-Semitism. See, for example, Robert Spenser's website dhimmiwatch.org, subsequently renamed jihadwatch.org.

59. Cohen, "The 'Convivencia' of Jews and Muslim in the High Middle Ages," 57.

60. David Nirenberg, *Communities of Violence: Persecution of Minorities in the Middle Ages* (Princeton, NJ: Princeton University Press, 1996), 9.

61. See my *The Invention of Jewish Identity: Bible, Philosophy, and the Art of Translation* (Bloomington, IN: Indiana University Press, 2010), 84–92.

62. Perhaps one of the most famous examples of this is the so-called "Jewish-Sufi" movement associated with the son of the great Moses Maimonides: Abraham Maimonides (1182–1237). For relevant context, see Paul B. Fenton, "Judaeo-Arabic Mystical Writings of the XIIIth–XIVth Centuries," in *Judaeo-Arabic Studies: Proceedings of the Founding Conference of the Society for Judaeo-Arabic Studies*, edited by Norman Golb (Australia: Harwood Academic Publishers, 1997), 87–102.

63. An elegant account of this may be found in Jonathan Boyarin, "Responsive Thinking: Cultural Studies and Jewish Historiography," in *Jewishness and the Human Dimension* (New York: Fordham University Press, 2008), 25–44.

Bibliography

Abbot, Nadia. *Studies in Arabic Literary Papyri*. Chicago: University of Chicago Press, 1967.

Abu-Nimer, Mohammed, Amal Khoury and Emily Welty. *Unity in Diversity: Interfaith Dialogue in the Middle East*. Washington, DC: United States Institute of Peace, 2007.

Accad, Martin. "The Gospels in the Muslim Discourse of the Ninth to the Fourteenth Centuries: An Exegetical Inventorial Table." *Islam and Christian-Muslim Relations* 14.1 (2003): 67–91; 14.2 (2003): 205–220; 14.3 (2003): 337–352; 14.4 (2003): 459–479.

Adang, Camilla. *Muslim Writers on Judaism and the Hebrew Bible: From Ibn Rabban to Ibn Hazm*. Leiden: Brill, 1996.

Anderson, Benedict. *Imagined Communities: Reflections on the Origin and Spread of Nationalism*. Rev. ed. London: Verso, 2006.

Andrae, Tor. *Muhammad: The Man and His Faith*. New York: Harper and Row, 1955 [1936].

Anonymous. "Review of the Covenant of Grace, and Baptism the Token of it, explained upon Scripture principles, by John Taylor, D.D. of Norwich." *The Monthly Review, Or, Literary Journal. By Several Hands* vol. 17 (1757): 346.

———. "The Covenant of Scripture." *The Danville Quarterly Review*, vol. 2 (1862): 35–57.

Arnal, William E. *The Symbolic Jesus: Historical Scholarship, Judaism, and the Construction of Contemporary Identity*. London: Equinox, 2005.

Arnaldez, Roger. *Averroes: A Rationalist in Islam*. Trans. David Streight. Notre Dame, IN: University of Notre Dame Press, 2000.

Asad, Talal. *Genealogies of Religion: Discipline and Reasons of Power in Christianity and Islam*. Baltimore: Johns Hopkins University Press, 1993.

Ashtor, Eliyahu. *The Jews of Moslem Spain*. 3 vols. Trans. Aaron Klein and Jenny Machlowitz Klein. Philadelphia: Jewish Publication Society of America, 1984.

Auerbach, Erich. *Mimesis: The Representation of Reality in Western Literature*. Trans. Willard R. Trask. Princeton, NJ: Princeton University Press, 1953.

Augustine. *City of God*. Trans. Marcus Dods. New York: Modern Library, 1950.

Azra, Azyumardi. "Trialogue of Abrahamic Faiths: Toward an Alliance of Civilizations." In *The Meeting of Civilizations: Muslim, Christian, and Jewish*, 220–229. Ed. Moshe Ma'oz. Eastbourne, UK: Sussex Academic Press, 2009.

Baer, Yitzhak. *A History of the Jews of Christian Spain*. 2 vols. Philadelphia: Jewish Publication Society of America, 1993.

Bayart, Jean-François. *The Illusion of Cultural Identity*. Trans. Steven Rendall et al. Chicago: University of Chicago Press, 2005.

Berg, Herbert. *The Development of Exegesis in Early Islam: The Authenticity of Muslim Literature from the Formative Period*. London: Curzon, 2000.

Boyarin, Daniel. *Border Lines: The Partition of Judaeo-Christianity*. Philadelphia: University of Pennsylvania Press, 2006.

Boyarin, Jonathan. "Responsive Thinking: Cultural Studies and Jewish Historiography." In his *Jewishness and the Human Dimension*, 25–44. New York: Fordham University Press, 2008.

Bulliet, Richard W. *The Case for Islamo-Christian Civilization*. New York: Columbia University Press, 2004.

Bulman, Raymond F. "The Historical Context." In *From Trent to Vatican II: Historical and Theological Investigations*, 3–18. Ed. Raymond F. Bulman and Frederick J. Parrella. New York: Oxford University Press, 2006.

Campbell, Rev. A., and Rev. N. L. Rice. *A Debate Between Rev. A. Campbell and Rev. N. L. Rice on the Action, Subject, Design and Administrator of Christian Baptism; Also, on the Character of Spiritual Influence in Conversion and Sanctification, and on the Expediency and Tendency of Ecclesiastic Creeds, as Terms of Union and Communion: Held in Lexington, KY., From the Fifteenth of November to the Second of December, 1843, a Period of Eighteen Days*. Reported by Marcus T. C. Gould, Stenographer, assisted by A. Euclid Drapier, Stenographer and Amanuensis. Lexington, KY: A. T. Skillman and Son, 1844.

Carrette, Jeremy. *Foucault and Religion: Spiritual Corporality and Political Spirituality*. London and New York: Routledge, 2000.

Carter, James. *Heart of Buddha, Heart of China: The Life of Tanxu, a Twentieth-Century Monk*. New York: Oxford University Press, 2011.

Carter, Judy, and Gordon S. Smith. "Religious Peacebuilding: From Potential to Action." In *Religion and Peacebuilding*, 279–301. Ed. Harold G. Coward and Gordon S. Smith. Albany, NY: State University of New York Press, 2004.

Charlesworth, James H. (ed. and trans.). *Old Testament Pseudepigrapha*. Garden City, NY: Doubleday, 1983.

Chidester, David. *Savage Systems: Colonialism and Comparative Religion in Southern Africa*. Charlottesville, VA: University of Virginia Press, 1996.

Chittester OSB, Joan, Murshod Saadi Shakur Chisti, and Rabbi Arthur Waskow. *The Tent of Abraham: Stories of Hope and Peace for Jews, Christians, and Muslims*. Foreword by Karen Armstrong. Boston: Beacon Press, 2006.

Cohen, Arthur A. *The Myth of the Judeo-Christian Tradition.* New York: Harper and Row, 1970.

Cohen, Mark R. "The 'Convivencia' of Jews and Muslim in the High Middle Ages." In *The Meeting of Civilizations: Muslim, Christian, and Jewish,* 54–65. Ed. Moshe Ma'oz. Eastbourne, UK: Sussex Academic Press, 2009.

———. *Under Crescent and Cross: The Jews in the Middle Ages.* Princeton, NJ: Princeton University Press, 1994.

Crone, Patricia. *Meccan Trade and the Rise of Islam.* Princeton, NJ: Princeton University Press, 1987.

———, and Michael Cook. *Hagarism: The Making of the Islamic World.* Cambridge: Cambridge University Press, 1977.

Daniel, Norman. *Islam and the West: The Making of an Image.* Edinburgh: Edinburgh University Press, 1960.

Davidson, Herbert. *Moses Maimonides: The Man and His Works.* New York and Oxford: Oxford University Press, 2005.

Denny, Frederick Mathewson. *An Introduction to Islam.* 4th ed. New York: Macmillan, 2010.

Donner, Fred M. *Muhammad and the Believers: At the Origins of Islam.* Cambridge, MA: Harvard University Press, 2010.

Douglas, Mary. *Purity and Danger: An Analysis of the Concepts of Pollution and Taboo.* New York and London: Routledge, 2002 [1966].

Dow, Daniel. *A Dissertation on the Sinaitic and Abrahamic Covenants: Shewing the Former to be Only Temporary, the Latter Everlasting.* Hartford, CT: Peter B. Gleason and Co, 1811.

Duara, Prasenjit. "The Historical Roots and Character of Secularism in China." In *China and International Relations: The Chinese View and the View of Wang Gungwu,* 58–71. Ed. Zheng Yongnian. London: Taylor and Francis, 2010.

Dubuisson, Daniel. *The Western Construction of Religion: Myths, Knowledge, and Ideology.* Trans. William Sayers. Baltimore: Johns Hopkins University Press, 2003.

Eliade, Mircea. *Patterns in Comparative Religion.* Trans. Rosemary Sheed. New York: Sheed and Ward, 1958.

Esposito, John L. *Islam: The Straight Path.* 3rd rev. ed. New York and Oxford: Oxford University Press, 2005 [1988].

———. *The Future of Islam.* New York and Oxford: Oxford University Press, 2010.

——— and Dalia Mogahed. *Who Speaks for Islam?: What a Billion Muslims Really Think.* New York: Gallup Press, 2007.

Essex, Keith H. "The Abrahamic Covenant." *The Master's Seminary Journal* 10.2 (1999): 191–212

Fakhry, Majid. *Averroes: His Life, Work, and Influence.* Oxford: Oneworld, 2001.

al-Faruqi, Ismail Raji (ed.). *Trialogue of the Abrahamic Faiths: Papers Presented to the Islamic Studies Group of the American Academy of Religion.* 3rd ed. Alexandria, VA: Al Sadawi Publications, 1991.

Feiler, Bruce. *Abraham: A Journey to the Heart of Three Faiths.* New York: HarperCollins, 2002.

Fenton, Paul B. "Judaeo-Arabic Mystical Writings of the XIIIth-XIVth Centuries." In *Judaeo-Arabic Studies: Proceedings of the Founding Conference of the Society for Judaeo-Arabic Studies,* 87–102. Ed. Norman Golb. Australia: Harwood Academic Publishers, 1997.

Firestone, Reuven. *Journeys in Holy Lands: The Evolution of the Abraham-Ishmael Legends in Islamic Exegesis.* Albany: State University of New York Press, 1990.

———. *Children of Abraham: An Introduction to Judaism for Muslims.* New York: Ktav, 2001.

Fischer, Eugene. "Kennedy Institute Jewish-Christian-Muslim Trialogue." *Journal of Ecumenical Studies* 19 (1982): 197–200.

Fitzgerald, Timothy. "Religion, Philosophy and Family Resemblances." *Religion* 26.3 (1996): 215–236.

———. *The Ideology of Religious Studies.* New York: Oxford University Press, 2000.

———. *Discourse on Civility and Barbarity: A Critical History of Religion and Related Categories.* New York: Oxford University Press, 2007.

——— (ed.). *Religion and the Secular: Historical and Colonial Formations.* London: Equinox, 2007.

Friedmann, Yohanan. *Prophecy Continuous: Aspects of Ahmadi Religious Thought and Its Medieval Background.* Berkeley: University of California Press, 1989.

Funk, Nathan C., and Meena Sharify Funk. "Peacemaking Among the Children of Abraham." In *The Meeting of Civilizations: Muslim, Christian, and Jewish,* 203–219. Ed. Moshe Ma'oz. Eastbourne, UK: Sussex Academic Press, 2009.

Geertz, Clifford. *The Interpretation of Cultures: Selected Essays.* New York: Basic Books, 1973.

Geiger, Abraham. *Was hat Mohammad aus dem Judenthume aufgenommen.* Bonn: F. Baaden, 1835. Translated into English as: *Judaism and Islam.* Trans. F. M. Young. Madras: MDCSPK Press, 1835; repr. New York: Ktav, 1970.

Gelernter, David. *Judaism: A Way of Being.* New Haven, CT: Yale University Press, 2009.

Gibb, H. A. R. "Pre-Islamic Monotheism in Arabia." In *The Arabs and Arabia on the Eve of Islam,* 295–306. Ed. F. E. Peters. Aldershot, UK: Variorum, 1999.

Goitein, Shlomo Dov. *A Mediterranean Society: The Jewish Community of the Arab World as Portrayed in the Documents of the Cairo Geniza.* 5 vols. Berkeley, CA: University of California Press, 1967.

Goldziher, Ignaz. "Über muhammedanische Polemik gegen ahl al-kitāb." *Zeitschrift der Deutschen Morgenländischen Gesellschaft* 32 (1878): 341–387.

Goodman, Martin, George H. van Kooten, and Jacques T. A. G. M. van Ruiten (eds.). *Abraham, the Nations, and the Hagarites: Jewish, Christian, and Islamic Perspectives on Kinship with Abraham.* Leiden: Brill, 2010.

Gude, Mary Louise. *Louis Massignon: The Crucible of Compassion.* Notre Dame, IN: University of Notre Dame Press, 1996.

Guinness, H. Grattan. *The Divine Programme of the World's History.* London: Hodder and Stoughton, 1888.

Gutas, Dimitri. *Greek Thought, Arabic Culture: The Graeco-Arabic Translation Movement in Baghdad and Early 'Abbāsid Society (2nd–4th/8th–10th Centuries).* New York and London: Routledge, 1998.

Harpigny, Guy. *Islam et Christianisme selon Louis Massignon.* Louvain-la-Neuve: Centre d'histoire des religions de l'Université Catholique de Louvain-la-Neuve, 1981.

Harrison, Peter. *"Religion" and the Religions of the English Enlightenment.* Cambridge: Cambridge University Press, 1990.

Hartzel, Elder Jonas. *A Dissertation on the First and Third Abrahamic Covenants, The Covenant at Horeb, and the New Covenant. Their Differential Peculiarities.* New York: T. Holman, 1865.

Harvey, L. P. *Islamic Spain, 1250–1500.* Chicago: University of Chicago Press, 1992.

Hawting, Gerald R. *The Idea of Idolatry and the Rise of Islam: From Polemic to History.* Cambridge: Cambridge University Press, 1999.

Heft, James L. (ed.). *Beyond Violence: Religious Sources of Social Transformation in Judaism, Christianity, and Islam.* New York: Fordham University Press, 2004.

Heninger, Joseph. "Pre-Islamic Bedouin Religion." In *Studies on Islam,* 3–22. Ed. Merlin L. Swartz. New York and Oxford: Oxford University Press, 1981.

Hentsch, Thierry. *Imagining the Middle East.* Trans. Fred A. Reed. Montreal: Black Rose Books, 1992.

Hibbard, Rev. F. G. *Christian Baptism: In Two Parts. Part First: Infant Baptism.* New York: Carleton and Phillips, 1856.

Hill, Brennan R., Paul Knitter and William Madges. *Faith, Religion and Theology: A Contemporary Introduction.* Revised and expanded. Mystic, CT: Twenty-Third Publications, 1997 [1990].

Hinze, Bradford E., and Irfan A. Omer (eds.). *Heirs of Abraham: The Future of Muslim, Jewish, and Christian Relations.* Maryknoll, NY: Orbis Books, 2005.

Hodgson, Marshall G. S. *The Venture of Islam: Conscience and History in a World Civilization.* Vol. 1: *The Classical Age of Islam.* Chicago: University of Chicago Press, 1974.

Horowitz, Elliot. *Reckless Rites: Purim and the Legacy of Jewish Violence.* Princeton, NJ: Princeton University Press, 2006.

Hoyland, Robert G. *Arabia and the Arabs: From the Bronze Age to the Coming of Islam.* London and New York: Routledge, 2001.

Hughes, Aaron W. "The 'Golden Age' of Muslim Spain: Religious Identity and the Invention of a Tradition in Modern Jewish Studies." In *Historicizing Tradition in the Study of Religion,* 51–74. Ed. Steven Engler and Gregory P. Grieve. Berlin: de Gruyter, 2005.

———. *Situating Islam: The Past and Future of an Academic Discipline.* London: Equinox, 2007.

———. *The Invention of Jewish Identity: Bible, Philosophy, and the Art of Translation.* Bloomington, IN: Indiana University Press, 2010.

———. "Science Envy in Theories of Religion." *Method and Theory in the Study of Religion* 22.2 (2010): 285–296.

———. *Theorizing Islam: Disciplinary Deconstruction and Reconstruction.* London: Equinox, 2012.

———. *Muslim Identities: An Introduction to Islam.* New York: Columbia University Press, 2013.

———. *The Study of Judaism: Identity, Authenticity, Scholarship.* Albany: State University of New York Press, forthcoming.

Hughes-Seager, Richard. *The Parliament of Religions: The East/West Encounter in Chicago, 1893.* Bloomington, IN: Indiana University Press, 1995.

Huntington, Samuel P. "The Clash of Civilizations?" *Foreign Affairs* 72.3 (1993): 22–49.

———. *The Clash of Civilizations and the Remaking of the World Order.* New York: Simon and Schuster, 1996.

Hurgronje, Christiaan Snouck. "La Légende Qoranique d'Abraham et la Politique Religieuse du Prophète Mohammed." Trans. G. H. Bousquet. *Revue africaine de Théologie* 95 (1950): 273–288.

Iggers, Georg. *Historiography in the Twentieth Century: From Scientific Objectivity to the Postmodern Challenge,* with a new epilogue by the author. Middleton, CT: Wesleyan University Press, 2005.

Janeway, Jacob Jones. *Letters Explaining the Abrahamic Covenant: With a View to Establish, on the Broad and Ancient Basis, the Divine Right of Infant Baptism and the Question Relative to the Mode of Administering this Christian Ordinance: Addressed to the Members of the Second Presbyterian Church, in Philadelphia.* Philadelphia: J. Maxwell, 1812.

Johnson, Nathaniel E. *Household Consecration.* New York: Ezra Collier, 1836.

Jukko, Risto. *Trinity in Unity in Christian-Muslim Relations: The Work of the Pontifical Council for Interreligious Dialogue.* Leiden: Brill, 2007.

Kennedy, Hugh. *Muslim Spain and Portugal: A Political History of al-Andalus.* London: Longman, 1997.

Khoury, Adel-Théodore. *Les Théologiens byzantins et l'Islam: Textes et auteurs. VIIe-XIIIe s.* Louvain: Nauwelaerts, 1969.

King, Richard. *Orientalism and Religion: Post-Colonial Theory, India, and the "Mystic East."* New York and London: Routledge, 1999.

Knowles, Michael. "The Galatian Test: Is Islam an Abrahamic Religion?" *New Blackfriars* 92.3 (2011): 318–321.

Kraemer, Joel L. *Maimonides: The Life and World of One of Civilization's Greatest Minds.* New York, Doubleday, 2008.

Kritzeck, James. *Sons of Abraham: Jews, Christians, and Moslems.* Baltimore: Helicon, 1965.

Kuschel, Karl-Josef. *Streit um Abraham. Was Juden, Christen und Muslime trennt—und was sie eint.* Munich: Piper Verlag, 1994. Translated into English as: *Abraham: Sign of Hope for Jews, Christians, and Muslims.* Trans. John Bowden. New York: Continuum, 1995.

Lamoreaux, John C. "Early Eastern Christian Responses to Islam." In *Medieval Christian Perceptions of Islam: A Book of Essays*, 3–31. Ed. John Victor Tolan. New York: Garland Press, 1996.

Lawrie, Swinton. *An Inquiry, Proving Infant-Baptism to be Untenable, As Well From the Abrahamic Covenant, As From the Scriptures At Large. Containing Also an Investigation of the Principles Which Bind Christians to Unite and Forbear with One Another.* Edinburgh: J. Ritchie, 1810.

Lecker, Michael. *Muslims, Jews, and Pagans: Studies on Early Islamic Medina.* Leiden: Brill, 1995.

van der Leeuw, Gerardus. *Religion in Essence and Manifestation.* 2 vols. Trans. J. E. Turner. New York: Harper and Row, 1963.

Levenson, Jon D. *The Death and Resurrection of the Beloved Son: The Transformation of Child Sacrifice in Judaism and Christianity.* New Haven, CT: Yale University Press, 1993.

———. "The Conversion of Abraham to Judaism, Christianity, and Islam." In *The Idea of Biblical Interpretation: Essays in Honor of James L. Kugel*, 3–40. Ed. Hindy Najman and Judith H. Newman. Leiden: Brill 2004.

Lewis, Bernard "The Roots of Muslim Rage." *The Atlantic Monthly.* September (1990): 47–60.

Lincoln, Bruce. "Theses on Method." *Method and Theory in the Study of Religion* 8 (1996): 225–227.

———. *Theorizing Myth: Narrative, Ideology, and Scholarship.* Chicago: University of Chicago Press, 1999.

———. *Holy Terrors: Thinking About Religion After September 11.* Chicago: University of Chicago Press, 2003.

Lopez, Donald S., Jr. *Prisoners of Shangri-La: Tibetan Buddhism and the West.* Chicago: University of Chicago Press, 1998.

Lowney, Chris. *A Vanished World: Muslims, Christians, and Jews in Medieval Spain.* New York and Oxford: Oxford University Press, 2005.

Mann, Vivian, Thomas Click, and Jerrilynn Dodds (eds.). *Convivencia: Jews, Muslims, and Christians in Medieval Spain.* New York: George Braziller, 1992.

Ma'oz. Moshe. *The Meeting of Civilizations: Muslim, Christian, and Jewish.* Eastbourne, UK: Sussex Academic Press, 2009.

Marcus, Ivan G. "Beyond the Sephardic Mystique." *Orim: A Jewish Journal at Yale* 1 (1985): 35–53.

Mason, Herbert. *Memoir of a Friend: Louis Massignon.* Notre Dame, IN: University of Notre Dame Press, 1988.

Massignon, Louis. *La passion de Husayn Ibn Mansūr al-Hallāj martyr mystique de l'Islam, exécuté à Bagdad le 26 mars 922, etude d'histoire religieuse.* 2nd ed. 4 vols.

(Paris: Gallimard, 1975). Translated into English as *The Passion of al-Hallāj: Mystic and Martyr of Islam*. Trans. with a biographical foreword by Herbert Mason. Princeton, NJ: Princeton University Press, 1982.

———. "Les trois prières d'Abraham, père di tous les croyants." *Dieu Vivant*, 13 (1949): 20–23. Republished in Louis Massignon, *Parole donèe*. 2nd ed., 257–272. Paris: Seuil, 1983. Translated in English as "The Three Prayers of Abraham." In *Testimonies and Reflections: Essays of Louis Massignon*, 3–20. Selected and introduced by Herbert Mason. Notre Dame, IN: University of Notre Dame Press, 1989.

Masuzawa, Tomoko. *The Invention of World Religions: Or, How European Universalism Was Preserved in the Language of Pluralism*. Chicago: University of Chicago Press, 2005.

Matory, J. Lorand. "Is There Gender in Yorùbá Culture?" In *Òrìsà Devotion as World Religion: The Globalization of Yorùbá Religious Culture*, 513–558. Ed. Jacob K. Olupona and Terry Ray. Madison, WI: University of Wisconsin Press, 2008.

McCalla, Arthur. "When Is History Not History?" *Historical Reflections* 20.3 (1994): 435–452

McMullin, Neil. "The Encyclopedia of Religion: A Critique from the Perspective of the History of Japanese Religions." *Method and Theory in the Study of Religion* 1.1 (1989): 80–96.

McCutcheon, Russell T. *Manufacturing Religion: The Discourse on Sui Generis Religion and the Politics of Nostalgia*. New York and Oxford: Oxford University Press, 1997.

———. *Critics Not Caretakers: Redescribing the Public Study of Religion*. Albany, NY: State University of New York Press, 2001.

———. *The Discipline of Religion: Structure, Meaning, Rhetoric*. London: Routledge, 2003.

———. *Religion and the Domestication of Dissent: Or, How to Live in a Less than Perfect Nation*. London: Equinox, 2005.

———. "Will Your Cognitive Anchor Hold in the Storm of Culture?" *Journal of the American Academy of Religion* 78.4 (2010): 1182–1193.

Mendes-Flohr, Paul. "Fin de Siècle Orientalism, the *Ostjuden*, and the Aesthetics of Jewish Self-Affirmation." In his *Divided Passions: Jewish Intellectuals and the Experience of Modernity*, 77–132. Detroit: Wayne State University Press, 1991.

Menocal, María Rosa. *The Ornament of the World: How Muslims, Jews, and Christians Created a Culture of Tolerance in Muslim Spain*. Foreword by Howard Bloom. New York: Back Bay Books, 2002.

Moltmann, Jürgen. *God for a Secular Society: The Public Relevance of Theology*. Trans. Margaret Kohl. Minneapolis: Fortress Press, 1999.

Muir, William. *The Life of Mohammad: From Original Sources*. Rev. by T. H. Weir. Edinburgh: John Grant, 1923.

Murphy, Tim. *Representing Religion: Essays in History, Theory and Crisis*. London: Equinox, 2007.

Newby, Gordon Darnell. *A History of the Jews of Arabia: From Ancient Times to Their Eclipse under Islam.* Columbia, SC: University of South Carolina Press, 1988.

Nirenberg, David. *Communities of Violence: Persecution of Minorities in the Middle Ages.* Princeton, NJ: Princeton University Press, 1996.

———. "Mass Conversion and Genealogical Mentalities: Jews and Christians in Fifteenth-Century Spain." *Past and Present* 174 (February 2002): 3–41.

Ochs, Peter and William Stacy Johnson (eds.). *Crisis, Call, and Leadership in the Abrahamic Traditions.* New York: Palgrave Macmillan, 2009.

Orsi, Robert A. *Between Heaven and Earth: The Religious Worlds People Make and the Scholars Who Study Them.* Princeton, NJ: Princeton University Press, 2005.

Peters, Francis E. *The Monotheists: Jews, Christians, and Muslims in Conflict and Competition.* 2 vols. Princeton, NJ: Princeton University Press, 2003.

———. *The Children of Abraham: Judaism, Christianity, Islam.* A New Edition with a Foreword by John L. Esposito. Princeton, NJ: Princeton University Press, 2006.

Plato. "The Seventh Letter." In *Plato: The Collected Dialogues.* Edited by Edith Hamilton and Huntington Cairns. Princeton, NJ: Princeton University Press, 1989.

Powers, David S. *Muhammad Is Not the Father of Any of Your Men: The Making of the Last Prophet.* Philadelphia: University of Pennsylvania Press, 2009.

Preus, J. Samuel. *Explaining Religion: Criticism and Theory from Bodin to Freud.* New Haven, CT: Yale University Press, 1987.

Pulcini, Theodore. *Exegesis as Polemical Discourse: Ibn Hazm on Jewish and Christian Scriptures.* Atlanta: Scholars Press, 1998.

Rauf, Feisal Abdul. *What's Right with Islam: A New Vision for Muslims and the West.* Foreword by Karen Armstrong. San Francisco: HarperCollins, 2004.

Reynolds, Gabriel Said. *The Qur'ān in Its Historical Context.* New York and London: Routledge, 2008.

———, and Samir Khalil Samir (ed. and trans.). *The Critique of Christian Origins.* Provo, UT: Brigham Young University Press, 2010.

Robinson, Chase. *Abd al-Malik.* Oxford: Oneworld, 2005.

Robinson, Neal. "Massignon, Vatican II and Islam as an Abrahamic Religion." *Islam and Muslim-Christian Relations* 2.2 (1991): 182–205.

Roclave, Pierre. *Louis Massignon et l'Islam.* Damascus: Institut française de Damas, 1993.

Rubenstein, Richard E. *Aristotle's Children: How Christians, Muslims, and Jews Rediscovered Ancient Wisdom and Illuminated the Middle Ages.* New York: Harcourt, 2003.

Sahas, Daniel J. *John of Damascus on Islam: The "Heresy of the Ishmaelites."* Leiden: Brill, 1972.

Said, Edward. *Orientalism.* New York: Vintage, 1978.

de Saussure, Ferdinand. *Course in General Linguistics.* Ed. Charles Bally and Albert Sechehaye. Trans. Roy Harris. LaSalle, IL: Open Court, 1983.

Seidensticker, Tilman. "Sources for the History of Pre-Islamic Religion." In *The Qur'ān in Context: Historical and Literary Investigations in the Qur'ānic Milieu,* 293–322. Ed. Angelika Neuwirth, Nicolai Sinai, and Michael Marx. Leiden: Brill, 2010.

Silk, Mark. "Notes on the Judeo-Christian Tradition in America." *American Quarterly* 36.1 (1984): 65–85.

Six, Jean-François (ed.). *Louis Massignon.* Paris: Éditions de l'Herne, 1970.

Sizgorich, Thomas. "Narrative and Community in Islamic Late Antiquity." *Past and Present* 185 (2004): 9–42.

Smith, Jonathan Z. *Imagining Religion: From Babylon to Jonestown.* Chicago: University of Chicago Press, 1982.

———. "Connections." *Journal of the American Academy of Religion* 58.1 (1990): 1–15.

———. *Drudgery Divine: On the Comparison of Early Christianities and the Religions of Late Antiquity.* Chicago: University of Chicago Press, 1990.

———. *Relating Religions: Essays in the Study of Religion.* Chicago: University of Chicago Press, 2004.

Solomon, Norman, Richard Harries and Tim Winter (eds.). *Abraham's Children: Jews, Christians, and Muslims in Conversation.* London: T & T Clark, 2005.

Soltes, Ori Z. *Mysticism in Judaism, Christianity and Islam: Searching for Oneness.* Lanham, MD: Rowman and Littlefield, 2009.

Stausberg, Michael (ed.). *Contemporary Theories of Religion: A Critical Companion.* London and New York: Routledge, 2009.

Stroumsa, Guy G. *A New Science: The Discovery of Religion in the Age of Reason.* Cambridge, MA: Harvard University Press, 2010.

Swidler, Leonard. *After the Absolute.* Minneapolis: Fortress Press, 1990.

———. "International Scholars' Annual Trialogue." In *Theoria to Praxis: How Jews, Christians, and Muslims Can Move from Theory to Praxis,* 30–41. Ed. Leonard Swidler. Leuven: Peeters, 1998.

———. "Preface: Beyond Violence through Dialogue and Cooperation." In *Beyond Violence: Religious Sources of Social Transformation in Judaism, Christianity, and Islam,* ix–x. Ed. James L. Heft. New York: Fordham University Press, 2004.

Taves, Anne. *Religious Experience Reconsidered: A Building-Block Approach to the Study of Religion and Other Special Things.* Princeton, NJ: Princeton University Press, 2009.

Thomas, David Richard (ed. and trans.). *Early Muslim Polemic Against Christianity: Abū 'Īsa al-Warrāq's "Against the Incarnation."* Cambridge: Cambridge University Press, 2002.

Tisserant, S. E. le Cardinal et al. *Abraham: Père des croyants.* Paris: Éditions du Cerf, 1952.

Tolan, John V. *Saracens: Islam in the Medieval European Imagination*. New York: Columbia University Press, 2002.

Trible, Phyllis, and Letty M. Russell (eds.). *Hagar, Sarah, and Their Children: Jewish, Christian, and Muslim Perspectives*. Louisville, KY: Westminster John Knox Press, 2006.

Trimingham, J. Spencer. *Christianity among the Arabs in Pre-Islamic Times*. London: Longman, 1979.

Varisco, Daniel Martin. *Reading Orientalism: Said and Unsaid*. Seattle: University of Washington Press, 2007.

van der Veer, Peter. *Imperial Encounters: Religion and Modernity in India and Britain*. Princeton, NJ: Princeton University Press, 2001.

Wansbrough, John. *The Sectarian Milieu: Content and Composition of Islamic Salvation History*. Oxford: Oxford University Press, 1978.

Wasserstein, David. *The Rise and Fall of the Party-Kings: Politics and Society in Islamic Spain 1002–1086*. Princeton, NJ: Princeton University Press, 1985.

———. *The Caliphate in the West: An Islamic Political Institution in the Iberian Peninsula*. Oxford: Oxford University Press, 1993.

Wasserstrom, Steven M. *Between Muslim and Jew: The Problem of Symbiosis under Early Islam*. Princeton, NJ: Princeton University Press, 1995.

———. *Religion After Religion: Gershom Scholem, Mircea Eliade, and Henry Corbin at Eranos*. Princeton, NJ: Princeton University Press, 1999.

Watt, W. Montgomery. *Muhammad at Medina*. Oxford: Clarendon Press, 1956

———. *Muhammad and Mecca*. Oxford: Clarendon Press, 1968.

———. *A History of Islamic Spain*. Edinburgh: Edinburgh University Press, 1977 [1965].

———. "Belief in a 'High God' in Pre-Islamic Mecca." In *The Arabs and Arabia on the Eve of Islam*, 307–312. Ed. F. E. Peters. Aldershot, UK: Variorum, 1999.

Wayland, Francis. *A Memoir of Life and Labors of Rev. Adoniram Judson, D.D.* 2 vols. Boston: Phillips, Sampson, and Co., 1853.

Werner, Roland. *Transcultural Healing: The Whole Human: Healing Systems Under the Influence of Abrahamic Religions, Eastern Religions and Beliefs, Paganism, New Religions, and Mixed Religious Forms*. Kuala Lumpur: University of Malaya Press, 1993.

White, Hayden. *Metahistory: The Historical Imagination in Nineteenth-Century Europe*. Baltimore: Johns Hopkins University Press, 1973.

———. *Tropics of Discourse: Essays in Cultural Criticism*. Baltimore: Johns Hopkins University Press, 1978.

Wiebe, Donald. *The Politics of Religious Studies: The Continuing Conflict with Theology in the Academy*. New York: Palgrave Macmillan, 1999.

Wittgenstein, Ludwig. *Philosophical Investigations*. Ed. G. E. M. Anscombe and R. Rhees. Trans. G. E. M. Anscombe. Oxford: Blackwell, 1953.

Wolfson, Elliot R. "That Old Time Religion." *Azure* 41 (2010): 97–108.

Worcester, Samuel. *Two Discourses on the Perpetuity and Provision of God's Gracious Covenant with Abraham and His Seed,* 2nd rev. ed. To which are annexed, *Letters to the Rev. Thomas Baldwin, D.D., on his Book, entitled The Baptism of the Believers Only, &c.* Salem, MA: Printed by Haven Pool, for the Author, 1807.

Ye'or, Bat. *The Dhimmi: Jews and Christians under Islam.* Trans. David Maisel. Rutherford, NJ: Fairleigh Dickinson University Press, 1985.

Index